THE SHAPE OF THE GOOD

The Shape of the Good

Christian Reflections on the Foundations of Ethics

C. STEPHEN LAYMAN

University of Notre Dame Press
Notre Dame

Copyright © 1991
University of Notre Dame
Notre Dame, Indiana 46556
www.undpress.nd.edu
All Rights Reserved
Manufactured in the United States of America

Reprinted in 2013

Library of Congress Cataloging-in-Publication Data

Layman, Charles S., 1950-
    The shape of the good : Christian reflections on the foundations of ethics / C. Stephen Layman.
        p.   cm. — (Library of religious philosophy ; v. 7)
    Includes bibliographical references and index.
    ISBN 13: 978-0-268-01752-1 (pbk.)
    ISBN 10: 0-268-01752-2 (pbk.)
    1. Christian Ethics.   I. Title.   II. Series.
BJ1251.L34   1991
241—dc20   90-50977
                                                                      CIP

∞ *This book is printed on acid-free paper.*

Contents

For Marla

Preface

This book is an introduction to ethical theory from a Christian perspective. As such it belongs to a long tradition of reflection on the foundations of ethics. It differs from other works in the tradition in several ways. First, in its theological orientation: unlike most contemporary introductory books on ethics, this one takes theological ideas very seriously. I have tried to argue for a perspective on ethics that any Christian (standing in the main historic tradition) could accept. On the other hand, I have not hesitated to discuss interesting theological ideas which, from a historical point of view, only a minority of Christians have endorsed.

Second, while theology is taken seriously, my formal training is primarily philosophical. This means that I discuss theological ideas only to the extent that they show promise of providing solutions to philosophical difficulties. It also means that I have worked hard to maintain clarity and rigor in the argument.

Third, unlike many introductory books on ethics, this one attempts to defend a particular point of view. This means that the book is, in effect, a sustained argument. I hope this provides a sense of direction which many introductory treatments lack. In any case I have avoided the tendency, common enough in the present philosophical climate, to produce a book that is almost entirely negative in its results. Chapters 5 and 6 develop a view which I endorse and call 'the Christian teleological view'. In outline, this view says that an act is right if and only if it promotes a certain kind of community—the kingdom of God. Thus, I am a *consequentialist*—one who holds that the consequences (results) of an act make it right or wrong—but not a *utilitarian*. That is, I do not hold that the right act is the one that produces the greatest possible balance of pleasure over pain in the world.

Fourth, unlike most recent introductions to ethics, this one attempts to give Aristotle his due. For all the recent discussion of "virtue ethics," it seems to me that few authors have clearly described how Aristotle's view relates to other major views of ethics in the Western tradition. It is common in some circles, for example, to regard "virtue ethics" as an alternative to a view of ethics in which principles or rules have an important place. It seems to me that this puts a most unhelpful slant on the issues. I hope I will have provided a useful corrective in my discussion of Aristotle in Chapter 5.

I do not pretend that this is a highly original book; it is rather an attempt to make important ideas in ethical theory available to Christian scholars and students who are not professional philosophers. I have tried to provide a helpful treatment of some of the most interesting contemporary ideas, along with a discussion of important ideas with a longer ancestry. And while I have borrowed heavily from other authors, I hope that the synthesis attempted in Chapters 5 and 6 is provocative. I am not aware of any philosopher who has proposed just the approach taken there.

One warning: while the book is an introduction to ethics, I do not think it appropriate for most entering university students. Ethical theory is abstract and can be appreciated only by those who have given some serious thought to particular moral issues (e.g., abortion, criminal punishment, war, suicide, etc.). Therefore, the book is aimed at faculty and more advanced university students who have done enough ethical thinking to develop a strong desire to see things put in systematic order. Philosophy speaks only to those who have reached a certain state of perplexity.

I am deeply indebted to my colleague Richard McClelland for reading the chapters of this book as I produced them. Richard's criticism, both oral and written, helped me to avoid many errors and infelicities. I am also indebted to Thomas V. Morris, who provided extensive and acute comments on the penultimate draft. Whatever the value of the book, it is much better for having undergone the careful scrutiny of these philosophers. It remains for me to thank the Glenmede Foundation for an Ethics Project Grant during the summer of 1987 which helped to make the book possible.

Introduction

Many people nowadays assume, as a matter of course, that ethical disputes cannot be settled through rational means. And it is not hard to see why they assume this. Notoriously, the participants in ethical discussions never seem to be swayed by the words of their opponents. Increasingly, an ethical "discussion" is regarded as no more than a genteel trading of opinions, or a heated clash of assertion and counterassertion, both sides feeling hopeless about convincing the other through evidence and logic. The very effort to give reasons is sometimes regarded as nothing more than an attempt to avoid the obvious: that at the bottom of every ethical dispute lie conflicting personal preferences utterly beyond the reach of reason.

[margin note: THE STATE OF ETHICAL DISCUSSION]

Furthermore, it seems to many that even if unambiguous moral principles can be found that bear on our problems, we still make no progress, since for each principle we invoke there seems to be a contrary principle with strong claims on our loyalty. Thus, in the debate over capital punishment, principles of retributive justice are immediately opposed to principles about the right to life. Both sets of principles seem relevant and weighty, and so the debate seems unresolvable. "That is a value judgment" is no longer just a way of identifying an important form of discourse, but a way of asserting that further discussion is pointless.

We are aware that by no means have all other cultures regarded moral judgments as mere personal preferences. How has our culture come to such a pass? Alasdair MacIntyre has suggested that our deep confusion about ethics is

1

the fallout from historical philosophical shifts in Western culture.[1] Ways of thinking about ethics tend to be deeply ingrained, so that a clean break with an older tradition is never made. Instead, each new philosophic age inherits moral concepts from its ancestors. But the various ages embody incompatible perspectives: they exalt competing virtues and endorse conflicting ends. As one major ethical paradigm, for example, feudal inegalitarianism, gives way to another, such as the individualism of the Renaissance (which in turn gives way to yet another, such as the utilitarianism of the nineteenth century) deep confusion results.[2] People find themselves strongly attracted to aspects of conflicting traditions, often without even realizing where the ideas come from or what role they played in their original philosophical setting. With a variety of ethical perspectives forming a kind of conceptual salad in our heads, it is little wonder that we have come to feel that there is nothing rational about ethical thinking.

But our despair about ethical dialogue is not merely the legacy of Western philosophy. We moderns are more aware of the ethical pluralism in the world than any previous age; we have had intense and debilitating conflicts with cultures in the East, and are keenly aware that these cultures embody values distinct from our own. Moreover, we are aware that these cultures exhibit considerable intellectual depth and practical vigor. And this awareness has produced cultural self-doubt in the West. A fear comes over many of us that perhaps our own moral traditions are narrow, or even fundamentally flawed. Who are we to pass judgment on the world, when we are confined to our own limited perspective?

Such uncertainty may also be symptomatic of a larger cultural shift away from a broadly Protestant consensus on values. It appears that American culture is experiencing a gradual breakdown of that consensus. Something of the same shift has already gone very far in western European countries, where the overt profession and practice of

Christian beliefs has for many generations been a minority force in the public culture. While the European experience is bound to be different from our own in various respects, erosion of such a consensus is likely to have the same effects wherever it occurs. In particular, such erosion makes it harder to find common ground on which to argue about moral issues. One might add that Protestantism has in all likelihood contributed to its own breakdown, since there is a conspicuous absence, in the Protestant tradition, of ethical theories comparable in range and power to, say, the moral philosophy of Thomas Aquinas. Thus, as various elements of the consensus have been challenged, Protestants have been unable to respond with a systematic, reasoned defense. And a retreat to dogmatic assertion only intensifies the suspicion that morality is a matter of personal preference.

This book is an attempt to provide a framework for the rational discussion of ethical issues. It is not, of course, an attempt to give an answer to every ethical question, but it does try to provide a rational way of approaching ethical questions in general. It is written primarily for a Christian audience, though I believe others will find the discussion lucid and instructive. I have drawn freely on mainstream Christian theological resources throughout the book. Indeed, the book is in large part designed to help Christians organize *their* thinking about morality. To some it may seem that this is bound to render the effort to provide a *rational* framework for ethical argument null and void. Aren't religious and theological disagreements even harder to settle than moral disagreements? So says the prevailing academic orthodoxy. But for several reasons I believe that it is unfortunate that contemporary scholars so often try to discuss ethical issues in isolation from religious and theological ones.

First, as a matter of fact religious views often influence a person's moral views. This is obvious in the case of religious persons who draw explicit inferences from their religious beliefs to moral issues. But the influence can be less direct, as in the case of the secular person influenced by cultural values that stem from religion. For example, a person's views about capital punishment, euthanasia, and abortion are often bound up with the view that human life is sacred. Nowadays, in Western culture the view that human life is sacred is widely held among secular as well as religious persons. For religious persons this view is apt to be consciously inferred from specific religious beliefs, such as that God loves all humans or that each human has a soul. But since our cultural belief in the sacredness of life is at least partly rooted, historically speaking, in such religious convictions, secular people are indirectly influenced by these religious ideas also. Thus, to ignore religious views when discussing moral issues is to leave highly *influential* ideas unaddressed.

Second, on some views of religion and ethics, the two cannot logically be divorced from one another—or at least, the two cannot be properly understood in isolation from one another. For example, it is sometimes claimed that certain religious ideas play an important role in the most adequate theories of morality. If this claim is correct, an examination of moral theory that omits such religious ideas would be impoverished. Moreover, the plausibility of the religious views in question would presumably be linked with the explanatory role they play in moral theory, so that the question of the rationality of religious and moral beliefs may be intimately connected. I am unwilling to assume, without discussion, that such conceptual connections between religion and morality do not exist.

Third, the omission of religious ideas from ethical texts is, in my opinion, often an expression (whether witting or unwitting) of intellectual bias. The truth is that the current climate in academia is largely unfavorable to religion; so much so, in fact, that academic writers can easily come to feel that religious ideas need not be taken seriously. But it is my view that, in every age, academics must think critically about such climates of opinion. Books about ethics which omit religious ideas leave an important aspect of the current climate of opinion unchallenged.

So, this book differs from many discussions of moral theory in that it takes religious ideas into account each step of the way. Another way in which this work differs from the typical introduction to ethics is that it makes no pretense of neutrality; a particular point of view is being argued for each step of the way. I have tried to be objective and even-handed, but I have not hesitated to say where I think the truth lies. I hope this gives the book a cohesiveness and urgency often lacking in standard texts. Too often, having plowed through a thick volume of contemporary philosophy, the reader is left with the conclusion that "none of the theories work." I think that philosophy can and must get beyond such negative results. If it is a mistake to expect infallible answers, it is equally a mistake to eschew provisionally adequate solutions.

Chapter 1 scrutinizes moral relativism and subjectivism. Since our culture exhibits a strong impulse toward these points of view, it is imperative that we understand clearly what these views are and what can be said for and against them. If relativism and subjectivism can be shown to have important philosophical demerits, their attraction will be reduced, and we can proceed to alternative perspectives with greater confidence.

Chapter 2 treats of the relation between God and ethics. This topic, often omitted or given cursory treatment in contemporary ethical texts, is obviously a matter of central concern for religious thinkers, and for Christians in particular. Indeed, it is here that the first steps toward a Christian view of ethics must be taken.

In Chapters 3 and 4 a series of major ethical perspectives is examined, among them egoism, utilitarianism, Kant's view, and Rawls's contractarianism. Chapter 3 is devoted to consequentialist views—views involving the claim that the consequences (results) of an act determine its rightness or wrongness. Chapter 4 is devoted to deontological views—views involving the claim that something other than the consequences of an act make it right or wrong.

Chapters 5 and 6 are given over to the development of a Christian moral theory. It is my belief that much of the popular urge toward relativism results from the lack of a systematic framework which reveals the connections between such important moral concepts as right and wrong, virtue and vice, rule and command, *telos* (goal) and intention, justice and love, and the concept of a human right. In Chapter 5 I describe a Christian view of ethics which links most of these concepts and contrast it with its nearest secular counterpart, namely, the view of Aristotle in his *Nicomachean Ethics*. In Chapter 6 I complete the task by describing a perspective on justice and human rights.

Obviously, a work this short cannot be exhaustive. I have tried to focus on the most important ideas and to avoid getting bogged down in analytic detail. My goal has been to produce a readable discussion of moral theory without indulging in oversimplification.

Relativism and Subjectivism   1

A foreign exchange student in a Third World country is shocked to discover that bribing is a common practice. She expresses dismay when her host bribes a policeman to avoid a traffic ticket. Her host replies, "What's right in our society may not be right in yours. Morality is relative." The exchange student nods uneasily, not wishing to appear close-minded or intolerant.

The realization that other peoples have different customs and different values is apt to be disturbing. In the early part of this century, for example, many Americans were shocked when explorers began to report the customs of the Eskimos.

> [Eskimo] men often had more than one wife, and they would share their wives with guests, lending them for the night as a sign of hospitality. Moreover, within a community, a dominant male might demand—and get—regular access to other men's wives. The women, however, were free to break these arrangements simply by leaving their husbands and taking up with new partners—free, that is, so long as their former husbands chose not to make trouble.[1]

It was not only with respect to marriage and sex that Eskimo customs were at variance with ours.

7

. . . the Eskimos also seemed to have less regard for human life. Infanticide, for example, was common. Knud Rasmussen, one of the most famous early explorers, reported that he met one woman who had borne twenty children but had killed ten of them at birth. Female babies, he found, were especially liable to be destroyed, and this was permitted simply at the parents' discretion, with no social stigma attached to it. Old people also, when they became too feeble to contribute to the family, were left out in the snow to die.[2]

The comparison between our culture and that of the Eskimos provides us with a particularly vivid example of cultural relativity. Some cultures are cannibalistic, some sharply restrict eating meat, some proscribe the consumption of alcohol—customs differ from culture to culture. These differences often lead people to claim that morality is in some sense relative. But just what does it mean to say that "morality is relative"? Usually at least one of two theses is meant, one of which seems to me true, the other highly objectionable. Let us examine both of them.

I. DESCRIPTIVE RELATIVISM

It can hardly be denied that different societies or cultures have different and conflicting moral beliefs. Some societies regard polygamy as right, others regard it as wrong. Some societies regard slavery as wrong, others regard it as right (think of the North and the South at the time of the American Civil War). Some societies—those steeped in Islam, for example—regard alcohol drinking as wrong, while others, such as the societies of western Europe, do not regard it as wrong. Note that we are here merely *describing* the beliefs of different cultures or societies; we are merely taking note of the apparent disagreements across societies on at least some ethical issues. Let us call this view *descriptive relativism* (DR):

(DR)   Concerning some moral issues the members
of distinct societies have different and logically
incompatible beliefs.

The first thing to note about descriptive relativism is that
it is not an ethical thesis. It does not say that any ethical
belief is true or false, it does not say that any act is right
or wrong. Rather, it is an anthropological or sociological
thesis. It merely says that the ethical beliefs of distinct societies logically conflict in some cases.

Two points need to be stressed about descriptive relativism. First, it should be obvious that the mere fact that
people disagree about moral issues in no way implies that
there is no moral truth binding on all humans. Human
beings can and do disagree on just about every subject
imaginable. Some cranks even reject the fundamental theses of modern science; but would anyone suggest that the
law of gravity might be true for some but false for others?
Surely not. Yet, our deep confusion about ethics has led us
to treat disagreements about morality in a way we would
never treat disagreements in other areas. Suppose, for example, that two cultures disagree about the existence of
God. We do not immediately lapse into talk about how religion is relative to cultures. Perhaps the majority of people
in China do not believe in God. So? That is not a good reason to think that God somehow exists for Americans but
does not exist for the Chinese. Rather we know that the
way of wisdom is to see which side in such a controversy
has the best evidence.

Second, the extent of moral disagreement between cultures is sometimes exaggerated, for at least three reasons.
(1) Because disagreements are more interesting than agreements, we often tend to focus on disagreements and to
overlook the enormous amount of ethical agreement between cultures. No culture allows its members to kill humans at will, to have sex with anyone at will, or to lie
and cheat at will. Although the specific rules may differ,
one can often see an underlying shared concern—e.g., the

value of life, fidelity, and truth. In fact, it is very doubtful that there could be lasting societies that did not value
such things as life and truth, for constant murdering and lying would surely destroy any society. (2) Sometimes what
may seem to be a difference of ethical perspective is a
difference of circumstance. The inhabitants of a desert
community may view it as wrong to throw out a glass of
potable water, while those living near an abundant supply
of water would not. Yet people in both communities could
agree on the underlying ethical principle that it is wrong
to waste scarce resources. (3) Sometimes what seems to
be a deep moral disagreement is more properly characterized as a factual or metaphysical disagreement. The ethicist
William Frankena discusses an interesting case of such disagreement:

> . . .the fact that in some primitive societies children be-
> lieve they should put their parents to death before they
> get old, whereas we do not, does not prove descriptive rel-
> ativism. These primitive peoples may believe this because
> they think their parents will be better off in the hereafter if
> they enter it while still able-bodied; if this is the case, their
> ethics and ours are alike in that they rest on the precept
> that children should do the best they can for their parents.
> The divergence, then, would be in factual, rather than in
> ethical, beliefs.[3]

In other words, if we believed that those who entered the
afterlife in a feeble state would remain feeble eternally, we
might look at euthanasia in a new light. But this would not
reflect a change in our deep-lying ethical principles, rather
a change in our view of the afterlife. James Rachels makes
a similar point:

> Consider a culture in which people believe it is wrong
> to eat cows. This may even be a poor culture, in which
> there is not enough food; still, the cows are not to be
> touched. Such a society would appear to have values very
> different from our own. But does it? We have not yet asked
> why these people will not eat cows. Suppose it is because

they believe that after death the souls of humans inhabit the bodies of animals, especially cows, so that a cow may be someone's grandmother. Now do we want to say that their values are different from ours? No; the difference lies elsewhere. The difference is in our belief systems, not in our values. We agree that we shouldn't eat Grandma; we simply disagree about whether the cow is (or could be) Grandma.[4]

Once again, what appears to be a difference in values turns out to be a factual or metaphysical disagreement—in this case a disagreement about reincarnation.

Descriptive relativism, then, seems to be a true anthropological thesis, though it occasions a variety of misunderstandings about ethics. Most importantly, perhaps, it is often confused with (or thought to imply) *normative* relativism.

II. NORMATIVE RELATIVISM

Does descriptive relativism imply that there is no universal moral truth? Many thinkers have claimed that there is no standard independent of social mores for judging right and wrong. For example, the famous American sociologist William Graham Sumner (1840–1910) once wrote that the

> "right" way is the way which the ancestors used and which has been handed down. The tradition is its own warrant. It is not held subject to verification by experience. The notion of right is in the folkways [customs]. It is not outside of them, of independent origin, and brought to them to test them. In the folkways, whatever is, is right. . . . When we come to the folkways we are at the end of our analysis.[5]

[margin note: ETHICS AS FOLK-WAYS]

I shall call this view *normative relativism* (NR). It has often been held by social scientists, and can be succinctly stated as follows:

(NR)   An act is morally right if and only if it conforms to the conventions of the society in which it is performed.

Three clarifications are needed here. First, note that (NR), unlike (DR), *is* an ethical thesis: it tells us what is right and wrong. Right acts are those permitted by the relevant conventions, i.e., the accepted beliefs about morality in the society in question. Wrong acts are those not permitted by the relevant conventions. In other words, when in Rome do as the Romans do. If I am living in Iran, it is not right to drink alcohol; if I am living in Moscow, a shot of vodka is morally permissible.

Second, a rather technical explanation of the logical phrase 'if and only if' is needed, since this phrase will be in frequent use throughout the book. If we dropped 'and only if' from (NR), we would have the claim that *an act is right if it is permitted by the relevant conventions.* By itself, this claim would allow acts which do not conform to the conventions to be right. That is, it merely guarantees that acts which do conform to the conventions are right— it makes no statement about the acts that do not conform. On the other hand, consider the claim that *an act is right only if it conforms to the relevant conventions.* This says, in effect, that if an act does not conform to the conventions, it is not right. This in turn is equivalent to the claim that *if an act is right, then it conforms to the relevant conventions.* More generally, an expression of the form "*P* if and only if *Q*" (where *P* and *Q* stand for sentences) implies two 'if-then' statements: "if *P* (is true), then *Q* (is true)", and, "if *Q* (is true), then *P* (is true)."

Third, note that descriptive relativism does not logically imply normative relativism. Many people think that the anthropological fact (assuming it is a fact) that cultures have conflicting moral beliefs somehow implies that what is right and wrong actually does vary from culture to culture. But we must insist on a distinction between what people *think* is right and what is right. Just because the people in a given society approve of slavery, it by no means follows (logically) that slavery is right, in that society or anywhere else; an entire society could very well be mistaken. Most

Americans would now agree, for example, that the conventions regarding slavery in the South prior to the Civil War were profoundly mistaken.

So, normative relativism does not follow from the truth of descriptive relativism. But couldn't it nevertheless also be true? To answer this question, we need to consider some objections to normative relativism. The first objection I shall call, following Fred Feldman, the 'Reformer's Dilemma'.[6] Most of us think that, at some points in history, moral reformers correctly observed that the conventions adopted by their societies were morally deficient (think of Old Testament prophets such as Amos, or of Wilberforce's attacks on the slave trade in England). But consider this phenomenon from the point of view of normative relativism. Suppose we are in society *S* where the conventions clearly endorse slavery. Along comes a "reformer" who says that slavery is wrong for reasons *x*, *y*, and *z*. We can safely ignore his reasons, given normative relativism, for we have an easy proof that the "reformer" is mistaken. We simply refer him to the conventions of our society, the contents of which are not in dispute, and point out that any effort to abolish slavery is clearly in error. In other words, if normative relativism is true, then it immediately follows that all would-be reformers are mistaken. But surely such people have not been mistaken in every instance. We can sum up the Reformer's Dilemma as follows:[7]

(1) If normative relativism is true, then anyone who advocates reform is in error.

(2) Not everyone who advocates reform is in error.

So,

(3) Normative relativism is not true.

The logic here is impeccable, i.e., if (1) and (2) are both true, then (3) must be true also. Can the relativist cast doubt on either (1) or (2)? Premise (1) seems undeniable. If we can agree on what the conventions are, anyone with moral views contrary to those conventions must be in error, according to the normative relativist. And a reformer would not be a reformer unless he were advocating views contrary to the conventions. Accordingly, the normative relativist cannot deny premise (1).

Premise (2) is the one most likely to come under attack. How does the critic of relativism know that (2) is true? Who gets to decide whether an alleged reformer has spoken the truth? These are fair questions, but it is slightly ironic that the relativist takes a skeptical tack at this point. He of course has not been loath to make sweeping claims about moral truth, for in asserting (NR) he is in effect claiming to know the truth about a host of ethical issues.

What is at stake here is an issue of philosophical method: once someone has asserted a particular moral hypothesis, what are the rest of us supposed to do with it? Just accept it uncritically? There are really only three things we can do. First, we can demand evidence for the hypothesis. The only real evidence the normative relativist typically provides is descriptive relativism, and, as we have seen, descriptive relativism does not imply normative relativism. Second, we can propose an alternative hypothesis. Ultimately, the best objection to one philosophical view is the availability of another view that explains the data more adequately. At the moment, however, we have not got another view to work with. Third, we can draw out the implications of the hypothesis, and show that some of these implications are implausible. That is what we are now doing in pressing the Reformer's Dilemma. To save his theory the relativist can verbalize the position that slavery, or at least slavery in slave societies, may after all be right. But such a position is highly implausible; most of us find the idea that one human should be allowed to own another profoundly objectionable. Yet, the normative relativist must endorse slavery, for on his view it is right in those societies which approve of it. And anyone who advocates reform in those societies is simply mistaken.

The Reformer's Dilemma brings to light another implausible feature of normative relativism. Notice how moral truth is arrived at, according to (NR). In essence, it is arrived at by taking a vote or opinion poll, for the conventions in a given society are just the beliefs about right and wrong held by *the vast majority of members of that society*. Yet, the participants in moral debates seldom act as if the correct answer were necessarily identical with the majority opinion. In the contemporary debate about capital punishment, for example, no one seems to think the *moral* issue could be settled simply by taking a vote or opinion poll. Rather, it is argued that the death penalty does (or does not) deter crime, that it does (or does not) fit the crime, that it is (or is not) mere revenge, etc. Now, admittedly, there may at present be no overwhelming majority either for or against the death penalty, since it is controversial. Nevertheless, it would be hard to deny that many things besides public opinion are relevant *as evidence* in the controversy. Even if we grant that opinion polls do provide *presumptive* evidence in a given case, they are not the only type of evidence relevant to moral issues, much less the decisive evidence in every case. So, (NR) implies a very dubious moral epistemology (i.e., theory of how we *know* what is right and wrong), since it implies that majority opinion is the only type of evidence relevant to moral issues.

A second objection to normative relativism emerges if we ask: What becomes of *descriptive* relativism on the normative relativist's account?[8] Suppose the members of society S_1 believe that slavery is right, while the members of society S_2 believe that slavery is not right. This *looks* like a disagreement, but, on the normative relativist's view, it really is not. For the normative relativist, moral issues are decided, in effect, by an opinion poll. So, to determine whether slavery is right in S_1, we merely ascertain whether the vast majority of people in S_1 believe slavery to be right. Since the vast majority of people in S_1 believe slavery is right, then it *is* right in society S_1. So, the members of S_1 and S_2 can agree that slavery is right for the members of S_1. Similarly, to find out if slavery is right in S_2, we ascertain the conventions in S_2. Since the vast majority of people in S_2 believe that slavery is *not* right, then slavery is *not* right in S_2. So, the members of both S_1 and S_2 can agree that slavery is not right for the members of S_2 . But what has become of the disagreement between S_1 and S_2 insisted upon by the *descriptive* relativist? It has dropped out of sight. For, on the normative relativist's view, the statement "Slavery is both right in S_1 and not right in S_2," is not a contradiction. In fact, it is a truth, given our assumptions about the conventions in the two societies. Therefore, although it appears that societies disagree about morality, in the final analysis their claims are logically consistent. Accordingly, the normative relativist implicitly denies *descriptive* relativism. But as we have already seen, descriptive relativism is almost certainly true. Hence, it appears that *normative* relativism is unacceptable.

A final observation about normative relativism. Obviously it is motivated by a tolerant, democratic spirit, and we all dislike intolerant dogmatic moralizing. Having been subjected to the preachments of a moral bigot for an hour, normative relativism may seem attractive—a breath of fresh air in a world of narrow-minded judgment. But it is easily shown that normative relativism is not a reliable defense against intolerance. Suppose society S is a very intolerant one in which the people approve of burning "infidels" at the stake for the most trivial departure from orthodox teaching; then the normative relativist must say that intolerance is right in S. Nor is this a merely academic possibility, as the Spanish inquisition and the recent revolution in Iran attest. Thus, while normative relativism may seem to spring from a concern for the toleration of diverse moral beliefs, it actually is incapable of justifying a principle of tolerance.

So, for a variety of reasons, I must conclude that normative relativism is false. Is there, then, no grain of truth in (NR) at all? For example, consider the issue of who is responsible for bringing up a child in case its mother dies. Some societies regard the father as primarily responsible, others regard the maternal grandmother as primarily responsible. Must we say that one of these types of society is correct, and the other simply mistaken? In Chapter 5, Section II, I argue that a "Yes" answer to this question is too simple, and that a *highly restricted* form of relativism is implied by the most promising moral theory I am aware of.

III. MORAL SUBJECTIVISM

People sometimes speak of "moral relativism and subjectivism" in one breath, as if these were the same thing. But while the normative relativist says that there is no moral truth *outside societal conventions*, he does insist that the conventions provide a method for obtaining the correct answers to moral questions—a method that transcends the subjectivism of individual opinion. The subjectivist, on the other hand, says that we have *no objective way* of getting at moral truth. Thus, while the normative relativist provides a means, however questionable, for settling ethical disputes (viz., appeal to the conventions), the subjectivist position amounts to moral skepticism. For the subjectivist, a moral judgement is similar to a matter of taste. Some people like oysters and some do not. Some enjoy playing chess and some do not. In such matters there seems to be no ground for claiming that one individual's preference is more justified than another. Similarly, according to the moral subjectivist, no particular moral judgment can be shown to be rationally preferable to another.

One important strand of philosophy in the twentieth century, logical positivism, has issued in an influential form of subjectivism. Proponents of logical positivism include, among others, the members of the Vienna Circle (e.g., Moritz Schlick, Otto Neurath, and Rudolf Carnap) and the

British philosopher A. J. Ayer. The heart of logical positivism is the *verification principle*. According to this principle, only two kinds of statements have truth value or
"cognitive meaning," that is, only two kinds of statements
are *either true or false*. First, there are *analytic* statements;
these are regarded as true (or false) by definition—e.g., "All
husbands are male" (true) and "Some husbands are unmarried" (false). The idea is that we can determine the truth
of these statements simply by knowing the meanings of
the terms employed ('all,' 'some,' 'husband,' 'unmarried,'
etc.), quite apart from *empirical confirmation*, i.e., without observation or experiment involving the five senses.
One does not, for example, have to conduct experiments
to find out if all husbands are male; it is just a matter of
knowing the definitions of the terms involved.

Second, there are *empirical* statements. These are statements which can be confirmed (or disconfirmed) through
the five senses, and especially through the methods used
in the natural sciences, for example, "Some husbands have
blond hair" or "The Sun is 93,000,000 miles from the
Earth." Using the verification principle, the positivists
claimed that metaphysical statements such as "God exists"
are meaningless. Such statements seem to be neither analytic nor verifiable through observation or experiment;
therefore, argued the positivists, such statements are cognitively meaningless. They do not even rise to the level of
falsehood! A speaker may use metaphysical sentences to
express emotion, but they are without *truth value*, i.e.,
they are neither true nor false.

Many positivists, among them Ayer and Schlick, argued
similarly that moral statements are cognitively meaningless.[9] For example, a statement such as "You ought to
keep your promises" does not appear to be analytic; one
cannot ascertain its truth value just by knowing the meanings of the terms. In fact, promise-keeping seems to admit
of exceptions—in a given case someone may be able to
help an accident victim only if she breaks her promise

to meet a friend for lunch. So, "You ought to keep your promises" is not true by definition.[10] Moreover, it does not seem that such a statement can be verified by observation or scientific experiment. In many cases I can see or hear how things *are*, but how can I *literally* see or hear how they *ought* to be? (What observable properties indicate "oughtness"?) Ayer concluded that moral statements are neither true nor false, but instead merely express emotions. For example, saying that stealing is wrong is like saying "Stealing—boo!" Or saying that we ought to keep our promises is like saying, "Hurray for promise-keeping!" Such statements lack cognitive meaning (truth value), but express important emotions. This view of moral statements is called *emotivism*, and can be summarized as follows:

(E)   Moral statements are neither true nor false, but merely express approval or disapproval.

Statements of the form "*X* is right (good, virtuous, etc.)" express approval; those of the form "*X* is wrong (bad, vicious, etc.)" express disapproval.

As we have just seen, one of the main arguments for emotivism involves the verification principle as a premise. However, that principle has now been thoroughly discredited. For convenience, let us abbreviate the verification principle (VP) as follows:

(VP)   A sentence is cognitively meaningful if and only if it is either analytic or empirically verifiable.

Many philosophers have argued that (VP) is self-defeating, since it seems to be neither analytic or empirically verifiable. One cannot discover that (VP) is true just by analyzing its constituent terms. It does not seem to be true by definition like, "All husbands are male" or "All bachelors are unmarried." Furthermore, it is not the type of statement that could be confirmed through the human senses. (Where would one look? What experiment would confirm it?) Thus, it appears that the positivist is caught in his own trap. In fact, it seems much more natural to reverse the flow of argument: since it seems obvious that there are many meaningful statements which are not meaningful according to (VP), (VP) is an unacceptable criterion of meaning.

In addition to appealing to the verification principle, emotivists may appeal to *descriptive* relativism or to ethical disputes in general as evidence for their subjectivist outlook. They may claim that where there are longstanding, unresolved disputes, objective methods for arriving at answers must be lacking. People may be stupid and cantankerous, but if the evidence is there they will eventually come to see it. Hence, the failures of individuals and cultures to agree about ethical issues provide evidence that there is no objective way to determine what is right and wrong.

A number of points are in order at this juncture. First, it is most implausible to claim that *all* ethical matters are in serious dispute. To take an obvious example, no culture has ever claimed that it is morally permissible to kill at will. Thus, descriptive relativism does not really support emotivism, which is a sweeping generalization about *all* moral beliefs.

Second, if we make universal agreement a condition for objectivity, virtually *all* our beliefs, not just our beliefs about morality, will fail to be objective. There are groups of people who will deny virtually anything. There really is a Flat Earth Society; there really are religious sects that deny the reality of human suffering. Thus, it is a philosophical error to suppose that a belief is well supported only if everyone accepts it. So, it would be a mistake to infer, for example, that *we do not know that genocide is wrong* simply on the grounds that certain groups, such as the Nazis, have approved of genocide.

Third, there are special psychological factors that tend to produce resistance to moral persuasion. In urging a person to accept a moral thesis, we are often in effect asking him to undergo a significant change in his behavior. *This change is not forced on him by physical necessity, and so it is often felt as an unnecessary burden* (think of trying to convince a group of slave owners that slavery is wrong). When people tell us we ought to do something or blame us for what we have done, then, if our consciences are pricked, we feel that something has cut across our wills. This experience is most unpleasant, and one way to reduce the unpleasantness is to defend ourselves with rationalization. The tendency to rationalize is much less pronounced in scientific matters, because the attempt to deny physical necessities is typically very impractical. So, there are good psychological reasons for expecting special difficulties in securing agreement on ethical issues; yet by itself disagreement implies neither emotivism nor any other form of subjectivism.

However, at this point the emotivist may claim that there is a deep and ineradicable philosophical problem which gives rise to ethical disagreements, namely, *the fact that moral words such as 'good' or 'right' cannot be satisfactorily defined or analyzed in terms of observable properties.* To appreciate the force of this claim, we must consider some attempts to define or analyze moral terms. Let's examine some of the main attempts to define or analyze the word 'good.'

On one view, sometimes called *subjective naturalism*, "X is good" means "I (the speaker) approve of X," while "X is bad" means "I (the speaker) disapprove of X."[11] It may seem that the emotivist would favor such an analysis of 'good,' but in fact subjective naturalism is logically incompatible with emotivism. If "Killing is bad" *means the very same thing as* "I disapprove of killing," then "Killing is bad" has a truth value, for subjective naturalism reduces moral language to language about the speaker's psychological states. And it is either true or false that the speaker feels a certain way about killing. Of course, the emotivist rejects the claim that moral statements have truth value. They *express* the speaker's feelings ("Killing—boo!"), but do not *state* that those feelings exist, just as a sentence like "Ouch!" may express a speaker's pain without actually stating that she is in pain. ("I am in pain" is either true or false, but it makes no sense to say that "Ouch!" is either true or false. So, "Ouch!" typically expresses pain, but does not actually state that the pain is occurring. Thus, "Ouch!" is not identical in meaning with "I am in pain," even though the fact that one is uttering the word "Ouch!" normally provides evidence that one is in pain.)

Now, subjective naturalism is highly problematic. First, as the Cambridge philosopher G. E. Moore pointed out, if "*X* is good" means only "I approve of *X*," the subjectivist lacks an adequate account of ethical disagreement.[12] Suppose I hold that slavery is good and you hold that it is not good. This certainly appears to be a disagreement, but it is not if we accept the suggested analysis of moral statements, since the statement "I approve of slavery and you do not approve of slavery" is not a contradiction. It could very well be true that I approve of slavery, and that you do not. So what are we arguing about? Apparently nothing. But any analysis of the word 'good' that leaves us unable to disagree about moral issues is absurd.

A second and slightly more subtle objection to subjective naturalism is due to A. C. Ewing.[13] It is plausible to suppose that if two statements mean exactly the same thing, then whatever proves one of them should also prove the other. For example, if I have given good evidence for "Joe is a bachelor," then presumably I have also given good evidence for "Joe is an unmarried adult human male," and vice versa. But suppose someone says,

(a) Racial discrimination is good.

According to subjective naturalism, this has the very same meaning as

(b) I (the speaker) approve of racial discrimination.

But couldn't we have good evidence for (b) without having good evidence for (a)? For example, suppose a psychologist carefully interviews the speaker and gives her a battery of psychological tests, concluding that she really does approve of racial discrimination. Would this type of psychological evidence provide good evidence for (a), the claim that racial discrimination is good? Surely it does not. So, the view that "*X* is good" *means the very same thing as* "I approve of *X*" must be false.

Hedonism suggests that goodness can be analyzed in terms of pleasure.[14] To say that something is good, from this perspective, is to say that it is pleasant in the long run. But pleasant *for whom* in the long run? Suppose a sadist finds torture pleasant in the long run for himself, while his victims find it highly unpleasant in the long run for themselves. Are we to say that the sadist's acts of torture are both good and bad? But it seems absurd to say that one and the same act is both morally good and bad. To avoid this absurdity, must we content ourselves with relativized expressions, such as "Torture is *good for the sadist* but *bad for his victims*"? This approach leaves us unable to say that the sadist's acts of torture are simply bad from the moral point of view. Moreover, don't we normally distinguish between the question of whether an act is *pleasant* (even in the long run) for someone and whether it is *good* or *right* from a moral point of view? If so, it is implausible to identify goodness with pleasure, or to define 'good' as "pleasant in the long run."

To avoid the difficulties of subjective naturalism and hedonism, others have tried to define 'good' in terms of what an ideal observer would approve, or in terms of what God does approve. The emotivist rejects these definitions on the grounds that they fail to define 'good' in terms of observable properties. How can we obtain evidence, through our senses, that a given act would be approved by an ideal observer or by God? We cannot, says the emotivist; such metaphysical analyses only turn morality into mysticism.

Furthermore, the terms 'ideal' and 'God' almost certainly have moral meaning packed into them. How can we define 'ideal observer' or 'God' without using evaluative terms? But if we have to use 'good' or some similar evaluative term in defining 'ideal observer' or 'God,' the proposed definitions of 'good' become circular and therefore unilluminating. For example, if "X is good" is defined as "God approves of X," but 'God' is defined as "an almighty, allknowing, perfectly *good* Being," then the proposed definition of 'good' becomes circular.

G. E. Moore is famous for suggesting that the word 'good' cannot be analyzed or defined in terms of nonmoral properties. Goodness is a unique moral property; it cannot be seen, smelled, touched, heard, or tasted. The emotivist rejects such a view, again on the grounds that it turns morality into mysticism. Moore has to claim that we intuit goodness in some extrasensory fashion, which makes no sense at all to the emotivist. Why don't we just admit that moral judgments are not factual but are merely subjective expressions of feeling?

It must be granted that the emotivist raises hard questions about the analysis of moral terms, and that most of the attempts to define such terms as 'good' and 'right' are clearly defective. However, I think it would be hasty to leap to emotivism on the basis of this evidence. What is needed is a more subtle analysis of moral terms. I believe that a promising analysis as been provided by the late J. L. Mackie, in his book, *Ethics: Inventing Right and Wrong.*[15] According to Mackie, 'good' means "such as to satisfy requirements . . . of the kind in question."[16] This definition may seem rather vague, but Mackie points out that it has to be, since the word 'good' is used in so many different contexts. The point is that when someone says, "This is a good knife," "That's a good sunset," or "She's a good person" certain standards or requirements are assumed even if they are not explicitly stated. The standards or requirements in question vary widely from case to case. Thus, a good knife is presumably one that cuts smoothly and stays sharp a long time, and a good sunset is presumably a very colorful one. But in saying that something is good we are implying that it has certain intrinsic characteristics or qualities (e.g., sharp, colorful), often without specifying what these characteristics or qualities are. In saying that "X is good" implies that X has certain qualities, Mackie is denying the emotivist view of moral language, since it will be either true or false, in any given case, that X has the implied qualities or characteristics.

But how does Mackie's analysis apply to the use of 'good' in moral contexts, such as "Promise-keeping is good," or "She's a good person"? Here we have to keep in mind that the requirements or standards in question cannot be described in moral terms, since that would turn Mackie's definition into a circular definition. For example, "She's a good person because she meets the requirement of usually doing what's morally right," is unilluminating. We must also keep in mind that, where morality is concerned, there is much disagreement over which standards to employ. Nevertheless, it is not difficult to find possible requirements that illustrate Mackie's proposal. Thus, in saying that promise-keeping is morally good, one requirement we may have in mind is that promise-keeping generally leads to harmonious relations between persons, whereas promise-breaking generally creates anger and resentment. When we say that someone is a good person, the requirement would be that she has certain character traits, e.g., that she is loving, wise, honest, and courageous. We may then need to provide noncircular definitions of these character traits; for example, a loving person may be one who typically shows a concern for the fulfillment of others.

So, it seems to me that the emotivist is wrong in claiming that statements of the form "X is good" have no truth value. As Mackie claims, 'good' is best defined as "such as to satisfy the requirements in question." And while the

standards or requirements relevant to assessing moral goodness are subject to debate, the emotivist has not shown
that they are beyond the reach of human knowers. And,
in fact, most of the traditional theories of ethics propose
that goodness or rightness can be assessed in terms of *features* of acts, persons, practices, etc., *which are accessible
(directly or indirectly) to human knowers.* This book is
given over to an examination of such theories.

Thus far I have been saying that the arguments *in favor
of* emotivism are not compelling. (1) The verification principle has been discredited. (2) The phenomenon of ethical
disagreement does not, by itself, imply emotivism or any
other form of subjectivism. (3) The emotivist analysis of
'good' has worthy rivals—indeed, in my opinion, Mackie's
analysis is a victorious rival. Now, to make our assessment
of emotivism complete, we must go on to a consideration
of some of its logical consequences.

First, as Yale philosopher Brand Blanshard pointed out, if
emotivism is true, then *one cannot make mistakes about
values.*[17] The Nazi who approves of killing all Jews cannot
be said to be mistaken. We may not like his emotional
response to genocide, we may even choose to scream our
opposing emotional response in his face; but we cannot
logically claim that the statement, "It is right to kill all
Jews," is an error. For if emotivism is true, moral judgments
are neither true nor false.

Again, we may think that disapproval is at least a *more
appropriate response* to genocide than approval. But why?
Because approval of genocide may lead to mass killing,
whereas disapproval makes it less likely to occur? But so
what? Who says it's *better* to avoid mass killing than to
promote it? 'Better' is a moral word. When we say that
something is good, better, or best, what we say has no truth
value, if emotivism is correct. In using the word 'better,'
we are merely expressing our emotions, which happen to
be positive, and the Nazi is free to express his own contrary
emotions.

Now, the idea that there can be no mistakes about values is pretty hard to swallow. Why isn't a person who claims, "Torturing people for fun is good," just as plainly in error as someone who claims that suffering is an illusion? Can we really believe that no one has ever made serious and fundamental mistakes about values?

Second, as Blanshard also observed, if emotivism is true, then moral judgments *always* express emotion. But do they? For example, if a modern American says, "It was wrong for Brutus to kill Caesar," is she necessarily expressing an emotion? Aren't moral judgments sometimes delivered as emotionlessly as ordinary factual statements? It is true, of course, that if another person disagrees, claiming that it was right for Brutus to kill Caesar, a debate may ensue. And the debate may become heated. But, then again, it may not. Moreover, a heated debate is just as likely to occur if someone disagrees with a purely factual statement. Historians may express strong emotions in arguing about exactly what happened in an ancient battle. Thus, the fact that a statement expresses emotion in a given case may have more to do with its being controversial than with its belonging to one particular kind of discourse (viz., moral) rather than another (e.g., historical). But the emotivist claims that moral statements always and necessarily express emotions.

Third, as Fred Feldman has noted, emotivism implies that we cannot apply logic to moral judgments.[18] As standardly conceived, logic is about the relationships between propositions—statements which are either true or false.[19] For example, "All humans are mortal and Socrates is human, therefore Socrates is mortal" is an example of what logicians call a *valid* argument. "All humans are mortal," "Socrates is human," and "Socrates is mortal" are each propositions—in this case, I take it, true propositions. An argument is a set of propositions, some of which (the premises) are intended to support another (the conclusion). To say that an argument is *valid* is to say that *if its*

*premises were true, its conclusion would have to be true
also.* Of course, a valid argument can have one or more
false premises. Thus, "All birds have beaks and George
Bush is a bird, therefore George Bush has a beak" is valid,
even though "George Bush is a bird" is false. (The conclusion follows logically, *given* the premises. Logicians reserve the term 'sound' for arguments that are valid and
have only true premises.) But, as standardly conceived,
logic cannot judge a set of statements or sentences to be
valid if those statements or sentences are neither true nor
false, and the emotivist insists that moral statements are
neither true nor false.

The problem for emotivism is that plenty of sets of moral
statements strike us as valid. For example,

Set A

    (1) Killing is wrong.

    (2) Booth killed Abraham Lincoln.

So,

    (3) Booth did something wrong.

It seems obvious that Set A is a valid argument. But in
saying this we imply that the premises and conclusion have
truth value. Yet, (1) and (3) are clearly moral statements.
So, the emotivist must deny that they have truth value, and
hence deny that Set A is a valid argument. In fact, for the
emotivist Set A becomes Set B:

Set B

    (4) Killing—boo!

    (5) Booth killed Abraham Lincoln.

So,

    (6) Booth's killing of Lincoln—boo!

Set B plainly is not an argument at all, let alone a valid one.
For (4) and (6) are not propositions, i.e., they are neither
true nor false. Thus the emotivist is led to deny that Set A
is even an argument, let alone a valid argument. To put it
mildly, this is difficult to accept.

By way of reply, some emotivists have suggested that logicians need to expand their concepts of argument, logic, and validity. Perhaps, they suggest, logicians need to consider the emotive connections between sentences, not merely the logical relations as standardly conceived. However, it is one thing to suggest a radical revision of logic and another to work out such a revision. Traditional logic asks the question, "If so-and-so were *true*, what would follow?" If we try to transcend this traditional idea of logical connections, defined in terms of truth and falsity, what will prevent us from turning "valid argument" into "effective propaganda" or "persuasive rhetoric"? It is fair to say that most philosophers have found the suggested revision of logic unattractive.

For a variety of reasons, then, I must conclude, along with the majority of contemporary philosophers, that emotivism is deeply flawed. However, the reader may feel that some of the emotivist's concerns merit further discussion. I concur; for it is my belief that much of the appeal of both subjectivism and relativism is due to the apparent absence of a compelling theory of morality that provides a helpful framework for ethical disputes. From this standpoint, one could view the remainder of this book, and particularly Chapters 2, 5, and 6 (in which I describe and defend a particular moral theory), as an extended reply to relativism and subjectivism. The best reply to any philosophical view is, in the end, the clear presentation of a better view—one that explains the phenomena more adequately, and thus results in fewer difficulties.

God and Ethics 2

What is the relation between God and ethics? Did God create moral obligation? Does God have moral obligations? Is ethics simply a matter of doing God's will? Could there be a purely secular ethic? Any viable theory of ethics must provide answers to these questions.

I. THE DIVINE MOTIVATOR VIEW

Some Christians seem to think that the only connection between God and ethics is that God supplies the motivation for ethical action: He promises to send the virtuous to heaven and the vicious to hell, and without such extrinsic, post-mortem reinforcements, we would have no reason to be moral. We might call this the 'divine motivator' view of the relation between God and ethics.

There are a number of problems with the divine motivator view. First, it seems clear that the fear of punishment and the desire for rewards are not by themselves adequate moral motives. Surely there is a defect in my love for you if my actions are motivated simply out of the desire to avoid eternal punishment or to gain eternal bliss. To love you is to care in a special way about what happens to *you*. But on the divine motivator view, to love you is to care in a special way about what happens to *me* (in the long run after death).

Second, it must be said that the negative side of the motivation tends to loom larger in the human mind than the positive. Where the fear of hell has played a large role in religious instruction one usually finds a conception of

31

God as a Cosmic Tyrant: "Do as I say or suffer forever; it's *your* choice." (The reader may recall Jonathan Edwards's famous sermon, "Sinners in the Hands of an Angry God.") In short, it is easy enough to instill the fear of hell, once a belief in hell is in place, but the most noteworthy effect of this fear seems to be a distorted view of the nature of God.

Third, the doctrine of hell is problematic. According to this doctrine, some sinners will be punished everlastingly. Moreover, as the doctrine is standardly conceived, once the punishment has begun (after death) there will be no way to escape it—not even by repenting or by ceasing to exist. This means that some persons will be everlastingly miserable with absolutely no chance (after death) of avoiding that misery. Now, there seems to be no way to reconcile this doctrine with what Christians say about God's love. According to Christians, God loves every human being; but if God loves humans, then it follows that He desires their long-term best interests. (One cannot claim to love another if one does not care deeply about what happens to that person in the long run.) Yet, it is obvious that being damned eternally is in no one's long-term best interest. Hence, love cannot be the motive for eternal damnation.

Some would claim that the doctrine of hell is fundamentally a doctrine of separation rather than one of punishment: "It is not that God *punishes* people eternally, rather, He merely *separates* Himself eternally from those who do not want to live with Him. After all, it wouldn't be right for God to force people to live with Him if they didn't want to, right? Thus, He has no choice but to leave unrepentant sinners to their own devices. Unfortunately, they find that living apart from God is miserable." The main problem with this line of reasoning is that, if God is omnipotent, He does have alternatives to eternal separation. The pains of hell might be reformative; or, if the damned *will* not repent, an omnipotent God can annihilate them, i.e., make them cease to exist. Surely it is better to cease to exist than to be *eternally* miserable. (Arguments to the contrary always wind up claiming, implicitly or explicitly, that "Hell isn't such a bad place after all.") But then it appears that divine love would prefer either reform or annihilation to eternal separation.[1]

At this point, some defenders of the doctrine of hell may claim that unrepentant sinners are sent to hell as a matter of *justice*, not love. This response is weak for two reasons. (1) It implies that the divine love and justice are incompatible, i.e., that God cannot always be loving because that would interfere with His being just. But, from a Christian point of view, God's love is constant; He never stops loving people, no matter how blatantly they sin. In other words, divine justice must be conceived of as an expression of (or at least as compatible with) divine love. So, a Christian cannot consistently defend the doctrine of hell by saying that God damns people out of His justice, not His love. Whatever punishments God administers in the afterlife must be compatible with His passionate concern for the long-term best interests of those punished. (2) It is doubtful that any plausible theory of justice would endorse eternal punishment for sins committed prior to death.[2] Some very cruel people, who have made life miserable for others, may deserve a lengthy period of punishment. We may even grant, for the sake of the argument, that some deserve thousands of years of intense punishment. But can anyone literally merit *unending* punishment? It is natural to suppose that each sin a person commits merits some finite degree of punishment. To take an analogy from the legal sphere, we normally suppose that a burglar deserves a few years of imprisonment, and that it would be unjust to imprison him indefinitely. However, to put the point crudely, if each sin an unrepentant sinner commits adds a finite number of years in hell, the total number of years in hell will be finite (assuming the number of sins is finite).

Some have tried to avoid this consequence by making the claim that every sin merits eternal damnation, *because it is an offense against an infinite Being.* Two points are worth noting here. (A) This claim is not biblical. Apparently, it has its roots in a medieval view of justice, in which the heinousness of a crime depends on the social status of the person against whom the offense is committed. On this view, for example, it is much worse to commit an offense against a lord than a serf, for a lord is higher in the great chain of being. Hardly anyone endorses such a view of justice nowadays; many feel that it is as bad or even worse to offend against persons having low social status. (It is noteworthy that the Bible condemns certain inegalitarian attitudes; e.g., James 2:1-7 offers a scathing criticism of those who show partiality for the rich and powerful.) Yet, the claim that every sin merits eternal damnation (because it is an offense against a Person having the highest possible status) seems to be an application of this questionable view of justice to theology.[3] (B) The claim that each sin merits eternal damnation is simply implausible. Can anyone seriously suggest that a child, upon its first disobedience to its parents, deserves literally unending punishment by virtue of that act alone? Or that a person who has just shoplifted for the first time merits everlasting misery by virtue of that one act of theft? It is inadequate to say, in response to these questions, that God's ways are not our ways, His thoughts not our thoughts, etc. (Isaiah 55: 8-9). For if it is true that such acts merit eternal punishment, then it must be true that we humans have no real grasp of the concepts of justice and love. ("It would be loving and just to punish someone eternally for a single act of shoplifting" is as blatantly false a statement regarding love and justice as one could contrive.) But if we have no real grasp of the concepts of love and justice, then Christians have no business preaching that God is loving and just.

Fourth, how good is the evidence that the promised rewards and punishments affect behavior? Studies in psychology suggest that delayed rewards and punishments have relatively little effect on behavior. Thus, one well-known criticism of our criminal justice system is that by the time criminals are incarcerated, the psychological link between crime and punishment has been lost. So, it is by no means clear that the fear of hell typically produces moral action; surely moral behavior is more commonly motivated by a desire to help others (or at least to avoid hurting them), by self-interest ("Honesty is the best policy"), or simply by the desire to do what is right.

Fifth, and most important, the divine motivator view leaves too many questions unanswered. Even if it is true, it tells us little about God's relation to ethics, for it tells us only that God sanctions morality by supplying rewards and punishments. It does not get at the more fundamental questions such as, "Could there be a right and a wrong if there were no God?" or "Does God have any moral obligations?"

Some of my criticisms of the divine motivator view may raise questions about the way the Bible is being used in this book, since those who defend the traditional doctrine of hell usually do so because they believe that doctrine to be biblical. Thus, a word or two about my use of the Bible may be appropriate before going on to further views concerning the relation between God and ethics. First, we must never allow a simple identification between what the Bible says and what it is commonly thought to say. By all accounts, the Bible is easily misinterpreted. Moreover, religious communities of all types tend to build up an accretion of beliefs, and in Christian communities it is common for people to suppose that whatever they believe about theology (or whatever is often asserted by church leaders) is biblical. But the large number of disagreements between Christian denominations surely indicates that many such beliefs are not biblical—either that or the Bible contains many conflicting doctrines.

I cannot here discuss in detail whether the traditional doctrine of hell is biblical. Of course it cannot be denied that the Gospel of Matthew represents Jesus as saying, of those who ignore the needy, that "they will go away into eternal punishment" (Matthew 25:46). But are we meant to read such passages literally? I submit that it would be a dubious principle of interpretation which encourages us to read the relatively fragmentary and underdeveloped passages concerning hell in such a way that they conflict with the major scriptural themes of divine love and justice. Perhaps the biblical passages on divine punishment admit of more than one interpretation, e.g., that eternal punishment is eternal *destruction* (the annihilation of the soul), or that punishment in the afterlife is not merely retributive but reformative (and hence not utterly inescapable).

Second, the author assumes that the Bible is authoritative for Christian theology, but not that it is infallible. To some this no doubt seems a contradiction. I submit, however, that treating sources of knowledge as *authoritative but not infallible* is a pervasive feature of the human epistemological situation. Experts in any field are commonly regarded as authoritative, but not infallible. For example, we often wisely accept a doctor's diagnosis without supposing that she never makes mistakes. And we place a tremendous amount of trust in our own senses, yet we know that they sometimes mislead us—there are optical illusions and hallucinations. Now, when authorities give conflicting claims, we cannot accept all that they say. If two doctors disagree about a diagnosis, we cannot (reasonably) accept both diagnoses. We may decide that one of the doctors has better credentials. Or we may consult a third doctor—a specialist—who has more authority in the relevant area. Or we may simply suspend judgment, if we can find no good reason for placing one authority over the other.

For reasons already given, I think that those who hold that the traditional doctrine of hell is biblical must hold that the Bible gives conflicting messages about God's love. On the one hand, in affirming His love for each person, it affirms His unceasing desire for each person's long-term best interest. On the other hand, if the Bible affirms the doctrine of hell (as standardly conceived), it affirms that God will treat some people in a way that is clearly not in their long-term best interest. (Indeed, what could possibly be less in a person's long-term best interest than being eternally damned?) So, if the Bible teaches the doctrine of hell, then it presents us with conflicting messages about divine love. Which of the messages should we take as authoritative? My own response would be that if such conflicts occur, we ought always to give precedence to major scriptural themes rather than to relatively underdeveloped or fragmentary materials. This would imply acceptance of scriptural teaching about God's love if it conflicts with the relatively fragmentary materials about the precise nature of divine punishment in the afterlife.

II. THE DIVINE COMMAND THEORY

All Christians agree that if an act is morally right, then it is God's will that we perform it. Moreover, they agree that if God wills that we perform an act, then that act is morally right.[4] But something crucial turns on the precise way in which God's will and moral rightness are connected. To paraphrase the question Socrates asked Euthyphro: Is an act right simply because God approves of it, or does God approve of a given act because it is right?[5] Divine command theorists take the first horn of this dilemma. More precisely, on the divine command theory (DC) of ethics,

> (DC) An act is morally right if and only if, and *because*, God wills that it be performed.[6]

Many ordinary Christians assume that (DC) is true, and it was held by such famous theologians as William of Ockham (c.1285-1349), Martin Luther (1483-1546), and Emil Brunner (1889-1966).[7] But the divine command view has been a minority position among Christian philosophers and theologians throughout church history. There are essentially two reasons for this. First, the problem of arbitrariness.

On the divine command view, acts are right *because* God wills or approves of them (the first horn of Euthyphro's dilemma). But if acts are right because God approves of them, then it follows that torture, rape, stealing, etc. would be right if God approved of them. This is, to put it mildly, hard to believe; surely torture, rape, stealing, etc. would not be right even if God did approve of them. But then it must be that God wills actions *because they are right* (the second horn of Euthyphro's dilemma), not that they are right because He wills them. We can sum up this problem as follows:

> (1) If acts are right because God approves of them, then torture would be right if God approved of it.
> (2) But torture would not be right even if God approved of it.

So,

> (3) Acts are not right because God approves of them.

The conclusion here, (3), follows logically from the premises (1) and (2). But are the premises true? Premise (1) seems undeniable. If it is God's approval that makes an act right, then if God approves of torture (or rape, etc.), it is right. Premise (2) is more likely to come in for criticism. Some people will say, "But God would never will something cruel like torture. He is, after all, a perfectly good Being." There are at least two important replies to this objection. First, it is not (strictly speaking) relevant. It might be that your friend Smith would never steal anything, but we can still reasonably ask, "If Smith *were* to steal something, should he make amends?" And presumably, the answer is "Yes." In other words, a purely hypothetical question can still have an answer. So, even if God would not approve of torture, it is still true, according to the divine command theory, that *if* He were to approve of torture, *then* torture would be right.

Second, and more importantly, what can the divine command theorist mean by saying that God is *good* (and hence would not approve of torture)? In general, to say that something is good is to say that it meets certain relevant standards. A good painting meets certain aesthetic standards; a good knife is one that cuts well; a good father is one that can be expected to behave in certain specified ways. A good Deity, then, is presumably one whose acts accord with certain standards. This is not to say that creatures *set* the standards. Of course they do not. It is merely to say that there must *be* some standards for the expression "God is good" to have any content. But on the divine command view it seems that there are no such standards. To say that God is good is apparently to say that God approves of His own acts, or that He wills whatever acts He performs. So, how can the divine command theorist confidently assert that God would not approve of torture since He is good? If God did approve of torture (rape, theft, etc.), He would still be good from the point of view of the divine command theory.

Now the point being made here is crucial and needs to be underscored: (DC) places no restrictions on what God can will, and hence no restrictions on what can count as good. Suppose someone tried to defend (DC) by saying, "We know that God would never approve of torture (lying, etc.) *because He is loving.* Love is the standard Christians have in mind when they say that God is good." Unfortunately, this defense is not available to the divine command theorist. For to say that God is loving is to say much more than that He approves of whatever acts He performs. A selfish or cruel person could conceivably approve of his own actions in every case. A loving person is, at least in part, one who manifests a concern for the fulfillment of others. So to say that God is loving is to say that there are restrictions on what God can approve (or will), *if He is to remain good.* A God who neglected His creatures or actively sought to undermine their fulfillment would not be good, according to Christian theology.

But what can restrict God's will? It would seem that there are only two possible candidates: something outside of God or some aspect of God other than His will. Obviously, the divine command theorist will reject the idea that something outside of God restricts His will. But could the divine command theorist hold, as some theologians have, that God's will is restricted by His own nature or character? For example, it has been claimed that God's nature is *unalterably* loving and just, and hence that God cannot violate his nature by performing an unloving or unjust act. Notice, however, that this view places the ultimate source of moral value outside of God's will, in his unalterable nature or character; from this perspective, it is God's inability to will acts *contrary to His loving nature* which guarantees the goodness of His commands. Thus, to place restrictions on God's will is to admit that something outside of His will determines what is right. So, the "unalterable nature" approach is not open to the divine command theorist.

It appears, then, that if the divine command theory is true, nothing prevents our ethics from being, at bottom, purely arbitrary; any set of ethical norms or principles could be true. It just happens that God approves of love— He might have approved of hatred, violence, lying, etc. Moreover, there is nothing to stop God from changing his will in the future. Presently, He approves of love, but next week He may approve of hate. To say this cannot happen is to imply that there are restrictions on God's will, and as we have just seen, the divine command theorist is unable to allow for such restrictions. It is even useless to allege that once God wills something, He cannot change His mind, for this is to suppose that God is obligated to be consistent or faithful. But what is to stop God from disapproving of consistency and faithfulness, if the divine command theory is true? Nothing.

Now, the divine command theorist may bite the bullet. He may say, "Perhaps torture would be right if God approved of it. God can make things right or wrong as

He pleases. Who are you to put limits on God?" But it is hard to see how torture could become right just by gaining the approval of a powerful person. How could torture be right while involving the suffering, degradation, and will to dominate which comprise it? (And any act not involving such negative features would not count as torture.) Thus, it again appears that the attempt to deny premise (2), "Torture wouldn't be right even if God willed it," puts the divine goodness in a disturbingly arbitrary light. In short, premise (2) stands up well under criticism.

Christians are rightly suspicious, of course, about any claim of the form, "Even God can't do that." Yet virtually all theologians agree that there are things God cannot do. He cannot, for example, bring it about that He both does and does not exist (at one and the same time). He cannot make a figure that is both perfectly round and perfectly square. He cannot *force* a person to repent *freely*. Similarly, it seems that He cannot make torture permissible. It just is not the kind of thing that could be made permissible, even by God.[8]

So, it appears that there are some moral truths which God, as an omniscient being, knows, and which He cannot make false. This leaves it open what makes such truths true, and in particular whether their truth is independent of God's own nature or is somehow guaranteed by His nature. Enough has been said, however, to indicate why it is unacceptable to view God's commands as merely arbitrary.

In addition to the arbitrariness problem, the divine command theory raises nontrivial epistemic questions, i.e., questions about our *knowledge* of ethics. For example, "Unless we have some way of knowing what God wills, (DC) fails to provide us with any practical direction. How, according to divine command theorists, can we know what God wills?" Two main answers have been offered to this question by Christians. First, some have claimed that we know what God wills *only* through special revelation, such as the Bible or church tradition. Special revelation is defined as a set of truths God has revealed which are not accessible to unaided human cognitive faculties—e.g., truths available through miracles, visions, or inspired writings. The contrast is with general revelation, which is defined as "truths available through the normal human cognitive faculties given by God." Second, some have claimed that we know the will of God through general revelation *as well as* special revelation. Both of these views lead to problems for the divine command theorist.

Let us begin by considering the view, held by some, that the Bible is the only source of information about God's will. If we assume that the Bible alone reveals God's will, we must acknowledge that there are many ethical issues the Bible does not discuss. Examples include contraception, genetic engineering, test-tube babies, and chemical warfare. Not only are these practices never mentioned in the Bible, but it is doubtful whether any biblical principle clearly forbids or permits them. So, this "Bible only" view leaves us without guidance on a range of significant moral issues. Moreover, as regards those moral issues which *are* treated in the Bible, significant problems of interpretation often arise. For example, what exactly does the Bible say about war? Christian theologians have been wrangling over that for centuries. What does the Bible teach about capital punishment? Again, it is not easy to sort this out. Some Christians think it is obvious that capital punishment is ruled out by the Sermon on the Mount; others appeal to the Old Testament to justify the practice. So, if the Bible is our sole source of knowledge about God's will, we have no way of knowing what to do in many moral situations.

One final snag in the "Bible only" view is this: the Bible itself teaches that moral truths are revealed outside the Scriptures. When the author of Proverbs says, "Go to the ant, O sluggard; consider her ways and be wise" (6:6), he is precisely saying that certain moral truths can be learned via observation and reflection—e.g., that laziness is a vice, not a virtue. So, the "Bible only" view runs into the embarrassment that the Bible (in effect) endorses general revelation. And so, if the Bible is authoritative, we cannot regard it as the only source of information about the will of God.

Some divine command theorists, still emphasizing the importance of special revelation, accept *church tradition* as a further source of knowledge about God's will. However, to appeal to tradition in this way is to make an appeal to authority, and not all appeals to authority are rational. In order for an appeal to authority to be rational, we must have good reasons for thinking that the authority in question is "in the know." In "mundane" matters, such reasons are often available—which explains why dictionaries, encyclopedias, textbooks, scientists, maps, and physicians are regularly consulted. The appeal to such authorities is rational, in part, because the relevant experts have based their judgments upon objective evidence. But arguments from authority are often misused, as when famous athletes make pronouncements about the nutritional value of breakfast cereals, or when scientists make pronouncements outside their special fields (e.g., on moral issues).[9]

Do we have reason to suppose that church traditions are based on objective evidence? Considerations of space do not permit a detailed discussion of this important question here. (Each claim to special authority must be evaluated on its merits, and hence there is no way to treat the matter adequately in short compass.) However, one can say that the appeal to tradition, unless it is accompanied by an explanation of how the relevant religious bodies or ecclesiastical authorities *know*, is weak. Moreover, it is plain that Christians cannot agree among themselves concerning whom the relevant authorities are. Eastern Orthodox Christians do not accept the authority of the Roman Catholic pope, and Roman Catholics do not accept the authority of the Protestant traditions. So, even people who believe in the same God find it very difficult to agree on which humans (or groups of humans), if any, can make authoritative pronouncements concerning the will of God.

Divine command theorists who endorse general revelation run into a different sort of problem. "General revelation" simply refers to the things we humans can learn through the powers of observation and reasoning God has given us. Now, what does come to us through these powers? Well, we do not just look at acts and "see" that God wills or does not will them. Rather, we see that some acts are beneficial, and some harmful, that some acts promote close personal relationships, and some do not, that some involve treating people equally, and others do not and so on. What this means, philosophically, is that the divine command theorist must combine (DC) with some other views about ethics if he is to have a theory of ethics with practical application. So, even if (DC) is true, we shall need considerable aid from philosophy and/or systematic theology if we are to arrive at reflective answers on a full range of moral issues. Fortunately, our first criticism of the divine command theory suggests how such aid might be possible. If God wills things because He sees that they are right, it is plausible to suppose that *acts have features in virtue of which they are right.* Perhaps we can learn to recognize these features. Though of course we could never see into things as clearly or as deeply as God, we might be able to "think His thoughts after Him" in a modest way—but adequate to the achievement of a moral life.

III. THE MODAL VIEW

Recall our paraphrase of the question Socrates asked Euthyphro: Are acts right because God wills them or does God will them because they are right? So far I have been arguing against a "Yes" answer to the first horn of this dilemma; that is, I have been trying to show that God cannot make just anything right by approving of it (or make just anything wrong by disapproving of it). And so it appears that I must take the second horn of the dilemma: I must say that God wills or approves of acts because they are right.

But does this imply that there is a standard of goodness independent of God's will? If so, won't it follow that God is obligated to will only what is in accord with that standard? And does that in turn imply a limitation on God? It may thus appear that the second horn of Euthyphro's dilemma is as problematic as the first.

Following Richard Swinburne, a contemporary British philosopher, I shall argue that there is a way out of the dilemma.[10] The way out turns on the *modes* in which a proposition can be true, and hence I call it the 'modal' view. Some propositions (statements) are *necessarily* true, according to most philosophers. These are propositions whose negations involve a logical or mathematical impossibility. For example, take the proposition "All dogs are dogs." This (admittedly trivial) statement is not only true, but necessarily true, because its negation "Some dogs are not dogs" involves a logical inconsistency. From the standpoint of logic, it just is not possible for something to both be a dog and not be a dog (at one and the same time). Similarly, "All husbands are male" and "Nothing can be red all over and green all over at the same time" are necessary truths. For nothing could be a husband without being a male spouse; and if something is red and green in the same respect and at the same time, then it is red and not red in the same respect and at the same time, which is logically impossible.

Necessity in one mode in which a proposition can be true. But not all truths are necessary truths. For example, "Some husbands own Fords" is true, but not necessarily true; it is logically possible that only women or bachelors should own Fords. (That is, there is no logical inconsistency in this supposition. We know it is false by observation, not by logical analysis.) Indeed, it is logically possible that there be no Fords at all. If Henry Ford had been killed early in life, or died of some childhood disease, perhaps there would now be no Ford automobiles. But, as a matter of fact, there are Fords, and some husbands own them. Such propositions, which are true but not necessarily true, are said to be *contingent* truths.

The simple examples I have given so far may mislead by suggesting that it is always easy to spot a necessary truth. It is not. For example, mathematical statements are usually thought to be necessarily true if they are true at all. "The square of the hypotenuse of a right triangle is equal to the sum of the squares of the sides" is thus thought to be a necessary truth. But it took mathematical genius to discover the Pythagorean Theorem. And the truth value of some mathematical statements is simply unknown. For example, Goldbach's Conjecture, that every even number greater than two is equal to the sum of two primes, has never been proved or disproved. But *if* it is true, it is presumably necessarily true. And a significant portion of philosophical debate is given over to the question of whether certain statements are necessarily true; for example, "Every event has a cause," "There could be no space unless there were physical objects," and "God exists."

Why does it matter whether a proposition is necessary or contingent? For our purposes, it matters because most Christian philosophers and theologians have held that God cannot, by willing it, make a truth necessary. Nor can He, by willing it, make a necessary truth false. In other words, necessary truths do not depend on God's will. This is so because if it is "up to God" whether a given truth is necessary, then there are no necessary truths. For example, if God could make "All husbands are male" *contingent*, then He could make it false. In other words, if this statement is contingent, then it must be within God's power to bring about a situation in which at least one husband is not male. But if God can bring about such a situation, it immediately follows that "All husbands are male" is not *necessarily* true, there being a possible circumstance in which it would be false; namely, the circumstance in which God creates a nonmale husband. So, if there are necessary truths, there necessity cannot result from divine volition.

God cannot make necessary truths false, because to do so He would have to be able to make contradictions true. For example, to make "All husbands are male" false, He would have to be able to make "Some husbands are not male" true, and hence He would have to be able to make "Some married males are not male" true. But even God cannot create nonmale males, round squares, or bad virtues. Nor can He cause himself both to exist and not to exist at the same time. In short, when Christian theologians and philosophers have said that God was omnipotent, they have usually qualified this by saying that God can do (roughly) those things which it is *logically possible* for Him to do. This is a wise qualification, because if God can make contradictions true, then anything goes. He can both love us and not love us, save us without saving us, damn us while giving us eternal bliss, and so on. Surely this is all nonsense—it simply does not make any logical sense to suppose that God (or anyone else) could do such things. The point, once again, is that necessary truths are true independently of God's will. He cannot make a statement such as "Some bachelors are married" true. Necessarily, all bachelors are unmarried. Of course, God can cause a man to be a bachelor; but in so doing, He must cause him to be unmarried. The conceptual link between *being a bachelor* and *being unmarried* is not something that can be broken by an act of will.

Please note that I am not denying that God could cause us to use the word 'bachelor' in a different way. We are really talking about concepts at this point, not about the words that express those concepts. The English word 'bachelor' might have been used to mean something besides "unmarried adult human male." Perhaps we might have used the word 'zanger' where we now use 'bachelor.' In that case the proposition we now express with the words "All bachelors are unmarried" would be expressed

by the words "All zangers are unmarried." The truth "behind the words" remains the same—an unmarried adult
human male cannot (at the same time) be married.

While it seems to me that God cannot by willing it
make necessary truths true (or false), He has a tremendous amount of control over which propositions are contingently true. For example, God did not have to create
anything. So, the fact that there is a universe at all is a
contingent truth, dependent on the will of God. Moreover, God could have created different creatures than He
has in fact created. So, "There are dogs" is a contingent
truth. Even propositions we make true by acts of free will,
such as "Jones lied about his qualifications for the job," are
permitted by God to be true. (God could have made the
statement false by stopping Jones's tongue as he was about
to speak.)

The question we are leading up to is this: Are moral
truths necessary or contingent? In a nutshell, Swinburne's
answer is that some are necessary and some are contingent. The necessary truths are true independently of God's
will, the contingent one's depend for their truth on
his will.

An example may help. Suppose I borrowed some money
from a friend, promising to pay it back by next Wednesday.
In such circumstances, the statement "I ought to pay my
friend the money by next Wednesday" would appear to be
a *contingent* truth. Its truth depends on certain contingent
facts, like the fact that I exist, the fact that I borrowed the
money, and the fact that I promised to pay it back by a
certain date. Presumably, these facts were not somehow
necessitated by logic; there may have been strong economic pressures on me, to be sure, but that is an entirely
different matter. Logically speaking, I might have borrowed
the money from someone else, promised to pay it back
Thursday instead of Wednesday, or simply gone without it.
So, it's a contingent truth that I ought to pay the money
back to my friend by next Wednesday.

Swinburne thinks that each contingent moral truth is explained by a more general necessary moral truth that applies to the situation in question. In the case we are discussing, it might be "One ought to pay one's debts" or "One ought to keep one's promises." Swinburne stresses that his view does not depend on whether he has managed to give any correct examples of necessary moral truths. He seems to think that although we may argue about *which* moral truths are necessary, we are bound to hold that *some* moral truths are necessary. And if we grant him this much, he offers us a shrewd response to Euthyphro's dilemma.

Does God approve of acts because they are right? Yes, in the case of acts that are "necessarily obligatory."[11] That is, some propositions of the form, "One ought to do X" are necessary truths. God cannot make them false, anymore than He can make "$1 + 1 = 2$" or "All dogs are dogs" false. This "inability" to make such statements false does not impugn His deity, for omnipotence does not imply an ability to do what is logically impossible. Thus, some acts— the necessarily obligatory ones—are such that God "sees" them to be right, and so wills that they be done. If God were to disapprove of such acts, He would be in error. But of course He does not disapprove of them, because He is omniscient and knows that they are right.

It is natural at this point to ask a very deep philosophical question: "What is the source of necessity? What makes necessary truths necessary?" It is fair to say that no one really knows. Philosophers have suggested a variety of answers. Plato himself thought that such truths were simply part of the structure of reality, independent of the physical universe. Some theologians have thought that these truths were in some way dependent on God's immutable *nature*, though not on His *will* (for reasons we have been discussing). It seems to me that we do not need to know the answer to this question, in order to accept the modal view. Suppose, for example, that Plato was right, that there are some necessary truths which do not depend on either

God's will or His nature. Would it somehow follow from this that god is not worthy of worship? It seems to me that it would not. He would still be omniscient and perfectly morally good. He would still be the almighty Creator of heaven and earth. He would still be Lord and Redeemer. Surely these qualities are sufficient to guarantee that God is worthy of worship. And after all, it is not as if the necessary moral truths were personal agents who are in a position to interfere with God's activities; they no more interfere with God's activities than mathematical truths do. They are simply truths about morality, independent of God's will, perhaps dependent on His nature, perhaps not.

Are some acts right because God will them? Yes, in the case of *some* "contingently obligatory" actions.[12] As Creator, God stands to us in a role analogous to that of our parents. He is our benefactor, and it is plausible to suppose that we owe a debt of gratitude to our benefactors. Moreover, as Swinburne points out, God, as Creator, is owner of the inanimate world, and the owner of property has the right to tell those to whom he has loaned it what they are allowed to do with it. So, as Creator, God has the right to make certain demands upon us, and those demands create obligations. Consider an analogy. When a mother demands that her child go to bed at a certain time, this (normally) creates an obligation for the child to go to bed at the specified time. And when a father loans his daughter the car, demanding that it be returned at a certain time, we (normally) allow that she has an obligation to return the car at the specified time. Similarly, God might demand that we keep the Sabbath or tithe; then, Sabbath-keeping or tithing would be obligatory, not because "One ought to keep the Sabbath" or "One ought to tithe" are necessary truths, but just because, as Creator, God has the right to make such demands. And since we owe him a debt of gratitude, these demands create obligations for us.

Perhaps it seems that I am now contradicting myself: "Wasn't it the point of the last section that God cannot create a moral obligation to do X just by willing X? Now you seem to be going back on that." No, I am not here reversing my position. The point of the last section was that God cannot make *just any act* right by approving it, not can He make *just any act* wrong by disapproving it. And I still insist on that. For example, God cannot make ingratitude to Himself right (and of course He would not do this because He is omniscient, and knows that creatures owe a debt of gratitude to their Creator). Or again, having promised to save us through faith in His Son, God cannot go back on His promise (while maintaining His moral perfection) simply by willing that promises no longer be kept. On the other hand, as we have seen, not every moral truth is a necessary truth. Whether we have an obligation to do X in some cases simply depends on whether God has demanded that we do X, just as whether children have an obligation in some cases depends on what demands their parents have placed on them. (Of course, since our debt of gratitude to God is much greater than our debt to our parents, God's demands have a special status.)

So, I endorse the main outlines of Swinburne's view of the relation between God and ethics, or what I here call the 'modal view.' However, I think that an adequate defense of the modal view must respond to the common allegation that there are no necessary moral truths. And I do not think this is a trivial task, since many suppose that there is an exception to every moral rule or principle. Consider one of Swinburne's examples, "One ought to pay one's debts." This seems not to be a necessary truth, because there are cases in which it seems that one ought not to pay one's debts. To take an extreme case, suppose I have promised to pay off a loan of two hundred dollars to my friend. He shows up on the agreed upon day and demands the money, saying he plans to buy a gun with the money and murder someone. And suppose I see he is not joking. Should I pay the debt as promised? Surely not. Many of our common moral judgments are generally true, but subject to exceptions. And that is a way of saying that they are not necessary truths, that is, true in every circumstance. The problem is that most, if not all, traditional moral rules conflict with others in certain special cases. This is a matter that we shall discuss in detail in Chapter 4. In the meantime, we shall examine a variety of principles which philosophers have defended as foundational and exceptionless moral truths; in Chapter 5 I shall defend my own candidate for this position. I believe, however, that it will greatly aid us to have a rough sketch of my proposed "Christian teleological view" before going any further.

IV. THE CHRISTIAN TELEOLOGICAL VIEW

Telos is the ancient Greek word for end, goal, or fulfillment. The general idea of a teleological view of ethics is that acts are said to be right or wrong according to whether or not they promote a certain end or goal. Different teleological theories recommend different ends. The *telos* of the Christian teleological view might be called "the Kingdom (or society) of God." From this perspective, God creates the human race for a certain end, namely, for harmonious relationships with God and with the other creatures God has made. God extends His love to humans freely, and so He seeks a freely chosen response of love on our part. Loving God involves loving the things He has made, and especially the other free creatures He has made. Moreover, it is in harmonious relations with God and with other free creatures that we find our highest good, our most complete fulfillment. To be unethical is to act in ways that hinder the realization of the Kingdom of God. And although the Kingdom of God cannot be fully realized this side of death, there is an earthly stage of the Kingdom which we can and must participate in now.

We may sum up the Christian teleological view as follows:

(CT)   An act is right if and only if it promotes the Kingdom of God.

Naturally, those who adhere to (CT) presuppose that God exists. So, in all likelihood, nontheists will find (CT) unattractive. And since this is a book on ethics, not a book on the philosophy of religion, I cannot provide a full discussion of the rationality of belief in God; however, in Chapter 5 I do offer reasons for supposing that belief in God is supported to some degree by philosophical reflections on the nature of morality. In the meantime, the nontheist may wish to bear in mind the possibility of a teleological view structurally similar to (CT), but not involving God. This secular analogue would claim that an act is right if and only if it promotes a well-functioning community of human persons. In Chapter 5 I shall argue that (CT) makes more sense of the moral life than this secular analogue does.

The reader will recall that we cannot take the modal view of the relation between God and ethics unless there are some necessary moral truths. And while a full discussion of the merits of (CT) must await Chapter 5, it will be useful to consider, at this juncture, whether (CT) is necessary if it is true at all. I believe that, from a Christian point of view, "One ought to promote the Kingdom of God" must surely be regarded as exceptionless. (How, from the Christian perspective, could it ever be permissible *not* to promote the Kingdom of God?) But someone might try to object that the principle is not necessary, because it presupposes the existence of creatures (members of the Kingdom) whose existence is not necessary, since God created them freely. In other words, "One ought to promote the Kingdom of God" was not true until God brought some creatures into existence. Hence, it is not *necessarily* true; God made it true by creating certain kinds of entities.

Putting this objection in other words may help to clarify it. The Christian teleological view implies that if an act does not promote the Kingdom, it is not right. Now, what about acts performed by God prior to creation? Did they promote

the Kingdom? If not, then they were not right, according
to this principle. Does this mean that God was obligated
to promote a Kingdom, and hence that He was *obligated*
to create (as the first step in promoting a Kingdom)? If so,
then what becomes of the standard Christian idea that God
created freely and not of necessity?

Obviously these questions lure us into highly abstract
metaphysical territory. I have two responses. The first assumes that traditional Christian view that God is a Trinity
of persons, the second does not. (1) If God is a Trinity of
persons, then God is a sort of community—three divine
persons in relationship. Thus, the divine persons were in
a position to promote a harmonious community among
themselves prior to (and without any intention of) creating
anything. If 'Kingdom' means 'community', the doctrine
of the Trinity allows that the members of the Trinity were
always promoting the Kingdom. That a harmonious community of divine persons existed prior to creation seems
to be implied by some passages in the Bible; for example,
the Gospel of John represents Jesus as praying, "Father,
glorify thou me in thy own presence with the glory which
I had with thee before the world was made" (17:5). So,
the doctrine of the Trinity suggests that the divine persons
have always been promoting a Kingdom (community) of
persons; it would not have been right for one of the persons of the Trinity to try to destroy the community of
divine persons. And while there is no obligation to create,
once the divine persons freely create other persons, then
a harmonious community of all persons must be sought.[13]
(2) Quite apart from the doctrine of the Trinity, there is
still reason to suppose that something in the logical vicin-
ity of (CT) is a necessary truth. Consider the conditional
(if-then) proposition: *Given certain circumstances, one
ought to promote a harmonious community among persons.* "Certain circumstances" is admittedly vague, but I
have in mind chiefly such circumstances as (a) there is
a plurality of persons and (b) it is *possible* to promote

harmony among them. Given these circumstances, I think
that many would accept "Promote harmonious relationships" as an exceptionless principle. Indeed, "If there is
a plurality of persons and it is possible to promote harmonious relations among them, then one ought to do so"
would be accepted as a necessary truth by many. From a
Christian point of view, it is difficult to think of circumstances in which it could be false. Could it *under any
circumstances* be right to promote discord—not simply as
a means to an end or as the foreseen (though unintended)
result of one's act—*but as the primary goal of one's acts?*
Not, I think, from a Christian point of view. I conclude that
we have here a necessary moral truth from the standpoint
of Christian theology. Moreover, as a conditional (if-then)
proposition, it apparently holds whether God is a Trinity or
not. Indeed, the conditional may be regarded as necessary
from a secular standpoint also, for on the assumption that
Plato was correct in speaking of truths being necessary independently of concrete existence, such a conditional may
be necessary even if there is no God.[14]

It seems, then, that the Christian teleological view can
be combined with the modal view of the relation between
God and ethics. For (CT)—or something very close to it—
appears to be a necessary truth. As we saw in the last
section, this means that God approves of some acts because they are right, i.e., because they are necessary for
the promotion of His Kingdom. And it is not the case
that these acts are right because God approves of them.
If God were to approve of acts that are destructive of
community, e.g., if God were to approve (in general) of
murder, rape, theft, and torture, He would be wrong in
so doing.

The Christian teleological view provides a framework
for discussing any ethical issue. The idea is that God has
indicated the overall goal He seeks, and has revealed certain key moral rules (often called "commandments") that
accrue to this goal; for the rest, he gives us minds to think

things out. Where simple rules conflict, we must do what seems most likely to promote the Kingdom of God. This is not to suggest that there are no hard cases in ethics; there are many situations in which it is difficult to see what is right, and hence there is always the potential for self-deception and sophistry. But we have hope of making headway only if we have a basic perspective from which to carry out our reflections.

Three features of the Christian teleological view are worth keeping in mind. First, a point about means and ends. Many crimes and wicked deeds have been rationalized by appeal to the principle that the end justifies the means. But notice that on the present view the end includes harmonious relations with God and our fellow creatures. This end, we might say, determines the means. That is, since the goal here is precisely harmonious personal and social relations (as opposed, e.g., to desire-satisfaction), the view contains some built-in resistance to facile rationalization (one cannot mistreat people, show them disrespect, cheat them, etc., and expect to have harmonious relations with them). This is not to say, of course, that horrible things cannot be done in the name of the Kingdom of God. History makes it abundantly clear that wicked deeds can be done in the name of Christian ends. But when such abuses occur, it is usually easy to identify a failure to think *clearly* within the Christian teleological scheme as lying at the root of the abuse.

Second, much of the working out of the Christian teleological view is an empirical matter. What institutions, practices, rules, and conditions of human existence in fact produce significant disharmony among God's creatures? It is these things the Christian is at war against. And it is from this base that a radical Christian critique of our culture's practices and institutions must be launched. But the Bible contains a basic vision, not a detailed ethical system. It seems plain that part of what God wants us to do is to learn to think ethically, to learn to see what forms of behavior (and social organization) advance His Kingdom, and what forms frustrate it.

Third, on the Christian teleological view, we see that ethical rules and principles are not designed to frustrate human nature, but to fulfill it. Jesus once said that the Sabbath was made for man and not man for the Sabbath (Mark 2:27). Do we dare say, with Frankena, that morality was made for humans and not humans for morality?[15] That is indeed the situation from the perspective of the Christian teleological view. And this book is an attempt to work out a partial system of ethics from that point of view. But we must now consider some of its main theoretical competitors.

Consequentialism 3

What makes an act right or wrong? This question has preoccupied philosophical ethicists through the centuries. Attempts to answer it have produced the great ethical perspectives—utilitarianism, contractarianism, egoism, and so on. While it is reasonable to regret that philosophers have at times been absorbed in this basic issue to the neglect of more practical ethical concerns, it is nevertheless important to be aware of the fundamental alternative views. We cannot think clearly about practical issues unless we have a sense for the more ultimate issues into which ethical disputes so often resolve themselves.

Consequentialists hold that it is the consequences of an act that make it right or wrong. When we judge that an act is wrong because of the harm it brings about, or that it is right because it relieves suffering, we are thinking in a consequentialist way. There are a number of types of consequentialism. The "Christian teleological view" outlined in the previous chapter is one type, which says that acts are right or wrong depending on whether they promote the Kingdom of God. In this chapter we will examine three well-known, alternative types of consequentialism: ethical egoism, act utilitarianism, and rule utilitarianism.

I. ETHICAL EGOISM

Roughly put, ethical egoism is the view that one ought always to act in one's own best interest. But what is in one's own best interest? Most ethical egoists, following

59

in the steps of such ancient Greek philosophers as Democritus and Epicurus, have answered, "Pleasure." That is, ethical egoists are typically hedonists. It would in principle be possible for an ethical egoist to say, "No, it is not pleasure that is in my best interest; it is knowledge or beauty or intimate personal relationships." But since, as a matter of historical fact, egoists have typically held that their own pleasure is in their best interests, that is the view we shall consider.[1]

It is convenient to formulate the basic thesis of egoism more precisely.[2] According to the ethical egoist, an agent (the one who performs the act) is doing the right thing, when he maximizes his own satisfaction. We might think of each act as producing a certain amount of "agent-satisfaction," where agent-satisfaction is determined as follows: add up all the pleasure the act would cause for its agent; next, add up all the displeasure or pain the act would cause for its agent; finally subtract the pain from the pleasure. Using the technical concept of agent-satisfaction, we can say that ethical egoism (EE) is the view that:

> (EE)   An act is right if and only if no alternative to that act produces more agent-satisfaction than it does.

To see how the view is supposed to work, consider an example: I am trying to decide whether to go on vacation to Hawaii. I consider the alternatives: (a) stay home and do nothing, (b) give the money to the poor, (c) take the vacation to Hawaii, (d) take a cheaper vacation, etc. Let's suppose that (c) would yield the most agent-satisfaction. Then it is the morally right thing to do. It would be wrong to do (a), (b), or (d). (If two alternatives would produce the same amount of agent-satisfaction, then either of them would be right from a moral point of view, assuming no other alternative has more agent-satisfaction.)

Several points of clarification are in order. First, in calculating agent-satisfaction, one must make reasonable estimates of expected pleasure. This requires taking the long

term into account. The egoist is an advocate of *enlight-
ened* self-interest, not a mindless party animal who cannot
see that today's binge is tomorrow's health problem. In
fact, the egoist's concept of pleasure can be quite refined.
It may include the aesthetic pleasures of the concert hall
and art museum, the pleasure of a good conversation with
friends, and the pleasures of the intellect—as well as those
of fine food and drink. There is something in ethical egoism to attract all of us.

Second, an egoist need not be an egotist; he need not
be prideful or have too high an estimate of himself. In fact,
since most people dislike egotists and shun them, the egoist who derives pleasure from the company of other people
will take care to cultivate a pleasing degree of modesty.

Third, it is often mistakenly supposed that egoists cannot
act altruistically. Thus, it is assumed that if the alternative
uses of $2000 are (a) an expensive vacation to Hawaii or
(b) giving money to the poor, the egoist must choose (a).
But it all depends on what gives the egoist pleasure. If it is
in her psychological make-up to derive the most pleasure
from giving to charity, her principles will require an altruistic act.

Is ethical egoism true? The main argument in favor of
it rests on a particular theory of human motivation. This
theory is called *psychological egoism* (PE):

> (PE)   A human being always acts so as to maximize
> his own satisfaction.

Note that psychological egoism is not an ethical principle;
it does not say that anything is right or wrong. Rather, as its
name implies, it is a psychological theory. It says, in effect,
that there is a psychological law governing human behavior, so that no matter how altruistic a person may appear to
be, she is in fact simply behaving so as to maximize agent-
satisfaction. (Mother Teresa just happens to enjoy helping
poor people, while most of us prefer other pleasures.)

Given *psychological* egoism, people cannot help but act
as the *ethical* egoist says they should act, so it appears

that any other view of ethics is unrealistic. For, according to many philosophers, "ought implies can." That is, if one ought to do something, one can do it. And conversely, if one cannot do something, then one is not obligated to do it. For example, there are situations in which one can save a drowning man only if one can swim a mile. But suppose one cannot swim a mile. Then, in such a situation one would not be obligated to save the drowning man, for one cannot save him.[3] Now, what happens if one tries to behave so as *not* to maximize agent-satisfaction? The attempt is bound to fail, for assuming (PE) is a psychological law, maximization of agent-satisfaction is just what human behavior is all about. Hence, insofar, as alternatives to ethical egoism require one *not* to maximize agent-satisfaction, they are unrealistic.

This defense is no more plausible than the motivational theory that underlies it. And there are at least three important objections to psychological egoism. First, psychological egoism is clearly meant to be a scientific theory, subject to confirmation through empirical methods. But it has never been scientifically confirmed. It is true that some well-known psychologists have put forward theories of human motivation which attempt to explain all human acts in terms of "selfish," unlearned primary drives (e.g., hunger, thirst, elimination, sex, and sleep). If we add to this the idea that an agent never gives up one primary reward unless he expects to gain another (and preferred) primary reward, we can derive psychological egoism (or something very close to it).[4] But these ideas are speculative and remain unconfirmed. Moreover, there are conflicting views vying for attention. For example, Abraham Maslow holds that humans will not act from higher motives such as benevolence until certain primary drives are satisfied, but once these primary drives are satisfied, it becomes possible to act on higher motives. The point is that the topic of human motivation is very much under debate among psychologists, and no particular school of thought has been able to gain a clear evidential advantage. Therefore, psychological egoism remains one among many competing hypotheses about the springs of human action; it has not got the status of a law.

Moreover, what frequently comes to light in discussions of psychological egoism is that its defenders tend to regard it, not as an empirical theory, but as something true by definition, like, "All bachelors are unmarried." Thus, it may be said that people can only do what they in some sense *want* to do, for how could one do something if one did not *prefer* it to alternatives? And hence, individuals never do anything without getting *something* out of it for themselves, *some* kind of payoff (because they want to perform the act). But these attempts at an "armchair" defense of psychological egoism are misguided, for even if the premises are true, they do not settle the issue in question. Psychological egoism is not the view that people always get some kind of payoff or satisfaction from their actions; it is the view that an agent always (and of psychological necessity) *maximizes* his own satisfaction. It is one thing to say that Mother Teresa gets some kind of satisfaction from ministering to the poor in Calcutta, and another to say that with each act she performs she is getting the most pleasure possible out of all her alternatives. So, the "armchair" defense of psychological egoism fails.

Second, psychological egoism seems to conflict with our commonsense understanding of human motivation. Many acts are motivated by benevolent inclinations, apart from a consideration of alternatives. If we did stop to think for a moment, we might very well judge that such acts are not apt to maximize our own satisfaction. For example, suppose I take a child to the beach because I think she will enjoy it. Further, suppose she enjoys it very much and I do not mind a day at the beach, but later it occurs to me that getting some work done or hiking in the mountains would probably have been a lot more satisfying for me. In such a case the natural interpretation is that I did not act so as to maximize my satisfaction—I simply acted on a benevolent inclination.

Third, it seems clear that we sometimes knowingly act so as to frustrate our own best interests. Think of what happens when people are trying to rid themselves of a habit. A smoker may very well *know* that it is not going to increase his long-term satisfaction to have another cigarette. In fact, he may know that smoking is apt to cause serious health problems that will reduce his overall satisfaction considerably and possibly even result in an early death. Yet many an informed smoker goes on smoking. Why? Because instead of acting so as to maximize agent-satisfaction, we humans often go for short-term gratification without much thought for the long term. From a Christian point of view, this is an important part of the psychology of sin. We find it hard to delay gratification and so we often wind up in self-defeating activities.

So, it seems that psychological egoism is a weak reed for the ethical egoist to lean on. Attempts to confirm it have been unsuccessful; moreover, it conflicts with common sense. But, now, if psychological egoism is in doubt, the best defense of ethical egoism is no longer available.

Fred Feldman, a contemporary American philosopher, has observed that people sometimes try to defend ethical egoism along lines reminiscent of Adam Smith's famous "invisible hand" defense of capitalism: Things work out best for everyone if each individual behaves in an entirely self-interested way, since each individual is the one most able to see to his own happiness, and, more often than not, do-gooders wind up actually interfering with the happiness of others. But this argument is not one the ethical egoist can consistently endorse. Note the premise: "Things work out best for everyone if . . .". Who cares about *everyone*? The whole point of egoism is that only the satisfaction of the agent matters; the satisfaction of persons other than the agent is irrelevant to morality (except, as we shall see, in those cases where the pleasure of others has an indirect bearing on the agent's pleasure). So, the attempt to defend ethical egoism on the grounds that *wide acceptance of it would increase the general welfare* is hopelessly confused.[5]

Attempts to provide support for ethical egoism, then, are rather unimpressive. Are there any positive reasons to reject (EE)? There are at least two. First, the idea that only the satisfaction of the agent is directly relevant to the rightness or wrongness of an act seems strange. Suppose two acquaintances, Smith and Jones, are quarreling. Jones finds himself possessed of a desire to hit Smith. Jones calculates the satisfaction hitting Smith would bring to him (Jones). Of course, Jones has to take into account the pain he will feel when his fist collides with Smith's teeth, and the possible pain resulting from Smith's counterattack. What is odd here is that neither Smith's pain nor the inevitable effect on the relationship between Smith and Jones comes into the calculation. Or if these factors are brought in, it is only indirectly—e.g., if Smith feels pain, then he is likely to counterattack. But it seems odd that such factors as Smith's pain and the probable deterioration of the relationship need not come into the story at all (except indirectly, if they happen to affect the amount of pleasure available to Jones).

This example illustrates an important difference between ethical egoism and the Christian teleological point of view. From a Christian point of view, the *telos* is not the private pleasure of the individual agent, but a special type of community. And since a certain type of community life is our highest good, we cannot separate the good of the individual from the good of the group. No individual can attain his highest good at the expense of others, for his highest good is participation in a well-functioning society under God's authority.

A second objection to ethical egoism is that, in certain cases, it endorses acts that are plainly cruel and selfish.

Suppose a con man works his way into the ranks of a relief organization. Once he is in charge of enormous sums of money, he considers the possibility of absconding with funds reserved for famine relief. He works out a scheme for doing this which includes a change of identity for himself, so that it is highly unlikely that he will ever be found out. What should he do? If he is hard-hearted (and let us assume that he is), the con man will not agonize over the horrible suffering of the famine-stricken people. And unless their suffering somehow reduces his own pleasure, there is no reason for him to take the suffering into account. In fact, it is completely irrelevant to the rightness or wrongness of the act (according to ethical egoism). On the other hand, five million dollars would certainly enable the con man to live out his days in considerable comfort and pleasure. Hence, according to (EE), the con man would be doing the morally right thing by taking the money. However, given the fact that his theft will result in horrible suffering for thousands of people, (EE) gives a blatantly incorrect answer in this case. Any ethical perspective that conflicts with our considered judgments this drastically is unworthy of acceptance.

II. ACT UTILITARIANISM

Utilitarianism is probably the most important form of consequentialism in Western culture. It has a firm grip on most of us, at least in some areas of our moral thinking. American senators and congressmen, for example, routinely employ utilitarian reasoning in discussions about social policy. The cost-benefit analyses so commonly used in the various departments of government are also utilitarian in style.

Jeremy Bentham (1748-1832) and John Stuart Mill (1806-1873) are the original exponents of utilitarianism. For them it was far more than an academic theory about ethics; it was the center of a vision of a new social order, and as a matter of historical fact utilitarianism has been an important instrument of social reform. For example, it was a force behind many reforms in the English penal system in the 1800s.

According to act utilitarians,

> (AU)   An act is right if and only if no alternative produces more utility than it does.

'Utility' is a technical term here, and is calculated as follows: First, add up the satisfaction of everyone affected by the act; then add up the dissatisfaction of everyone affected by the act; finally, subtract the sum of the dissatisfaction from the sum of the satisfaction.[6]

Several comments may help to clarify (AU). First, what is meant here by satisfaction? Utilitarians do not always agree about the answer to this question. For Bentham and Mill, satisfaction meant pleasure, dissatisfaction meant pain. But more recent utilitarians typically have preference-fulfillment in mind. They hold that our best estimate of whether a person's desires are satisfied is the extent to which his preferences are fulfilled. The advantage here is epistemological; we can ask a person what his preferences are in a given situation, and observe whether his preferences are met. (And often we can make reasonable assumptions without asking. For example, it is a fair bet that most people on most occasions prefer to go on living, prefer to remain healthy, prefer not to be robbed, beaten, etc.) This may be a more objective process than trying to guess just what degree of pain or pleasure another individual is feeling at the moment.

Second, to get a feel for how (AU) is supposed to apply, consider a simple case. My brakes fail as I am driving down a steep hill. The street is a narrow one with buildings on both sides. I have three main alternatives. On the left is a sidewalk crowded with people. If I swerve left it seems clear that I will kill or injure at least half a dozen people. Straight ahead a pedestrian is crossing the street; it is clear that I will strike her if I stay on course. On the right there is a row of parked cars without occupants. I am not going

very fast, so I could plow into the parked cars without
serious injury to myself.

Let us assume that the people involved in the situation
have the ordinary preferences not to be injured or killed.
We might diagram my alternatives as follows:

A_1 = swerve left (injuring or killing six   = 1.
      pedestrains)

A_2 = stay on course (injuring or killing one   = 2.
      pedestrian)

A_3 = swerve right (incurring slight injuries to = 3.
      myself and damaging several cars)

The numbers on the right indicate the relative utilities of
the three alternative acts, 3 indicating the most utility—
actually, in this case, the least disutility—and 1 the least
utility (or most disutility). Since A_3 will produce the least
dissatisfaction for all affected, A_3 is the right thing to do,
according to act utilitarians. It would be wrong to do A_2,
and even worse to do A_1 . (Note that not all of my alternatives are listed. I could, for example, throw up my hands
and hide my eyes, or jump out of the car, or just sit there
and do nothing. But it does not matter that these alternatives are unlisted, since they presumably have less utility
than A_3.)

Third, notice how act utilitarianism differs from ethical
egoism. Instead of considering only agent-satisfaction, we
now consider the satisfaction of everyone affected by the
action. While act utilitarians would agree that each person's welfare is a good to that person, they would add that
the concept of the *general welfare* is central to the moral
point of view. Notice too that act utilitarianism is distinct
from normative relativism. The normative relativist tells us
to act in accord with the conventions of the society we
are in; we can't challenge the conventions. But the utilitarian is free to challenge the conventions, and, indeed, *must*
do so whenever acting in accord with the conventions
has less utility than some alternative (but unconventional)
action.

Fourth, notice that employing (AU) involves predicting the consequences of our actions. Obviously, we humans are not infallible at that game. What we have to do is take the alternative with the most *expected* utility (or least expected disutility), and we have to be as *reasonable* as possible in forming our expectations. But it would be an error to reject (AU) on the grounds that we humans cannot know the future. As Butler said, probability is the guide of life. In many cases we know that the act we are contemplating is likely to frustrate or fulfill certain preferences. For example, in most situations we know that people prefer to be shown common courtesy, cured of diseases, relieved of intense pain, told the truth, and so on.

Many people find act utilitarianism plausible. Since it says that the welfare of *each person affected by an act* is relevant to the moral assessment of the act, it almost seems like the required view for a people of democratic spirit: Each person counts for one, and no person counts for more than one. Where tough choices have to be made, we have a clear and impartial rule that maximizes the general welfare. This certainly *sounds* reasonable. Moreover, some philosophers claim that (AU) is supported by sound argument. Among them is J. J. C. Smart, a well-known contemporary proponent of utilitarianism. Smart claims that:

> the chief persuasive argument in favour of utilitarianism has been that the dictates of any deontological ethics will always, on some occasions, lead to the existence of misery that could, on utilitarian principles, have been prevented.[7]

By 'deontological ethics' Smart means any view according to which rightness is determined solely by appeal to rules, such as "Keep your promises," rather than by appeal to the consequences of acts. Smart illustrates his point by giving an example in which breaking a promise seems to prevent more misery than keeping it. His example involves breaking a promise to give a large sum of money to a wealthy sports club in order that the money might be given to a hospital badly in need of medical equipment. Haven't we lost sight of what morality is all about if we "live by the rules" when we know that another approach to morality produces less misery? Smart thinks so. If we care more about keeping rules than about relieving human misery, we are simply being legalistic.

This argument is open to a number of objections. For example, deontologists may claim that it assumes the point to be proved, since Smart's appeal to human misery involves the assumption that the consequences of an act determine its rightness. Obviously, no deontologist can share this assumption. Alternatively, deontologists may challenge Smart on his own terms, by claiming that history provides abundant evidence of the misery produced by those who hold that "the end justifies the means." Keeping a rule can lead to bad consequences in some cases, but in the long run deontological systems are apt to produce less misery than consequentialist ones. However, since I shall consider what deontologists have to say for themselves in the next chapter, I do not wish to focus on these objections at the moment. Rather, I want to stress that Smart's argument is incomplete even if his criticism of deontological ethics is correct. For his argument contains the hidden assumption that the best alternative to deontological ethics is act utilitarianism. But while it is often assumed that some form of utilitarianism is the only serious rival to a deontological ethic, I wish to challenge this assumption in two ways. First, in this chapter I shall present a series of arguments designed to show that utility is not an adequate *telos* for human action. Second, in Chapter 5 I shall argue that the Christian teleological view has a number of advantages over utilitarianism.

Let us now examine five standard objections to act utilitarianism. In some cases the nature of the objection is most easily communicated through a rather contrived example. Some readers will be bothered by the contrived nature of the cases; but no one is suggesting that the cases are common or even that they have ever occurred. All that matters logically is that the cases be possible. Such contrived cases are often important for the purpose of clarifying the meaning of an ethical principle, because ordinary moral cases frequently involve unclarities or complexities which reduce their effectiveness for illustration.

(1) *Duty and Supererogation.* An act of supererogation is an act "above and beyond" the call of duty, i.e., an action that is morally praiseworthy but not a duty. Not everyone agrees that there *are* acts of supererogation, but if there are, a problem arises for act utilitarians. Suppose that a complete stranger is in need of a kidney transplant. No donor can be found. The doctor points out that I could save the stranger's life—at the cost of the kidney, a painful operation, and considerable interference with my career. Without minimizing my sacrifice, it is plausible to suppose that there is more utility to be gained by donating the kidney than by not doing so: Two lives will in all likelihood contain more satisfaction than mine alone, even subtracting the dissatisfaction that will accrue to me as a result of the operation, and the stranger will die without a kidney transplant. It follows that I have a duty to donate my kidney, according to act utilitarians.

Now, to most people this seems odd. Most of us think that it would be morally praiseworthy should I decide to donate my kidney in this situation, but hardly a duty. We could not reasonably *demand* such a sacrifice, as we demand that one pay one's debts or keep one's promises. In short, most of us believe that there are supererogatory acts, and that giving a kidney in this case would be one of them. But according to the act utilitarian, it is a moral duty to take the course of action with the highest utility.[8] Hence, there are no acts of supererogation in the act utilitarian scheme. But, if we believe that there are indeed some supererogatory acts, then we cannot consistently uphold act utilitarianism.

(2) *Promising.* Many philosophers hold that the practice of making and keeping promises points to a serious

problem for act utilitarians. But we should note that in most ordinary cases promise-keeping has a high utility. There are many goals that can be accomplished in the world only if people can be counted on to keep their promises. Moreover, when one breaks a promise, one risks damage to one's own reputation for trustworthiness. Some philosophers have even claimed that, in breaking a promise, an individual risks damaging the general institution of promise-keeping (on the grounds that, generally speaking, the more we keep our promises, the better the institution works). But there is a class of promises which seem to fall outside this type of justification.

Suppose my grandfather, to whom I am very close, is on his deathbed. I am deeply indebted to him for countless reasons, e.g., he made great financial sacrifices in order that I might get a college education. My grandfather says he is about to ask me to make a very solemn promise. He reveals that during the war he had an illegitimate son in France, and goes on to explain that, until this very moment, he has been the only person who knew this, since the child's mother died during the war. My grandfather exacts a solemn promise from me that I will find his illegitimate son and give him a large sum of money, $10,000—my entire life's savings. With tears in his eyes my grandfather asks me to make a solemn promise that I will deliver the money to his son, emphasizing that only in the knowledge that I will keep this promise can he go in peace to the grave. He also makes me promise to keep his secret. Finally, he reminds me of the considerable personal debt I owe him for my education.

Within a week my beloved grandfather passes away. Soon thereafter private detectives track down his son in France. To my dismay, however, the son, though good-hearted, is a wastrel. I immediately see that an alternative act will have higher utility than keeping my promise. In particular, I could use the money as down payment on a house. This would bring my family an enormous amount of satisfaction—more satisfaction, in all likelihood, than could be produced through the imprudent, wasteful ways of the illegitimate son. Being a good act utilitarian, I decide to break my promise and buy a house.

What is the point of this case? (Since we shall need to refer to this case in subsequent chapters, let us call it the "Deathbed Promise Case.") Most people think that the fact that I made a promise—indeed, an especially solemn promise—is highly relevant to the rightness or wrongness of my action in this case. (Even if they think I ought to buy the house, they are apt to think that the fact that I made a promise is morally significant.) If I break my promise, I will have sacrificed a most important ethical principle. But if act utilitarianism is true, the fact that I made a promise *carries no weight at all in this situation*. No one knows about the promise but me. The one to whom I made the promise is dead and gone. I should simply consider the consequences of my act and forget about history (past agreements). But can we really take promising this lightly?

(3) *Criminal Justice.* Many philosophers have held that act utilitarianism would require unjust punishment in certain (admittedly rare) criminal cases. In particular, it is held that (AU) will endorse framing an innocent person in some cases. One such case, which, for purposes of reference we shall call the "Case of the Framed Tramp," runs as follows.[9] A white woman is raped by a black man in a small town. The police have no suspects. A band of white racists threatens to lynch one black man per day until the culprit confesses. Since this band of racists has committed acts of terrorism before, everyone knows the threat is real. The local sheriff lacks sufficient staffing to provide adequate protection for the black community, and his requests for help from higher authorities are denied.

There is a black tramp drifting through town. No one knows him, but many suspect him of the crime. The sheriff, by the merest stroke of luck, happens to know the tramp is innocent, having seen him sleeping in a ditch at the time the crime occurred. But only the sheriff knows the tramp is innocent. (Omitting the tramp himself, of course, whose testimony will be essentially ignored. The rape victim is unable to identify her assailant beyond saying that he was black.) The sheriff realizes he could easily frame the black tramp, thus staving off a series of lynchings. Of course, it will mean years of imprisonment for the innocent tramp, but the disutility of sending the tramp to prison is clearly less than the disutility of even one lynching, let alone a series of them.

It does seem likely that there could be cases of this type, however rare, and it appears that act utilitarians would have to endorse framing innocent persons in such cases. But the deeper point is that act utilitarianism lacks the theoretical resources for giving our sense of justice its due. That a course of action involves "punishing" an innocent person would seem to be an important moral consideration against performing it on any occasion.[10] The tramp, as a person innocent of the crime, does not *deserve* to be imprisoned for it. Yet considerations of *just desert* do not come into the act utilitarian scheme, except insofar as they affect utility. This suggests that act utilitarians have not given concerns about justice a proper place in their thinking about the moral life.

(4) *Distributive Justice*. What is a *just* distribution of goods like? How unequally can wealth be distributed before *unfairness* enters the picture? Let's consider a highly idealized situation. Suppose there is a small society of one hundred people living on a tiny island, whose chief industry is a form of basket weaving. Under the present system each person works an eight-hour day, earning a modest but adequate living. The islanders are happy and content with their lot. Further, let us imagine that we can measure units of satisfaction (call the units, "sats"), and that on the present standard of living 10 "sats" accrues to each of the one hundred islanders per year. Summing the units

of satisfaction for the entire island for a year, we get a total of 1000 "sats."

A new chief comes into power on the island. He is a utilitarian who wants to restructure the economy. He notices that by making fifty islanders work ten-hour days, while fifty work six-hour days, a redistribution of "sats" will take place. The fifty islanders on short days will experience a marked increase in satisfaction, due to the increase in leisure time and decrease in drudgery: a new total of 15 "sats" per worker per year, or 750 "sats." Of course, the fifty islanders working longer days will experience a marked *decrease* in satisfaction, due to the tedium of the work and the relative lack of leisure. They will slide to a total of 5 "sats" per worker per year, or 250 "sats." But the total amount of satisfaction on the new scheme remains the same as that on the old—1000 "sats."

No one can pretend that this idealized case—call it the "Islanders' Case"—is realistic, but taken as a sort of economic parable, an important point emerges. Even if the new chief could effect these systemic changes, wouldn't it be wrong to do so? Isn't it clear that the present scheme is more just—*fairer* than the chief's new proposal? To most people, in any case, it seems clear that the move to the new system would be a move for the worse. But not according to act utilitarianism, for the sum of satisfaction remains the same. This may cause us to wonder whether there is something fishy about these sums of satisfaction, and the next objection focuses on this very point.

Before leaving the issue of distributive justice one last point needs to be made. Some people think that utilitarianism is the view that an act is right if and only if it promotes "the greatest happiness *for the greatest number*." Hence, they see utilitarianism as requiring a fair distribution of goods. But as Frankena points out, this formulation is defective, for it amounts to two principles, not one.[11] It tells us

(a) to produce the greatest sum of happiness that we can, and

(b) to distribute happiness as widely as possible.

In other words, this principle is a combination of the principle of utility and a principle of distributive justice. There is a very good reason, however, suggested by the Islanders' Case, for not identifying utilitarianism with such a two-principled ethic. Suppose the new chief's proposal were to provide a slight advantage in overall utility, say, 1001 "sats." Then which of the two principles are we to follow? The above formulation insists that the agent act on both principles, but that is not possible. For (a) tells us to act on the chief's proposal, while (b) tells us to maintain the *status quo*.

(5) *Sums of Satisfaction.* Utilitarianism makes sums of satisfaction relevant to moral decision making. Many philosophers think that this is fundamentally misguided. For example, suppose someone has in her possession one unit of a powerful painkilling drug. Traveling in a war-torn country, she comes upon six soldiers injured by artillery bombardment. One of the soldiers is seriously burned and in a great deal of pain. The other five are in pain also, but to a lesser degree. Let us assume that she knows the following medical facts: (a) None of the soldiers will die of his injuries, (b) it will take the entire unit of the drug in her possession to ease the pain of the burn victim, and (c) it will take only one-fifth of the unit to ease the pain of each of the five other soldiers. In other words, she must choose between relieving the burn victim's pain and the pain of the other five soldiers. Seeing her uncertainty, one of the five (who has recently been reading a book on utilitarianism!) speaks out: "Now look here. While none of us individually is in nearly as much pain as the burn victim, the moral point of view requires that you maximize utility. And of course each one of us prefers painlessness to his present state. Let's say the five of us are each in x amount of pain. Then this burn victim is in (at most) $3x$ amount

of pain. Your choice is therefore between relieving $5x$ or $3x$ amount of pain. Simple arithmetic makes your choice clear. No individual's pain is the issue. It is the sum of satisfaction that is at issue. Hence, we must insist that you use the drug to relieve our pain, and allow this burn victim to go on suffering. It's your moral duty."[12]

Let us call this the "Sums-of-Pain Case." To the argument in favor of giving the drug to the five men (rather than to the burn victim), I am immediately inclined to point out that no one is feeling that *sum* of pain, there being no single center of consciousness to which that sum of pain, $5x$, belongs. What seems relevant, then, is not the sum of pain but the fact that the burn victim is suffering far more intensely than anyone else in the situation; this seems like a strong reason in favor of giving him the drug. But since utilitarians claim that the sum of pain is relevant, they have to insist that the burn victim be neglected in favor of the five soldiers who are in far less pain. This seems absurd.

At this point it is only fair to note that some utilitarians would claim that I have misrepresented their position.[13] That is, some utilitarians claim that the proper *telos* is *average* utility and not *overall* utility. To determine the average utility of an act we simply divide the utility (as defined above) by the number of individuals affected by the act. To determine which act is right, we compare the average utility of the alternatives, and an act is right if (and only if) no other act has a higher average utility. Does this reformulation make a difference? Perhaps. For example, as I have defined utility, it could apparently be increased in some cases simply by increasing the population. Thus, assuming the production of goods (food, housing, education, etc.) does not lag behind population growth, utility might be increased just by increasing the number of individuals in the world. A greater number of satisfied individuals results in a greater sum of satisfaction, even if the average utility ("the standard of living") remains the same. Yet, it seems

odd to think that population growth (under such conditions) is *morally obligatory*. Average utilitarianism would
avoid this odd result.

However, I do not think that average utilitarianism
avoids the difficulties I have been discussing. Consider,
for example, the Sums-of-Pain case. Let us stipulate that
the satisfaction of removing x amount of pain is one "sat."
(And assume that this figure takes into account any dissatisfaction resulting from medical procedures, such as the
pain of a hypodermic injection.) The utilities of the two
alternatives could be represented in a diagram as follows:

	Alternative A (Help the Five)	**Alternative B** (Help the Burn Victim)
Soldier 1	1 sat	−1 sat
Soldier 2	1 sat	−1 sat
Soldier 3	1 sat	−1 sat
Soldier 4	1 sat	−1 sat
Soldier 5	1 sat	−1 sat
Soldier 6	−3 sats	3 sats
Utility	2 sats	−2 sats

The *average* utility of Alternative A is 1/3 "sat," while that
of Alternative B is -1/3 "sat." Thus, if we take average utility as the *telos*, we shall still conclude (against our better
judgment) that Alternative A is right. The concept of average utility is similarly unhelpful as regards the "Islanders'
Case," the gist of which might be diagrammed as follows:

	Alternative A	**Alternative B**
Person 1	10 sats	15 sats
Person 2	10 sats	15 sats
Person 3	10 sats	5 sats
Person 4	10 sats	5 sats
Utility	40 sats	40 sats

While alternative B is less fair than Alternative A, both alternatives have the same *average* utility (10 "sats"). In other
words, the concept of average utility fares no better at
capturing our convictions about distributive justice than

does utility. As far as I can see, *average* utilitarianism is of no use in rebutting any of the objections discussed in this section.

Thus, it seems to me that each of the five objections here described is damaging to the act utilitarian's cause. Together they provide good reasons for rejecting this particular form of consequentialism.

III. RULE UTILITARIANISM

Some philosophers, impressed by objections of the type we have just seen, have proposed an alternative form of utilitarianism. These philosophers believe that act utilitarianism has morally unacceptable implications because it allows the principle of utility to be applied to individual acts *without regard for the fact that these acts fall into certain important classes.* For example, in the previous section, we saw that in applying the principle of utility to isolated acts, one simply ignores the fact that the acts are instances of "promise-breaking," "punishing the innocent," or "treating persons equally." And notice that corresponding to such *classes* of acts are some traditional moral rules, such as, "Keep your promises," "Punish only the guilty," and "Treat like cases alike." So, perhaps the act utilitarian's error is that he ignores the importance of judging *classes* of acts, as opposed to individual acts.

It is interesting to note that even Bentham and Mill did not think the principle of utility should be applied in a case-by-case fashion; they saw a place for secondary rules. Thus, Mill warns against testing "each individual action directly by the first principle." For

> it is a strange notion that the acknowledgment of a first principle is inconsistent with admission of secondary ones. To inform a traveler respecting the place of his ultimate destination is not to forbid the use of landmarks and direction-posts on the way. The proposition that happiness is the end and aim of morality does not mean that no road ought to be laid down to that goal.[14]

Making the most of such plausible remarks, the rule utilitarian proposes that

> (RU)   An act is morally right if and only if it is required by an *optimal* set of rules,

where an optimal set of rules is one which, if sincerely believed in by most people, would produce at least as much utility as any of its competitors. A few remarks clarifying the notion of an optimal set of rules are needed at this point.

Note that an optimal set of rules is not defined as one such that, if everyone *conformed* to the rules in the set, utility would be maximized. If it were defined this way, it appears that rule utilitarianism would collapse into act utilitarianism, for to conform to (AU) is simply to perform all and only those acts which maximize utility. So, as a matter of logic, it has to be granted that *if* people conformed to (AU), utility would be maximized. The problem is that people seem unable to conform to (AU) entirely. For one thing, it is hard for humans to know, in many ordinary cases, which act does maximize utility, since our capacity for predicting the consequences of our actions is quite limited. For another, when people are allowed to employ (AU) in a case-by-case fashion, there is much opportunity for rationalizing. It is easy to allow personal preferences to enter the picture when we are trying to calculate the relative utility of several alternatives. So, if we could just pick any rule we liked and assume that people would live up to it, (AU) would be the one to pick in order to maximize utility. But we cannot reasonably make the assumption that people will conform to (AU).

But, then, what sorts of rules *will* be in the optimal set? Several factors must be kept in mind, if we are to arrive at a reasonable set of rules. (1) No matter what rules people accept, they will not conform to these rules entirely; people always fall short of their standards. That is why we speak of rules people *sincerely believe in*, not rules they conform to perfectly. (2) If we select unrealistically high standards, our set of rules will fail to be optimal, for if people find that they cannot approximate the conduct prescribed by the rules, they will eventually quit trying. (3) The rules must be challenging if utility is to be maximized. We are looking for rules which will "bring out the best" in people, even though people do not live up to them perfectly. And in order to bring out the best in people, an optimal set of rules needs to be both easily remembered and easily *applied*—unlike (AU), for instance. This means that the list of rules must be relatively short, and that applying the rules must not involve complicated calculations. The rule utilitarian claims that, by keeping these factors in mind, we can arrive at a set of rules such that, *if most people sincerely endorsed it*, utility would be maximized.

Rule utilitarianism has some apparent advantages over act utilitarianism. By giving greater attention to specific rules, the rule utilitarian has a plausible reply to a number of objections that plague act utilitarianism. For example, the rule utilitarian will probably insist that the optimal set of rules contain such items as "Keep your promises (unless doing so will cause serious harm)," "Never punish the innocent," and "Treat people as equals whenever possible." With these rules in the optimal set, the rule utilitarian may not fall prey to the problems concerning promising (the Deathbed Promise Case), criminal justice (the Framed Tramp Case), and distributive justice (the Islanders' Case) described in the previous section.

Nevertheless, there are serious objections to rule utilitarianism. First, a problem arises regarding the nature of the "rules." Thus, while Mill favored the use of secondary rules, it is unclear just what *sort* of rules he had in mind. There are two possibilities. (a) *Rules of Thumb*. A rule of thumb is a generalization from experience that serves as a handy guide, but can be overridden at any time by a direct application of (AU), the primary principle of utility. Since rules of thumb can be overridden at any time, a rule utilitarianism involving rules of this type seems equivalent to act utilitarianism (and hence inherits all the problems of act utilitarianism). (b) *"Practice" Rules.* In a famous essay, John Rawls pointed out that not all rules are rules of thumb.[15] Some rules define a *practice.* A practice is any form of activity specified by a system of rules. Games such as baseball or football are good examples of a practice. Thus, baseball is defined in terms of its rules; if one is not playing by such rules as "Three strikes and you're out," one is not playing baseball. Of course, the rules of a game can change in various ways over time, but the point is that the game is constituted by its rules. Players cannot stop at each juncture and ask whether a rule is useful in *this* case or not. If players were constantly asking questions such as, "Is the three-strikes-and-you're-out rule useful this time?" the game would bog down completely. Rawls suggests that rule utilitarians regard moral rules as "practice" rules. The question then becomes whether certain social practices such as promise-keeping or punishing only the guilty maximize utility. If these practices produce more utility than the alternatives, we ought to enter into these practices. But entering into these practices necessarily involves obeying the rules. So, we are not to ask in each new case, "Should I obey this rule?" Rather, having seen that the practice maximizes utility, we are to obey the rule even if we can see that in a particular case more utility would be produced by breaking it.

Even if the rules are of the practice sort, however, important difficulties remain. Like the act utilitarians, rule utilitarians make utility (or average utility) the *telos.* But recall the Sums-of-Pain case from the previous section. If the rule utilitarian is thinking clearly, his optimal set of rules will contain a rule implying that we ought to help the five men with less severe wounds rather than the burn victim. Such a rule would maximize utility, but, for reasons given in detail in the previous section, it is surely not a correct moral rule. The problem here seems to me quite fundamental. I think the Sums-of-Pain case shows that utilitarians have identified the wrong *telos*. If I am right, then no amount of refining their position will overcome this basic flaw.

Another problem arises if we ask what is to be done when the rules conflict. Such cases are common, and we shall consider a number of specific examples in Section III of the next chapter. But for the moment, consider the problem in the abstract. Suppose I can keep a promise only by breaking another important rule, e.g., to save a life whenever possible. What is to be done? Both rules are now to be regarded as "practice" rules. But if they conflict I cannot obey both. The usual utilitarian response is to say that, in cases of conflict, we revert to (AU), the primary principle of utility. In other words, one of the optimal rules is "in cases of conflict, revert to (AU)." But then, if cases of conflict are common—and I shall argue that they are in the next chapter—(RU) is virtually indistinguishable from (AU).

Finally, recall that in order to show the superiority of rule over act utilitarianism, the rule utilitarian typically includes many conventional (i.e., traditional) moral rules in the optimal set. But then one begins to wonder whether rule utilitarianism is not just a philosophical way of defending the status quo. Won't rule utilitarians in each society simply defend the conventions of that society? But, as we have seen, some societies endorse highly objectionable moral practices. On the other hand, if rule utilitarians endorse an *ideal* set of rules (at variance with convention), the alleged advantage of (RU) over (AU) is called into question. For if the ideal code is quite different from the conventional code, the ideal rules presumably move us in the direction (AU). But then, why suppose that (RU) will back up our convictions about promise-keeping, punishing only the guilty, and treating people equally?[16]

*   *   *   *   *

Let's take stock. This book begins with some reflections on the fact that, in modern times, morality tends to be regarded as a matter of personal preference, not amenable to rational method, and hence that one person's ethical opinion is as good as another's. In the first chapter I pointed out that this idea is open to serious objections, but I also admitted that the best response to it would be a developed moral theory—one that explains how ethical decisions can be made in a principled way. In the second chapter I took the first steps toward such a theory, by proposing a view about the relation between God and ethics. The Christian teleological view, outlined at the end of Chapter 2, says that acts are right if and only if they promote the Kingdom of God. Of course, much remains to be done in the way of fleshing this basic idea out. (I shall return to that task in Chapter 5.)

One way to make a philosophical idea clear is to contrast it with its alternatives. In this chapter I have been examining the main secular forms of consequentialism in order to allow us to best appreciate their contrast with the distinctively Christian teleological view. Standard objections to these secular views have also been summarized, to indicate why I cannot endorse them. My criticism of these secular views has two main elements. First, I have emphasized that each of them has unacceptable implications for moral decision making; in short, these views give us bad advice. Second, I have argued that these unacceptable implications have their ground in a defective *telos*, be it agent-satisfaction or utility. In the next chapter we shall consider some views of ethics which are not teleological in structure. Philosophers who back these views claim that it is a mistake to evaluate acts in terms of their consequences.

Deontological   4
Views

Some philosophers hold that an act can be right (or wrong) by virtue of something other than its consequences. These philosophers are called 'deontologists', from an ancient Greek word *deontos* meaning "that which is binding or right." *Pure* deontologists, like the great Prussian philosopher Immanuel Kant (1724–1804), hold that the consequences of an act have no bearing on its moral rightness whatsoever. *Mixed* deontologists, on the other hand, allow that the consequences of an act can be relevant to its rightness. These philosophers would insist, however, that at least in some cases, features of an act other than its consequences make it right. Some examples may help to identify the concerns of the deontologists.

(1) Suppose I have just found out how the pollution control devices on my car could be circumvented. Detaching the control devices will significantly increase my gas mileage. Let's also suppose that I could detach the pollution control devices without anyone else finding out. I reason that the pollution from *just one* vehicle would not harm anyone, and hence that the consequences of disconnecting my control devices would be insignificant. Should I disconnect them? Many would argue that I should not, along the following lines: "True, the consequences of your act are not in themselves significant. And since you will

perform this act in secret, you won't be providing a bad example for others. But what if everyone did this? Then the air pollution would be horrible. Surely you will admit that you wouldn't want other people to act this way. Hence, you shouldn't either."

Note that this argument does not involve the claim that my act will result in significantly bad consequences; it is not even being claimed that my act will influence other people to behave in harmful ways. The arguer thinks it would be wrong to disconnect my pollution control devices *even if I am the only one who does so*. The idea seems to be that one should not perform a certain type of act unless one is willing that everyone else should do the same. We expect others to shoulder a certain burden of restraint, so we shoulder it too; anything less would constitute a failure of responsibility. Arguments of this type are commonly used in discussions about littering, cheating on one's taxes, and draft dodging. One could regard Kant's moral theory as a philosophical refinement and elaboration of the approach to ethical decision making which centers on the question, "What if everyone did that?"

(2) Recall the case of the Deathbed Promise from the previous chapter. There it turned out that the consequences of breaking a promise were preferable to those of keeping it. Some deontologists would say: "But you must not simply look forward to the effects of your actions, as consequentialists do. You must also look backward to the fact that you made a promise. Historical considerations, and particularly past agreements, are just as relevant to morality as the future." As we shall see, contract theories of ethics regard agreements as the central concept in ethics.

For some deontologists, concerns about history arise in discussions of social justice. Thus, it is sometimes claimed that American whites should make reparations to American blacks because the ancestors of the whites oppressed and enslaved the blacks. Once again the point is that historical (or backward-looking) considerations—in this case past inequities—can render an act obligatory. Forward-looking considerations (i.e., the consequences) are not the only ones relevant to moral decision making. As we shall see, some rule deontologists (e.g., W. D. Ross) stress the importance of such backward-looking considerations as reparation and gratitude.

(3) Recall the case of the Framed Tramp (also from the previous chapter). There it turned out that the consequences of punishing an innocent person were preferable to the consequences of preserving his liberty. But in this case a plausible and commonly accepted moral rule applies: "Punish people only if they deserve it, and only to the degree that they deserve it." Some people would claim that acts are right (or wrong) simply by virtue of conforming to (or violating) such standard rules. And since a man who has not committed a crime does not deserve to be punished for it, he should not be. But then, from this perspective, it appears that conformity to a rule, and not the consequences of the act, determines its rightness. This is the fundamental thesis of such rule deontologists as W. D. Ross and Norman Geisler.

Deontologists agree only in the negative thesis that consequentialist views are false. That is, all deontologists affirm that (at least in some cases) features of an act other than its consequences make it right. But if asked to describe the positive "right-making" feature of acts, different deontologists give different answers. Let us now turn to an examination of the three most influential forms of deontology.

1. KANT'S CATEGORICAL IMPERATIVE

In his *Groundwork of the Metaphysic of Morals* Immanuel Kant sums up the demands of morality as follows: "Act only on that maxim through which you can at the same time will that it should become universal law."[1] This technical sounding statement is one formulation of Kant's famous "categorical imperative." Taken in context, it seems clear that Kant regarded this dictum as the single, exceptionless, foundational principle of ethics. But what exactly does it mean?

A maxim is a kind of rule. Apparently Kant thought that, for each of our acts, there is a corresponding rule or principle. Such rules need not be verbalized—indeed, one may not even be conscious of the rule one is acting on—but still we are always acting in accord with some principle or other. Here are some examples. Suppose Jones needs a pen but has not got any cash on hand, so he shoplifts a pen. Jones's maxim would then be something like: "Whenever I need a pen but haven't got the money to pay for it, I shall steal one." Or suppose I am bored and decide to see a film. My maxim might be: "Whenever I am bored and feel that seeing a film would relieve my boredom, I shall see a film."

Kant is saying that one must never act on a maxim unless one is willing for everyone else to act on it—unless one is willing that "it should become universal law." To illustrate: If my trip to the cinema is to pass Kant's test, then I must be able to will that "Whenever *anyone* is bored and feels that seeing a film would relieve his boredom, he will see a film."

One of Kant's own examples helps to clarify what is meant by "willing" a maxim to be universal law. Suppose I need a large sum of money. Further, suppose a banker is willing to loan me the money, but I know I will not be able to pay the money back. Should I borrow it? No, according to Kant. For my maxim is: "Whenever I need money and can get some by borrowing it, then (even though I know I can't pay the money back) I shall borrow the money and promise (falsely) to repay it." Now, asks Kant, what would happen if everyone acted on this maxim? Plainly, the institution of loaning money would break down; it would be impossible to borrow money, because those who have it would be unable to trust those who want to borrow it. So, if my maxim became universal law, there would be no institution of borrowing. But then my maxim could not be a *universal* law for my maxim presupposes the existence of the institution of borrowing, yet there would be no such institution if everyone adopted my maxim. I want to borrow money, but I am in effect willing the institution of borrowing out of existence. Hence, what I am willing is irrational because it is inconsistent, and Kant rules out such inconsistent "willings." So, when we "will a maxim as universal law," we must be "willing" a logically consistent state of affairs.

Why is Kant's proposed ethical principle called the "categorical imperative"? The contrast is with hypothetical imperatives. An imperative is hypothetical if it applies to an agent only if that agent has a certain desire or goal. Examples of hypothetical imperatives would be: "If you want to be trim, you must exercise regularly," or "if you want to pass calculus, you must do your homework." These are hypothetical imperatives because the "if-clauses" may or may not apply to a given agent. It is not necessarily required that one want to be trim, or want to pass calculus. But, according to Kant, moral obligations are not like this. They fall on us irrespective of our wants, inclinations, and desires. It is not a question of whether we want to be moral or not. Everyone must be ethical in all circumstances—the moral imperative is categorical, not hypothetical.[2] Thus, according to Kant, the "moral game" is not something a rational being can opt out of (while remaining rational); rational beings are always subject to the demands of the categorical imperative.

In spite of its initial plausibility, Kant's first formulation of the categorical imperative is highly problematic, for three reasons. First, it appears to create some absurd "duties."[3] For example, suppose I act on the following maxim: "Whenever I get dressed, I shall put my left shoe on first." Can I will that such a maxim be "universal law"? Why not? It certainly will not hurt anything if all persons adopt this maxim, yet it would seem absurd to suppose that putting one's left shoe on first is a moral obligation. (Those bothered by the fact that not everyone has a left foot need only consider the following closely related maxim: "Whenever I have two feet and am getting dressed, I shall put my left shoe on first.") Or, consider the following maxim: "Whenever I feel like a vacation, I shall go to Venice, Italy." I cannot will this to be universal law, because if everyone tried to act on it, Venice would be overrun with vacationers. In fact, most humans would not be able to get near the city for all the congestion. So, I am obligated not to act on this maxim. But that seems absurd. What is wrong with planning to take all one's vacations in Venice?

These examples may seem like mere verbal tricks, unworthy of Kant's serious and interesting proposal. But they bring up the point that a great deal depends on how the maxims are formulated; and Kant has not clarified that for us. In the absence of clear instructions about formulating maxims, Kant's principle permits bizarre results.

Second, Kant's procedure appears to permit some immoral practices. Suppose I live in a country where nearly everyone pays his taxes. And suppose that, as a highly placed official in the Internal Revenue Service, I am one of the very few people in the country who can easily get away with not paying his taxes. I act on the maxim: "Whenever I can avoid paying my taxes without harming my country and without getting caught, then I shall do so." Since nearly everyone in my country pays his taxes, my failure to pay my taxes will not harm the country. (Any individual's income tax is a mere drop in the bucket.) Moreover, since so few of my countrymen have (or could have) the kind of position I do—one that makes nonpayment possible with impunity—I can reasonably will that everyone *in my circumstances* act on the maxim. Yet, it would seem immoral for me not to pay my taxes, and to use my power to cover up the act.

Third, it seems that insensitive or uncaring people can will that clearly unacceptable maxims should be universal law. Frankena considers the case of a person who adopts the maxim, "Whenever others are in need, I shall not help them." While only a very tough person, entirely free of self-pity, could will such a maxim consistently, perhaps some "rugged individualists" would be able to do so. Or suppose an agent endorses maxims which, if made universal law, would permit the depletion of our natural resources within one generation (e.g., whenever I need some fire wood, I shall chop down the nearest tree). We might point out the disastrous effects of such policies on future generations. But suppose our agent does not care about future generations. Can we prove that it is somehow *inconsistent* of him not to care about them? Surely not. As Philippa Foot remarks, "The fact is that the man who rejects morality because he sees no reason to obey its rules can be convicted of villainy but not of inconsistency."[4]

The issue of future generations enables us to contrast Kant's view with the Christian teleological view. On the Christian teleological view, the goal (*telos*) is a well-functioning creation in harmony with the Creator. Each creature has a role to play in the larger scheme. Within this scheme it would be unthinkable for a human being so to exploit the environment for his own private ends that he made it uninhabitable for creatures yet to be brought into existence. To behave in this way would clearly be to step out of the role God intended, and therefore to hinder the formation of that harmonious Kingdom which the rules of morality are designed to promote. But Kant does not require that an individual, in formulating his maxims, be constrained by such teleological considerations. In fact, as a deontologist, he explicitly rejects every teleological approach to ethics. However, unless it is granted that our highest good as individual persons is bound up with the role we play in the life of the wider community of persons, and unless our maxims must be constrained by such teleological considerations, reason permits individuals to act on all manner of anti-social desires and inclinations. So, from a Christian point of view, Kant's first formulation of the categorical imperative is not an acceptable moral principle.

At this point it is only fair to say that Kant formulated his categorical imperative in a variety of ways. While we cannot examine them all, let us consider one further attempt:

> Act in such a way that you always treat humanity, whether in your own person or in the person of any other, never simply as a means, but always at the same time as an end.[5]

It is clear that Kant regards this second formulation of the categorical imperative as equivalent to the first. And both formulations are intended to express the single, exceptionless, foundational principle of ethics. But of course the two formulations sound quite different, and since this second formulation contains none of the troublesome language about maxims, perhaps it will prove more fruitful than the first.

What exactly is Kant saying? In a nutshell, this second formulation of the categorical imperative (CI) says that

> (CI)   An act is right if and only if the one performing it does not thereby treat any person simply as a means.

In more ordinary language, Kant is saying that we must not use people. The implied tribute to the dignity of persons makes this formulation of the categorical imperative sound promising, but, before passing judgment, we must get a better understanding of the terminology.

What does Kant have in mind in using the terms 'means' and 'ends'? Some things are valued as means, others are valued as ends. For example, money is valued as a means, since it enables those who have it to acquire such things as food, clothing, and shelter. Now, suppose someone asks why food is valued. We will answer that it is a means to health and pleasure. But why are health and pleasure valued? We are apt to be stumped by this question. We do not value pleasure, for example, because of anything it leads

to. We value it for its own sake. In other words, pleasure, unlike money, is intrinsically good. Thus, by insisting that we treat persons as ends, Kant seems to be saying that each person is an intrinsic good (and hence ought be valued as such). Persons are not to be valued, like money, simply as a *way* of attaining intrinsically good things.

But exactly what does it mean to treat a person as an intrinsically good thing? We should first note that Kant is not saying that we may never treat persons as means. When we listen to an entertainer sing, we are treating her as a means to our enjoyment. When we listen to a lecture, we are using the speaker as a means to gaining knowledge. When we ask a subordinate to perform some task, we are using him as a means to getting the job done. There is nothing wrong with such activities on Kant's view; rather, we err when we treat persons *merely* as means to our ends. But how do we determine whether we have treated someone merely as a means? Here again, Kant leaves us without much in the way of clarification, and a serious problem arises.

It appears that there is no way to describe what is meant by "treating persons as ends" without presupposing that we already know a great deal about morality. Treating persons "merely as means" seems to be closely connected with *disregarding their preferences.* But Kant cannot say that we are treating persons merely as a means *whenever* we disregard their preferences. There are many cases in which we ought to disregard a persons preferences, because he wants something immoral. For example, if Jones prefers to rape or steal, Smith is perfectly justified in stopping Jones; Smith need not feel as if Jones's preference for raping or stealing is on a par with legitimate preferences. Preferences are not all equal. But then, how do we sort out the legitimate from the illegitimate preferences? Certainly (CI) is no help at this juncture. What is needed is a detailed moral code (which would indicate which preferences are legitimate and which are illegitimate). But Kant is supposed to

be providing us with a philosophical procedure for determining what is right and wrong, not relying on any moral
code adopted independently of (CI). It thus appears that
(CI) is parasitic on some independent moral code, for we
have to be able to make all sorts of value judgments about
people's preferences in order to apply (CI). So, even if
(CI) is true, we must have moral knowledge independent
of (CI) in order to apply it. But if (CI) is parasitic on some
other moral principles, then *Kant has not given us the
single, foundational ethical principle he promised.*

The most favorable conclusion one can draw is that (CI)
is a radically incomplete theory of morality. Furthermore,
even if (CI) is true, we are left without a knowledge of
the source or roots of moral obligation. Perhaps the value
judgments we make in determining which preferences to
honor (in our effort to treat people as ends) are more fundamental than (CI). Kant has done nothing to exclude such
a possibility. So, even if (CI) is true, our search for the foundations of ethics is left unfulfilled.

It thus appears that both of the most common ways of
formulating the categorical imperative fail to be convincing
as foundational moral principles. Since I doubt that there
is any way of formulating this central Kantian notion that
succeeds in avoiding the problems raised here, I find Kant's
approach to deontology unsuccessful.[6]

II. CONTRACTARIAN VIEWS

A second deontological approach to ethics grounds obligation in a social contract. Traditionally, the social contract
view has been a theory of the justification of the state.
On this view, legal or political obligation results from an
agreement or contract made between persons living in the
"state of nature." (Persons are said to be living in the state
of nature if they have not yet formed themselves into a
society.) As the story is usually told, life in the state of
nature has little to recommend it. It is a harshly competi-
tive existence, with each person striving to fulfill his own

needs and desires in disregard for the needs and desires of others. In the words of the great contractarian Thomas Hobbes (1588-1679), life in the state of nature is a "war of every man against every man"—a life "solitary, poor, nasty, brutish, and short."[6] To escape this wretched existence, individuals long ago agreed to live by a set of rules beneficial to all. Rules against murder, theft, false witness, and adultery, for example, were seen to be to the advantage of all individuals. In essence this social contract says, "Don't harm me and I won't harm you." On the contract view, acts are judged to be (legally or politically) obligatory by virtue of conforming to a set of mutually advantageous rules agreed upon *in the past* by individuals living in the state of nature.

There is a devastating reply to this attempt to justify the state. Namely, there is no evidence (historical or anthropological) to suggest that people ever did live in state of nature, much less that they ever got together and made an explicit agreement to live by certain rules. The state of nature is a myth, and if it is a myth, then no contract was ever made; hence, there are no political obligations. Thus, in its traditional form, complete with the assumption that humans once lived in a state of nature, social contract theory fails utterly to explain the source of obligations—political or otherwise.

This fatal objection to traditional contract theories, however, has not stopped contemporary theorists from being intrigued by the concept of a social contract. Philosophers such as John Rawls, author of an influential work entitled, *A Theory of Justice*, have tried to produce a modified contractarian view.[8] Recently, Fred Feldman has shown how Rawls's theory of justice might be turned into a general theory of morality.[9]

Contemporary contractarians make no effort to deny that the state of nature is a myth. The historical status of the state of nature is regarded as irrelevant by contemporary theorists because the social contract is now regarded as *purely hypothetical.* On this modified contractarian view, our moral obligations are determined by the set of rules we *would* adopt if we *were* to make an explicit contract with others. The idea is that correct moral rules properly command our obedience, because they are just the set of rules individuals would agree to in order to secure their mutual advantage, if given the opportunity to negotiate a set of rules with everyone else.

A question immediately arises: Why should we suppose that individuals would agree on *any* set of rules? Wouldn't individuals, in their familiar, cantankerous way, just insist on rules that enhance their own position? For example, why would extremely poor people agree to a rule against stealing from the very rich? Such a rule would not seem to be in the interest of the poor. In fact, it would seem that the freedom to steal from the very rich would be to the advantage of the poor. On the other hand, wouldn't the rich favor very strict rules against theft, to protect their own interests? In such a fashion, irreconcilable differences would emerge at every turn. And as a matter of fact, the history of humanity is replete with such disagreements— laws and legal systems are notorious for protecting the powerful and rich at the expense of the weak and poor, from antiquity to the present.

Contemporary contract theorists admit that agreement is most unlikely unless certain restrictions are placed on the kinds of considerations individuals may employ in negotiating for a set of rules to live by. Rawls has produced a rather elaborate list of such restrictions, which may be roughly summarized as follows:[10]

(a) Individuals may not take into account their actual role or status in society. The decision to accept a set of rules is thus made behind a "veil of ignorance." This means, for example, that one's wealth (or poverty) must not be taken into account in negotiating the moral contract, that one's race may not be taken into account, and that one's vocational status must be ignored. The decision to adopt a set of moral rules must be made on the assumption that one could wind up with *any* actual role or status in society.

(b) Individuals must try to select those rules which would secure the highest level of welfare for themselves. Together with the veil of ignorance, this restriction in effect builds in a concern for the best interests of each person involved in the contract. By hypothesis, I do not know where I will wind up in the social order; so I will endorse a set of rules that will be to my advantage wherever I wind up.

(c) The negotiations for the moral contract must be rational; they must be logically consistent and in accord with the evidence. For example, they must be in accord with general facts about human nature. We are making a set of rules for humans, not for Martians or angels.

(d) Agreement on the contract must be unanimous. No one can be expected to live by a code that he would not agree to under the stipulated conditions.

(e) It must be understood by all parties that the contract cannot be revoked once it is made. The agreement is a solemn one, not taken up in a frivolous or experimental way. It will not be easy to live by any code we adopt, and we must commit ourselves to living by it, however difficult that turns out to be.

Conditions (a) through (e) describe a set of circumstances under which people could negotiate a moral code. Rawls calls this set of circumstances 'the Original Position'. The concept of the Original Position plays a role in Rawls's theory analogous to that of the state of nature in traditional contract theory. Let us say that a Hypothetical Moral Code is one that would be agreed upon in the Original Position. In a nutshell, then, the contractarian view of ethics says that

> (C) An act is right if and only if it conforms to a rule that would be included in the Hypothetical Moral Code.

The controlling moral vision of the contractarian is opposed to the idea that the consequences of an act make it right. Yet, one can become confused about the role expected consequences may take in shaping opinion in the Original Position. It is perhaps conceivable, for example, that people in the Original Position might select rules such as, "Promote the general welfare" or "Promote one's own welfare." These rules are clearly formed with certain consequences in mind. Nevertheless, even if these rules were adopted in the Original Position, the theory would remain deontological, because it is not the actual consequences that make an act right, but simply the fact that it conforms to a rule which all parties would accept in certain hypothetical circumstances.

It must be said that the notion of a social contract is a fruitful heuristic device, one that can free up our thinking about morality. It seems especially helpful in thinking about justice. Thus, it is plausible to suppose that a system of rules all parties would agree to in advance, under Rawls's stipulated conditions, would get high marks for fairness. Nevertheless, there are some deep problems with the hypothetical-contract approach to ethics.

Let us first consider an objection pressed by Ronald Dworkin, a philosopher well known for his work in jurisprudence.[11] This objection is analogous to the standard objection to traditional contract theories. As Dworkin puts it: "A hypothetical contract is not simply a pale form of an actual contract; it is no contract at all."[12] Some of Dworkin's examples help to make his point vivid. Suppose I have a painting in my possession, and suppose I would have accepted $100 for it, had someone offered me that amount last Monday. But suppose on Tuesday an art specialist informed me that the painting is a Picasso worth $10,000. Now it is Wednesday, and someone offers me $100 for the painting. What sense would it make for him to say: "But look, it's only fair that you accept $100 for the painting, *because you would have accepted that amount on*

Monday, as you yourself admit. So, here's my check, and please hand over the painting"? Plainly, such an argument has no weight at all. But, if I had actually signed a contract last Monday, or even made an explicit oral promise, then the buyer would have a reasonable argument in his favor. (It might not be a decisive argument, but it would at least have *some* force.) An actual contract is a relevant moral consideration; a hypothetical contract is not.

Another one of Dworkin's examples is worth quoting at length:

> Suppose that you and I are playing poker and we find, in the middle of a hand, that the deck is one card short. You suggest that we throw the hand in, but I refuse because I know I am going to win and I want the money in the pot. You might say that I would certainly have agreed to that procedure had the possibility of the deck being short been raised in advance. But your point is not that I am somehow committed to throwing the hand in by an agreement I never made. Rather you use the device of a hypothetical agreement to make a point that might have been made without that device, which is that the solution recommended is so obviously fair and sensible that only someone with an immediate contrary interest could disagree.[13]

So, while the concept of a hypothetical contract may free up our moral intuitions (by helping us to get emotional distance from our private interests), it cannot be the foundation for morality. A hypothetical contract is no contract at all.

It may help us to appreciate Dworkin's objection if we briefly compare the role of agreements in a Christian moral perspective with the role of agreements in hypothetical-contract theory. The notion of an agreement, or covenant, plays a major role in the biblical picture of the relation between humanity and God. But of course the idea that humans could bring *morality itself* into existence via a social contract (whether actual or hypothetical) is foreign to the biblical view. Also, the fundamental covenants in the Old and New Testament are not agreements between equals—rather they are agreements between God and humans. (Think of the covenant made at Mt. Sinai, recorded in Exodus 20–24, or the new covenant instituted at the Last Supper—"for this is my blood of the covenant which is poured out for many for the forgiveness of sin"—Matthew 26:28.) On the Christian view, it is an enormous compliment to human beings that God deigns to enter into covenants with them. Moreover, it is in the Christian scheme a matter of signal importance that agreements between God and humans have actually taken place. If these covenants are "merely hypothetical," then Christianity is false, for according to Christianity certain covenants between God and humans are not only actual but pivotal historical events. Finally, morality does not come into existence via the biblical covenants (though some special obligations, such as the obligation to keep the Sabbath, do arise through a covenant). Given the nature of God and the nature of human beings, there could not have been a time when we were not responsible to God. God's love has *always* been extended to us. It has *always* been possible to sin by rejecting the offer of divine love. The possibility of turning against God either directly or by mistreating some aspect of creation is in the very nature of things as God made them, prior to any particular historical agreements.[14]

A second objection to the hypothetical-contract view emerges if we ask: "Exactly who gets to participate in the hypothetical agreement?" Rawls's answer is, in essence, "Those who have the capacity to heed moral considerations (e.g., rules and principles), and those who have this capacity *potentially* (e.g., infants)." Peter Singer, a philosopher well known for his views about animal rights, thinks that this answer reveals an indefensible bias in contract theory; for nonhuman animals cannot take part in the negotiations in the Original Position, since they lack the capacity to heed moral considerations—even potentially.

Yet most people will agree that nonhuman animals can be, and indeed often are, subject to abuse. Dogs, cats, and chimpanzees can feel pain, and they have an interest in avoiding it. So, the class of beings who can enter into contracts is only a part of (i.e., a proper subset of) the class of beings who can be abused. Hence, the contract is an inadequate device for grounding morality. There are creatures having moral standing (e.g., the right not to be abused) who are unable to enter into contracts.[15]

Rawls agrees that it is morally wrong to abuse animals. But he claims that the treatment of animals falls outside the range of a theory of justice, and Rawls himself purports to offer us no more than a theory of justice. However, we are presently considering whether Rawls's contract approach can provide us with a *complete* moral theory, and Singer's objection strongly suggests that it cannot. Since participants in the Original Position must have a capacity to heed moral considerations, nonhuman animals are excluded from the Original Position. But then, the contract approach seems inherently incapable of explaining our moral relations to nonhuman animals. We may add that not only are nonhuman animals left out of the hypothetical contract, but so are those humans, such as the severely mentally defective, who lack the capacity (even potentially) to heed moral considerations. Rawls admits that this may present a problem, but he assumes that it will not force a fundamental revision of his theory.

Perhaps we can get some perspective on these issues if we look at the treatment of animals from a Christian point of view. According to Christian theology, humans are meant to be stewards of creation. In other words, the *telos* God seeks involves more than human beings. It involves the whole of creation, each creature having a role to play in the overall scheme. Humans are meant to play a role in nurturing and regulating the lower forms of life. Clearly, the wanton killing or torturing of nonhuman animals is a rejection of this role, not a way of fulfilling it. So, from a Christian point of view, it is a mistake to suppose that moral standing is grounded solely in the capacity to form agreements or contracts. In Chapter 6 (Section VI) I shall argue that sentient animals have the right not to be abused, and that justice consists, in part, in respecting such rights.

A third objection to Rawls's theory involves the claim that even if we assume his elaborate restrictions on negotiations in the Original Position, the parties would still not be able to come to agreement. Rawls himself insists that everyone would agree on the following two principles of justice for societies:

> 1. *The Principle of Liberty*: Each person is to have the same "basic rights and duties," or more precisely, "Each person is to have an equal right to the most extensive total system of equal basic liberties compatible with a similar system of liberty for all."[16]

> 2. *The Difference Principle*: "Social and economic inequalities [differences], for example inequalities of wealth and authority, are just only if they result in compensating benefits for everyone, and in particular for the least advantaged members of society."[17]

There has been much discussion of these principles in recent philosophical literature, and the Difference Principle has been a particular focus of attention. It is commonly regarded as the heart of Rawls's theory of justice.

The Difference Principle says, in effect, that the rich may get richer, provided that the increase in their wealth benefits the least advantaged members of society (e.g., by creating jobs, increasing wages, improving the welfare program, etc.). The rich may not get richer if their increased wealth *in no way* improves the lot of the very poor. The Difference Principle also applies in the workplace. Suppose an employer wants to increase efficiency or production by increasing the wages of some employees who have especially difficult jobs. (Presently, let us suppose, all employees make the same wages.) This is permitted if the increased wages increase profits, so that all the employees receive at least some increase in their wages. It is not permitted if, in effect, the raises are being taken from the pockets of the other employees. Thus, according to the Difference Principle, inequalities can be permitted only if the social system is not a "zero-sum game", i.e., only if the store of goods available (wealth, status, power, etc.) can be increased.[18] (If a social system is a zero-sum game, then distribution is like slicing a pie—one person can get a larger piece only if someone else gets a smaller piece.)

Many have questioned whether all parties in the Original Position would accept the Difference Principle. Rawls defends this principle by claiming that the parties in the Original Position, being rational, would seek to "maximize the minimum."[19] For instance, behind the veil of ignorance, one does not know whether one will be poor or rich, so one will choose a principle that will protect one from the worst, i.e., a principle that will make the minimum (the lowest economic level to which one can sink) as high as possible. This view of rationality is called the "maximin" strategy, for short. But there are at least two reasons for doubting that all parties would choose the Difference Principle.

(1) Does the Difference Principle permit large differentials in wealth and poverty? It does not clearly rule them out. For example, would the Difference Principle permit economic differentials similar to those present in contemporary free market economies? Even if we consider only idealized systems in which the poor *are* better off as the rich get richer, there may still be doubt about the fairness of large economic differentials. How can one person's contribution or effort be worth so much more than another's? Thus, it seems that parties in the Original Position might select some principle of justice other than Rawls's Difference Principle, one that puts a limit on the extremes of wealth and poverty.

(2) Robert Nozick, author of *Anarchy, State, and Utopia*, attacks the Difference Principle from another angle. Observing that the Difference Principle speaks of levels of income, but not of reward merited by contribution, he asks, in effect, "Why should members of the lowest economic class benefit from economic growth if they haven't produced it?" That is, according to Nozick, if a surplus of goods is created by special effort, those who make the effort are *entitled* to at least some of the surplus. The surplus should not be distributed as if no one *deserved* or *merited* any part of it. Yet the Difference Principle distributes goods to the least advantaged groups regardless of their contribution to the productive process.

Nozick suggests that we think of goods (wealth, status, etc.) as a pie that can be made to expand by the efforts of some people. How should the pie be divided? We must ask:

> Who is it that could make the pie larger, and would do it if given a larger share, but not if given an equal share under the scheme of equal distribution? To whom is an incentive to be provided to make this larger contribution? Why doesn't this identifiable differential contribution lead to *some differential entitlement*?[20]

To support his claim that Rawls's concept of the Original Position leaves no room for entitlement, Nozick remarks that

> if things fell from heaven like manna, *and no one had any special entitlement to any portion of it*, and no manna would fall unless all agreed to a particular distribution [in the Original Position], and somehow the quantity varied depending on the distribution, then it is plausible to claim that persons . . . would agree to the *difference principle* . . .[21]

But of course goods do not in general fall like manna, but are produced by effort. And according to Nozick, those who make the effort *deserve* to be rewarded in a way that others do not. The point is that *fairness* and *contribution* seem to be linked in some way, and Rawls's Difference Principle fails to take this link into account. If the parties in the Original Position would select a principle of distribution that took account of one's contribution, then they would not select the Difference Principle.

There are, then, diverse reasons for thinking that the parties in the Original Position would not agree on the Difference Principle. But this is a principle Rawls insists *all* would agree upon. If his arguments fail in this central case, what reason do we have to suppose that the parties in the Original Position could agree on a complete set of moral rules? Please recall: for Rawls, the Difference Principle is a correct principle of justice if and only if all parties in the Original Position would agree to the Difference Principle. And it does seem doubtful that they would. Thus, it appears that Rawls's attempt to characterize morality as *a set of rules humans would agree to under ideal conditions for negotiation* does not succeed. We shall return to an examination of some issues raised in this section, especially issues regarding justice, fairness, and entitlement, in the final chapter.

III. Pluralistic Deontological Views

So far all the views we have examined have had one thing in common: each identifies *exactly one* feature or characteristic which all (and only) morally correct acts have. For act utilitarians that single, right-making feature is *maximal utility*; for Kantians it is *conformity to the categorical imperative*; for contractarians it is *conformity to the Hypothetical Moral Code*; and so on. Philosophers call such views "monistic." The alternative to moral monism is the claim that there is a plurality of "right-making" features, which cannot be reduced to any single common characteristic. Such views are said to be "pluralistic."

In this section we shall discuss three forms of pluralism. Each of these views is deontological, because what makes an act right on these views is simply the fact that it conforms to a rule. These deontologists would readily grant that following a rule may have good consequences in many cases. Some of them might even grant the theoretical possibility that following a certain rule would *always* have good consequences. But they would insist that it is not the consequences that make an act right; acts are right (or wrong) simply by virtue of conforming to (or violating) correct moral rules.

A. The Ten Commandments

Some ordinary Christians seem to be pluralistic deontologists, for they seem to assume that the Ten Commandments represent a complete list of moral rules. We could state the Ten-Commandments view (TC) succinctly as follows:

> (TC)   An act is right if and only if it conforms to the Ten Commandments.[22]

Such a view is pluralistic if (1) each of the Ten Commandments is regarded as a rule proscribing a certain *kind* of action (e.g., stealing or adultery), and (b) these kinds of actions are not thought of as *reducible to any one type of act*. Christians who hold that the Ten Commandments are just a summary of love are monists. For them the foundational moral principle is "An act is right if and only if it is loving." A monistic Christian view will be discussed in the next chapter. For the moment, we want to examine pluralistic views. So, we are considering a view which says that "stealing," "adultery," "murder," etc., are kinds of acts which are always wrong, and that these kinds of acts cannot be subsumed under some more general "wrong-making" heading (such as "not utility maximizing" or "not loving").

There are very serious problems with (TC). First, it seems that one can do some very immoral things while abiding by the Ten Commandments. Consider some examples: (1) The Ten Commandments tell us not to commit murder, but they do not tell us not to beat people up or maim them. So, is it moral to beat or maim people, as long as one does not kill them? (2) The Ten Commandments rule out bearing false witness against our neighbor, i.e., telling lies that will put our neighbor in legal trouble, but how about lying to get oneself out of embarrassing situations—when so doing will not put anyone else in a bad light? For example, in order to avoid problems with her father, a teenager says she wrecked the car because a deer ran in front of her on the highway. In reality, she lost control of the car because she was absorbed in a conversation with some friends. (3) The Ten Commandments rule out adultery, but not sexual intercourse outside of marriage (see Exodus 20:14). So, according to (TC) one can have sexual intercourse at will provided all parties are unmarried. (4) Or how about the person who constantly abuses animals, torturing and killing them at will. The Ten Commandments do not seem to say anything about our treatment of animals. To sum up, it seems that one can abide by the Ten Commandments and still do some things that are clearly wrong.

It may be objected that these examples involve a very literal interpretation of the Ten Commandments, and that the spirit of the Ten Commandments goes far beyond the literal meaning. Perhaps so. But then of course we have to ask, "What *is* the complete set of (literally stated) moral principles, if the Ten Commandments do not really give the whole story? Just how many commandments are there altogether?" Unless the pluralistic deontologist provides us with a complete set of rules, we simply cannot evaluate his theory, for one cannot evaluate a theory if it has not even been stated.

It must be said that some Jewish deontologists, unlike their Christian counterparts, have been willing to offer a complete set of rules, taken from the Torah (first five books of the Old Testament). The complete list contains some 613 rules. However, if anyone is willing to assert that there are 613 basic right- or wrong-making features of actions, it seems that pluralism has gotten out of hand, for at least two reasons. First, one wants to say there must be some end that this plethora of rules is designed to promote, or at least some way of classifying the rules into a few revealing subgroups—otherwise the list of rules is simply too unwieldy for practical use. At stake here is the issue of legalism. Many people think that the attempt to live by an elaborate set of moral rules inevitably produces a distorted outlook. One winds up overly concerned with obedience to the rules, like a motorist who is so preoccupied with safety rules that he cannot remember when to make important turns. Second, the point of having a theory is to explain a complex phenomenon in terms of relatively few basic concepts. A theory with 613 basic concepts is by this standard most unsatisfying.

We shall discuss a deontological position that posits a *manageable* number of basic classes of duty momentarily. But it should be clear that the other mode of simplification—in which a plethora of rules is justified in terms of a *telos*—results in a consequentialist rather than a deontological view of ethics. As we saw in Chapter 3, rule utilitarianism is a consequentialist view of this type. In such a scheme the rules do not correspond to basic right- or wrong-making features of acts. So, ethical theories which countenance long lists of rules seem driven in one of two directions: either the rules are justified in terms of a *telos*, in which case the approach is not deontological, or some manageable set of rules is taken to be an adequate summary of the longer list.

So far we have argued that (TC) permits highly unethical acts. But there is another problem with (TC): It is not always *clear* what behaviors (TC) permits and proscribes. For example, the sixth commandment is often translated as follows: "Thou shalt not kill." But aren't there cases in

which killing is right? Suppose that a policeman can stop
a rape or a murder only by killing an assailant. In such a
case, wouldn't killing be the right thing to do? Most people
say that the answer is, "Yes." Now, it may be responded (I
think quite properly) that the sixth commandment is better
translated as, "Thou shalt not murder." But this response
only raises the question, "What is murder?" The best definition of 'murder' seems to be 'unjustified killing.' But
when is killing justified? How about capital punishment,
war, abortion, self-defense? Again, it seems clear that no
simple rule will be adequate. But then (once again) we
must ask the pluralistic deontologist to produce a complete set of rules; we cannot evaluate a theory if it has not
been stated.

Here is one last problem with (TC), directed at those
who emphasize the *spirit* of the Ten Commandments. The
ninth commandment, "Thou shalt not bear false witness,"
is often understood (by those who emphasize the spirit
of the Ten Commandments) as a general rule against lying.
But it seems that there are cases in which lying is right. For
example, suppose some thugs are trying to murder a friend
of mine, but they do not know where he is. Suppose I *do*
know where he is. The thugs threaten me with torture if I
don't tell them where my friend is hiding. It occurs to me
that a plausible lie will send them on a wild-goose chase
while I and my friend secure police protection. Wouldn't
a lie be perfectly ethical in a case like that? It seems that
people like these thugs, who show a complete disrespect
for the rights of others, do not deserve the truth. The point
is that some acts seem to be obviously right, even though
they violate what is often regarded as the spirit of the Ten
Commandments. Anyway we look at it, (TC) seems to be
a very naive and simplistic theory of morality. We need a
view that can address the highly complex questions the
moral life forces us to ask.

B. Ross's Rule Deontology

According to one famous pluralistic deontologist, W. D. Ross, there are seven fundamental right-making features that acts can have.[23] They are as follows:

1. *Fidelity*. Duties of fidelity have their basis in promises, either explicit or implicit. So, if I have agreed to do something, I ought to do it.

2. *Reparation*. Duties of reparation have their basis in a previous injury inflicted by the person having the duty—an injury that can be rectified. Thus, if I have taken money that belonged to you, I should pay it back.

3. *Gratitude*. Duties of gratitude have their basis in some previous benefit received. Thus, if you saved my life or bailed me out of a tough financial jam, I ought to repay you in kind (by benefiting you if and when you are in need).

4. *Justice*. Ross thought that we all have the duty to prevent unfair distributions of goods (food, money, shelter, clothing, etc.). So, for example, if a deserving fellow employee is being overlooked for promotions or raises, I ought to correct the situation if I can.

5. *Beneficence*. Ross thought that we all have a duty to help others achieve a greater degree of virtue, intelligence, and pleasure. Thus, if I can help a child learn to read or write (one who is otherwise likely to remain illiterate) I should do so.

6. *Self-improvement*. Ross thought that we all have a duty to make ourselves more virtuous and intelligent. Thus, one should always be making an effort to learn more, and to improve one's moral character.

7. *Nonmaleficence*. This is the duty to perform any act that would prevent an injury to another person. For example, if I can save you from being injured by pushing you out of the way of an onrushing automobile, I should do so.

A question immediately arises. Don't these duties sometimes conflict? For example, suppose I promise to meet you at a restaurant for lunch, but on the way I come upon the scene of an accident. An injured person needs my help. Helping him will involve missing my appointment with you, and indeed, his needs are so urgent that I will not have time even to call you to explain what has happened until later in the day. Am I to keep my promise (fulfill the duty of fidelity) or help the accident victim (fulfill the duty of beneficence)? Surely I ought to help the accident victim. But I can do that only by breaking my promise to you. I cannot fulfill both duties.

Ross's answer to this problem is that his seven categories represent *prima facie* duties. To say that something is a *prima facie* duty is to say that it is an actual duty unless other moral considerations intervene. Another way to put it is this: if one has a *prima facie* duty to perform act X, then X has a right-making characteristic—i.e., there is at least one moral reason in favor of performing X. But of course one right-making feature might be outweighed or overridden by another, as in the case above. Ross himself speaks of one's duty as having "the greatest balance of *prima facie* rightness."[24] We can state his ethical theory, then, as follows:

> (R) An act is right if and only if (a) it is a *prima facie* duty and (b) no alternative act is a weightier or overriding *prima facie* duty.

It should be noted that several of Ross's *prima facie* duties are backward-looking. That is, the rightness of the act is based more upon what has happened in the past than upon what will happen in the future. For example, duties of reparation have their basis in a past injury, duties of fidelity in a past agreement, duties of gratitude in a past kindness. As a deontologist, Ross thinks that consequentialists are unable to give an adequate account of these backward-looking *prima facie* duties.

Many philosophers have argued that Ross's view leaves us unable to determine what our actual (as opposed to *prima facie*) duties are in many cases, for Ross does not tell us how to determine which *prima facie* duty has more weight when two of them conflict. And conflict cases are quite common. For example, suppose I have promised to give $1000 to a charity, but an old friend, to whom I owe a debt of gratitude, shows up in need of just that amount of cash; and suppose I do not have enough money both to keep my promise and to help my friend. According to Ross it is self-evident that I have *prima facie* duties of fidelity and gratitude in such a case. But he does not claim that it is self-evident that o..e of these *prima facie* duties is weightier than the other. In fact, he offers no procedure for dealing with such conflict cases, other than advising us to reflect very carefully when confronted with such a choice. As Alan Donagan, a professor of philosophy at the California Institute of Technology, points out, "it is fraudulent to describe" such a process of

> moral deliberation as one of 'weighing' or 'balancing' con-
> siderations. For that metaphor to be appropriate, there
> must be a procedure for ascertaining the weight of each
> consideration, either comparatively or absolutely, a proce-
> dure analogous to that of putting objects on a balance or
> scale.[25]

But Ross has not provided us with such a procedure, so we are given no guidance in cases where *prima facie* duties conflict. And it must be emphasized that conflict cases are extremely common. For example, *prima facie* duties of beneficence apply in most any situation one can be in. (There is almost always something one can do to increase the pleasure of others.) Yet one cannot be forever securing the pleasure of others. There are the duties of self-improvement to attend to, as well as those of justice, reparation, fidelity, etc. So, one problem with Ross's deontological position is that it effectively leaves us without guidance in all cases in which *prima facie* duties conflict.

A second problem with Ross's view emerges if we ask, "Where do Ross's seven *prima facie* duties come from? How does he know that those seven (and just those seven) kinds of *prima facie* duty obtain?" Ross's answer is that these seven considerations are self-evident *prima facie* duties. He does not claim that it is self-evident that there are *only* seven basic types of duty, for he allows that his list of duties might not be complete. But he does insist that each of his seven categories represents a self-evident *prima facie* duty.

Is this claim to self-evidence plausible? To say that a statement is self-evident is to say that if one grasps the concepts involved, one sees that it must be true. For example, "Round squares do not exist" is self-evident—nothing beyond an understanding of the concepts involved is needed to know that the statement is true. But there is reason to doubt that statements such as, "Fidelity is a *prima facie* duty," are self-evident. Suppose a hit man makes an agreement with a mafia boss to kill an innocent person. Does the hit man have a *prima facie* duty to kill the person in question? If Ross says the hit man does have a *prima facie* duty to kill, he can hardly claim that this is self-evident. In fact, many would say that such a wicked promise has no moral weight at all; the hit man's promise does not result in a *moral reason* for killing an innocent person— not even a reason that is outweighed by others. It just is not self-evident that we can give ourselves even a *partial* moral reason to do something wicked or cruel simply by promising to do it.

On the other hand, suppose Ross says that the hit man does *not* have a *prima facie* duty to "make the hit." This is problematic, because Ross cannot deny that the hit man has entered into an agreement with the mafia boss, and if an agreement has been made, how can Ross's category of fidelity fail to apply? If Ross says that in some cases agreements have absolutely no moral force at all, the apparent simplicity of the statement "Fidelity is a *prima facie* duty" turns out to be deceptive, for the concepts involved are revealed as complex. If agreements constitute *prima facie* duties only in certain circumstances, then the word 'fidelity' masks a complicated concept of agreement-under-such-and-such-circumstances. And the statement, "Fidelity is a *prima facie* duty," translates into something like this: "Agreements under such-and-such circumstances constitute a morally relevant, though not necessarily a decisive reason for performing an act." Now this statement may be true. But is it self-evident? Can we know that it is true just by understanding the concepts involved? Most of us probably feel we lack a firm grasp of the circumstances under which an agreement is morally binding, and a self-evident statement must be clear and simple. Thus, the apparent clarity and simplicity of Ross's basic principles seems illusory upon examination.

So, Ross must either affirm or deny that the hit man has a *prima facie* duty to make the hit. And either way his claim that the basic principles of morality are self-evident is called into question.

Let us consider one final objection to Ross's theory. Feldman asks, how does it happen that "in every case of moral conflict, the act that we think is obligatory is the very one that Ross thinks is the most stringent prima facie duty?"[26] Any divergence between one's opinion about what is right and one's opinion about which *prima facie* duty is overriding seems to be ruled out by definition. Thus, it appears that the phrase "overriding *prima facie* duty" is just a synonym for 'duty.' If so, Ross's theory boils down to this: an act is right if and only if (a) it is a *prima facie* duty and (b) no alternative act is a duty. This seems rather trivial. To determine whether act X is right, clause (b) says I must first determine that the alternatives to X are not my duty. But if I already had access to such extensive information about those things that are *not* my duty, I would scarcely be in need of a moral theory. In effect, Ross is saying: "X is your duty if and only if there is something to be said in favor of doing X and no other act is your duty." And this really does not tell us very much. So, Ross's theory seems unilluminating upon scrutiny.[27]

For a variety of reasons, then, Ross's deontological position seems unattractive. The idea that conflicting *prima facie* duties can be weighed is spurious. The claim to self-evidence is implausible. And conceptual analysis suggests that Ross's theory is, at bottom, rather trivial.

C. Hierarchicalism

Some deontologists have broached theories that avoid at least some of the problems inherent in Ross's view. For example, Norman Geisler, an evangelical philosopher, has suggested that the problem of conflicting duties could be handled by arranging norms in a hierarchy.[28] As an illustration, views of this type might claim that duties of fidelity are the highest ranking duties; next would come duties of reparation, which outrank all duties except those of fidelity; duties of gratitude would outrank all duties except those of fidelity and reparation, and so on.[29] (The lowest ranking duty would be in force only when no other duties were applicable.) On this hierarchical view, clear direction is provided in cases when duties conflict, since one's duty is specified by the highest ranking norm applicable in a given situation.

Another possible virtue of Geisler's view is that he avoids the controversial notion of a *prima facie* duty. From Geisler's perspective "when any two or more . . . values happen to conflict, a person is exempted from his otherwise binding obligation to a lower norm in view of the pre-emptory obligation of the higher norm."[30] Thus, for Geisler, only the highest ranking norm in a given situation provides a moral reason to act. Lower ranking norms do not count as right-making features of an act. This gives the hierarchicalist a way (at least in principle) of avoiding the absurdity of saying that if one promises to kill an innocent person, one has a moral reason in favor of murder. Succinctly stated, then, the hierarchical view (H) says that

> (H) An act is right if and only if it fulfills the highest ranking applicable norm.

We do not, however, have a complete description of hierarchicalism until we are told what the correct hierarchy of norms is. And the precise ranking of norms is critical. To illustrate, if we treat fidelity as the highest ranking norm, then if we promise to kill someone, it is indeed our duty to do so! Hence, we must be careful to order the various norms correctly. Unfortunately, Geisler's own list of norms is radically incomplete. For example, his list contains no analogues for Ross's duties of fidelity, reparation, or gratitude.[31] As far as I know, Ross's list of duties is the most compelling any pluralist has offered. But severe problems arise for the hierarchicalist on Ross's scheme. For reflection on cases strongly suggests that in some cases one norm, such as justice, will outrank another, such as fidelity; while in others, the ranking will be reversed (in this case, fidelity will outrank justice). Feldman offers the following illustration:

> Suppose a judge has promised to be very lenient in the sentencing of a political ally who has committed a serious crime. The judge should not keep the promise. Rather, he should see that justice is done. In other cases, it might be more important to keep a promise than it would be to insure a just distribution of goods.[32]

For example, an aging father has promised to will a valuable object to one of his children, and has nothing of quite the same value for his other children, though they are equally deserving. He could sell the object and distribute the money equally among his children, but he feels he should honor his promise. The other children would like to have the object, but they respect the promise, and are not covetous.

There might be similar reversals in the case of gratitude and fidelity. For example, suppose someone owes me a debt of gratitude—at risk to my own life, I once helped him to drive away a mugger. I show up needing (and requesting) his professional services for next Tuesday afternoon. But last week he promised to attend a party that afternoon.

He cannot both attend the party and provide me with the help I need. Timing is crucial, and I need his help Tuesday afternoon. The person giving the party is reasonable, and will understand if he breaks his promise. What should he do? Now, in this case gratitude surely outranks fidelity—he should help me even though it means missing the party.

But in another case the ranking may be reversed. Suppose some one owes me a debt of gratitude—I once worked his shift at the factory when he felt burned out and needed some time off. Now I ask him to work my shift in the coming week, because I am having some guests and would like a little extra time off. However, a month ago he promised his twelve-year-old daughter that he would take her to New York next week, where she will take part in a music competition. It is an important promise, and he feels he cannot let her down. Moreover, his debt to me is not all that great. So, in this case fidelity surely outranks gratitude—he should keep his promise to his daughter. Again, this case strongly suggests that the attempt to produce a serial ordering of norms seems doomed from the outset. The moral life is too complicated to be reflected in a simple hierarchy of rules.

Consider one further example. On some occasions it seems that beneficence outranks self-improvement; while in others self-improvement outranks beneficence. Whenever I spend money, time, or effort on improving myself, I am using resources that could be used by others. For example, if I decide to spend my time and money getting a college education, I am using resources that could be used to benefit others (I could spend the time helping famine victims, or donate the money so that others might be educated.) Obviously, there are times when it is appropriate to engage in beneficence, and times when it is appropriate to engage in self-improvement. But this means that neither of these duties is always above the other in a simple hierarchy of norms. The situation is more complex than the hierarchicalist supposes.

It is worth contrasting the hierarchical approach to moral decision making with the Christian teleological approach. The Christian teleologist (and indeed, consequentialists in general) will approach cases of the type under consideration by asking which act is more likely to promote the *telos*. But this type of consequentialist thinking is not permitted by the hierarchicalist. Moral decisions are to be made simply in terms of which norm outranks the others. The problem is, this way of proceeding runs roughshod over the subtleties of the moral life.

Feldman has remarked on another problem for the hierarchicalist: conflicts of duty can take place in the same rank.[33] For example, suppose I owe a debt of gratitude to two people, Jones and Smith. Jones saved me from drowning once, while Smith once helped me paint my house. Smith calls to ask me to help him do a rush job of painting a room in his house. He is in a hurry because some guests are arriving tomorrow, and he has no one else he can turn to on such short notice. While I am on the phone with Smith, Jones rings the doorbell. He is facing a final deadline on an important project which must be completed by midnight. I have expertise of a type Jones needs to finish his project, and he has no one else he can turn to on such short notice. What should I do? For a hierarchicalist who accepts gratitude as a fundamental duty, there seems to be no answer, for I owe a debt of gratitude to both Smith and Jones. Nevertheless, intuitively, I owe a greater debt to Jones than to Smith, since Jones saved my life and Smith merely helped me paint my house. Thus, it appears that I should explain to Smith that I have a more pressing duty to help Jones. (I cannot fulfill both duties.) So, again, it appears that the hierarchical approach attempts to impose a simple framework on a phenomenon that is anything but simple. For this reason I find hierarchicalism unacceptable.

*   *   *   *   *

In this chapter I have examined the major deontological alternatives to the Christian teleological view. Though each of the deontological views presents us with an interesting perspective on morality, it seems to me that none of them provides us with an acceptable foundation for moral thinking. Having surveyed and criticized the alternatives, we can now turn to an examination of the Christian teleological view.

Ethics and   5
the Kingdom
of God

I. THE VALUE OF AN ETHICAL THEORY

What is the value of having an ethical theory? This is a question that occurs to most people as they work through any systematic treatment of ethical theory. It is the more pressing since ethical theories do not automatically provide answers to every controversial moral issue. For example, none of the theories we have considered gives an immediate answer to such contemporary moral problems as, "Is abortion always wrong?", "Is genetic engineering permissible?", "Is affirmative action just?", "Is euthanasia ever right?"

But even though ethical theories do not provide immediate answers to every moral issue, they do play an important role in ethical reasoning, in at least three ways. (1) They suggest a strategy for approaching complex moral issues. They tell us what sorts of things we will need to know to settle any moral question. Thus, the egoist tells us to focus on the satisfaction of the agent, while the utilitarian insists that we take into account the satisfaction of everyone affected by the act. In short, each ethical theory gives us a *framework* within which to carry out our thinking about

121

particular moral issues. Without such a framework we are apt to become hopelessly confused.

(2) Each ethical theory expresses a picture or vision of the moral life. It is hard to make this idea of a vision or picture precise, but there can be no doubt that the utilitarian's way of representing the moral life has an entirely different "feel" than the contractarian's or the pluralistic rule-deontologist's. And the vision of the moral life associated with an ethical theory is one of its most important features; for in the end, what one holds about specific moral issues may be less important than one's general moral orientation. From this point of view, the inability of groups in our society to agree about specific issues (such as abortion, extramarital sex, or military involvement in the Third World) may be merely a symptom of (and hence less important than) the fundamental divergences in ethical orientation which fuel the disagreement.

(3) Having a theory of ethics—and hence a vision of the moral life—can help us to avoid bias. Nearly all of us grow up with a more or less random list of moral concerns, which is delivered to us by our parents or other authorities along the way. But often our concerns, and capacities for moral outrage, are oddly selective. One person may be opposed to abortion, but unconcerned about her country's reckless use of military force. Another may be outraged by pornography while scarcely giving a thought to racial injustice or world hunger. Yet another may deplore his country's selfish foreign policy while finding adultery unobjectionable. Having a general ethical theory is one way to combat this natural human tendency to be selective about issues. Once we have a firm grasp on a particular ethical vision, there will be a tendency, if we are intellectually honest, to become clearer and clearer about the implications of that vision.

In addition to serving as a guide for practical moral decision making, an ethical theory will usually tell us what *makes* an act right or wrong. This is not quite the same thing as having a moral criterion (a way of telling what is right or wrong). For example, if I know that God disapproves of an act, then of course I know the act is wrong. But as we have seen, it is another thing altogether to say that the act is wrong *because* God disapproves of it (or *by virtue* of divine disapproval). The marks by which we happen to know that an act is right (or wrong) might conceivably differ from the features of the act that (metaphysically) account for its rightness (or wrongness). To illustrate: a child may know that something is wrong because her parents have told her it is wrong, without being able to identify the aspect of the action that actually makes it wrong (e.g., that it may be harmful to her). But the major ethical theories we have discussed can be understood as attempts to provide both a criterion for ethics and an explanation of the features of an act that account for its rightness (or wrongness). While, from a practical point of view, it is a criterion of ethics that we seek, from a theoretical point of view we naturally would like to know what truly makes an act right or wrong.

II. The Kingdom of God

A. Overview

With these remarks about the value of ethical theory in mind, it is now time to elaborate the Christian teleological (CT) view of ethics sketched in Chapter 2:

> (CT) An act is right if and only if it promotes the Kingdom of God.

This view is of course consequentialist, but it differs markedly from the other consequentialist views we have examined. Since the *telos* here is not agent utility or utility, but the Kingdom or society of God, (CT) gives us a radically different vision of ethics than that offered by egoism or utilitarianism. As a rough approximation, it tells us that the *quality of relationships* (with God, other humans, nature, and ourselves) is the controlling concept in ethics, rather than pleasure, satisfaction, obedience to rules, etc. Thus, (CT) is intimately bound up with the Christian view of the meaning of life: God has created humans freely, and freely bestows his love upon them; He seeks a free response of love in return. This drama of love between God and humans is the ultimate source of meaning in human life, according to Christian theology, and personal relationships obviously play a central role in the drama. But we must now move from these generalities to a more detailed account of the nature of the Kingdom of God.

First, the Kingdom or society of God consists in *harmonious* relations between God and humans, between individual humans, between groups of humans, between humans and the creation order (both animate and inanimate), and between each individual human and himself or herself. When Jesus was asked, "Which commandment is the first of all?" he responded, " '. . . you shall love the Lord your God with all your heart, and with all your soul, and with all your mind, and with all your strength.' The second is this, 'You shall love your neighbor as yourself' " (Mark 12:30-31). Now as commandments go, one could certainly complain that these two are not very specific or clear; love is a pretty vague concept. But Jesus is not endorsing a system of ethics in which obedience to a detailed moral code is the focus. Rather, He is offering us a vision of the moral life in which relationships are what count—harmonious relationships. Often He refers to this as the Kingdom of God, and it is that vision of a community of God and all His creatures which Jesus continually holds before us: "Seek ye first the kingdom of God. . ." (Matthew 6:33). His parables are again and again attempts to paint a picture of a society of humans under God's leadership.

It needs to be said that by 'harmonious relationships' I do not mean relationships which appear to be peaceful due to their superficiality. Sometimes the appearance of harmony is maintained at the cost of resentment, due to the fear of what will happen if individuals share their true feelings, aspirations, and ideas. So, while harmonious relationships are free of bitterness, resentment, and malice, they are not necessarily free of confrontation and disagreement, as long as the confrontation and disagreement occur in a context of respect and mutual esteem. And while the human capacity for deep relationships is limited—one can only know a few people intimately—the capacity for relationships with significant reciprocity is enormous. There is a wealth of satisfaction in relating to people we do not (and cannot) know intimately when such relations are characterized by respect, good will, and a desire to give as much as one takes. So, by 'harmonious relationships' I do not mean superficially peaceful ones, but relationships characterized by a genuine reciprocity or mutual exchange.

Second, the Kingdom of God is not a collective in which the individual is sacrificed for the group. Rather, the individual is fulfilled by participating in the kingdom. This ethical perspective is communitarian, in that it says that the individual cannot be fulfilled apart from the group. But it is equally true to say that there can be no establishment of the kingdom at the expense of individuals, for the kingdom is frustrated whenever (and to whatever extent) individuals are hindered from realizing their potential as creatures of God.

One can think of the Kingdom or society of God as comprised of persons living out roles to which God has called them. Here it is useful to refurbish the old (but often misunderstood) language of vocation. Nowadays the word 'vocation' often means 'career.' But it has another, richer meaning: 'the set of roles and tasks to which one has been called by God.' On this picture of ethics, the ideal is a community of persons each doing their God-intended part (or living out the role to which God has called them). To find one's vocation is to find both fulfillment and, in an important sense, to find oneself. I shall elaborate on the concept of vocation momentarily (Subsection C below), because it plays a central role in my understanding of the Kingdom of God.

Third, it is important to recognize that the Kingdom of God has a historical dimension: there is a degree to which it can be fulfilled this side of death or judgment. But the complete establishment of the kingdom will come in the afterlife.[1] At that time, the degree of delight for participants in the kingdom will rise dramatically, according to Christian theology.

Fourth, we may ask what forms of harmonious relationship are typical of the Kingdom of God. At the most general level, personal, social, and economic relations are involved. Every sort of wall of hostility is to be broken down. For "there is neither Jew nor Greek, there is neither slave nor free, there is neither male nor female; for you are all one in Christ Jesus" (Galatians 3:28), and "in Christ Jesus you who once were far off have been brought near in the blood of Christ. For he is our peace, who has made us both one, and has broken down the dividing wall of hostility" (Ephesians 2:13-14). No barrier to genuine reciprocity is to be left standing.

Thus, marriage is crucial because it is the fundamental institution for achieving harmony between the sexes. Families unite the generations, and are a means for cultivating in children character traits which promote the Kingdom of God. Nations typically unite people through the means of shared culture (language, art, myth, tradition). And while nationalism—a nation's preoccupation with itself—has often led to war, there is a proper love for the good things in one's own culture that can create a healthy bond between large social groups. Economic systems and social conventions are important also, for if these are unjust or oppressive, disharmony between persons or groups results.

Fifth, the church is meant to provide a picture of the kingdom "before the watching world."[2] Of course, it can only provide such a picture if it provides its members with genuinely fulfilling forms of social connectedness. The relation between the church and the world is of profound importance. Too often Christians have tried to equate the church with the Kingdom of God, but history continually undercuts this pharisaical assumption. Important movements for justice and benevolence have frequently come from outside the church. Indeed, one sometimes sees the church resisting what it ought to be approving in the world—one thinks of the blanket condemnation feminism has received in some parts of the American church and of the attitudes white Christians in South Africa frequently display toward those who resist apartheid. The church cannot be at peace with those attitudes and movements in the world which hinder the Kingdom of God; but it cannot be at war with those aspects of the world that promote it.

Sixth, from the standpoint of the Christian teleological view, harmonious relations between the various levels of being are also aspects of the kingdom. Thus, it is not only important that harmonious relations exist among humans, it is vital that harmonious relations exist between humans and God. We humans are to be, as it were, drawn up into the divine society (of Father, Son, and Holy Spirit), humble participants in an eternal community of love. Beyond this, there is a proper ordering of relations between humans and the rest of creation. This ordering has traditionally been described in terms of *stewardship*. That is, humans are to nurture and regulate the lower orders of creation, such as nonhuman animals and plants. I shall have more to say about the treatment of animals in the next chapter.

One possible misunderstanding needs to be laid to rest before we go any further. Someone might claim that the notion of the Kingdom of God is itself an ethical one. "Haven't you surreptitiously packed a lot of ethics into your description of the *telos*? And if so, doesn't this violate the whole idea of a teleological theory? Isn't it the project of a teleological theory to explain moral obligation in terms of nonmoral goods, such as pleasure or satisfaction? After all, if we already knew what was morally good we probably wouldn't be so desperately in need of a theory of moral obligation!"

I would (somewhat tentatively) agree that a teleological or consequentialist view is meant to explain moral obligation in terms of nonmoral good. I say "somewhat tentatively" because I am not sure that the distinction between moral and nonmoral good can be sharply drawn. But perhaps we can get some rough idea of the distinction. Try to imagine yourself on a moral holiday, in which you've decided to ignore all moral restraints (anything you regard as a moral rule or ethical consideration). What would you "go for" on such a holiday? What ends would you seek? No doubt you would want to retain (or regain) your health. Probably you would seek some physical pleasures—food, drink, and/or sex. Beyond this, you would probably enjoy some experiences of beauty, both in nature and in works of art. Thus it does appear that, even if one were to drop what are ordinarily regarded as moral constraints, there are still ends one would seek, still things one would value. Let us call these "nonmoral goods."

But it seems to me that these considerations do not amount to an objection to the Christian teleological view. For most of us, if on a moral holiday, would also want some satisfying personal relationships. Granted, we are unlikely to have any such relationships unless we treat people ethically, but that is not relevant at the moment. What is relevant is that, even on a moral holiday most of us would value such things as companionship, intimate romantic relationships, and close friendships. But, then, these are clearly forms of harmonious relationships, which concept is the fundamental building block of the concept of the Kingdom of God. In fact, the Kingdom of God consists in creatures in various forms of harmonious relationships with each other and with their Creator. So, it appears that the Kingdom of God is a "nonmoral good" in the sense needed to ward off the objection.

B. Relationships, Demands, and Obligations

A central feature of relationships is the fact that persons place *demands* (expectations, requests, commands) upon each other. These demands are the raw materials out of which relationships are constructed. A failure to meet a demand frequently strains a relationship; but of course, we cannot and should not meet all the demands placed on us. Sometimes conflicting demands are made of us; sometimes demands are unreasonable; sometimes they are hostile or destructive. Thus, it is not always in our power to achieve harmonious relations with others. They may create barriers over which we have no control by making illegitimate demands or by failing to satisfy entirely legitimate demands.

Demands can create obligations if relationships are valued, because there can be no worthwhile relationships if we entirely ignore the demands (expectations, requests, etc.) of others. Robert M. Adams, a philosopher at UCLA, has provided a helpful discussion of the relation between demands and obligations.[3] As Adams points out, parental demand is the first type of demand most of us become aware of. Before we understand rules of any type, we sense the demands of our parents, and know what it is to satisfy and to frustrate those demands. At a very early age we experience the alienation that comes from a refusal to meet parental demand—the sense of guilt on our side, the anger on the side of the parent:

> In our first experience of guilt its principal significance was an action or attitude of ours that ruptured or strained our relationship with a parent. There did not have to be a failure of benevolence or a violation of a rule; perhaps we were even too young to understand rules. It was enough that something we did or expressed offended the parent, and seemed to threaten the relationship. This is the original context in which the obligation cluster of moral concepts and sentiments arise. We do not begin with a set of moral principles but with a relationship . . . which is immensely valued for its own sake . . .[4]

Adams immediately adds that

> we do not really have obligation concepts until we can
> make some sort of distinction, among the things we do
> that strain relationships, between those in which we are
> at fault or wrong and those in which we are innocent or
> right (not to mention those in which we are partly wrong
> and partly right). We begin to grasp such a distinction as
> we learn such facts as the following: Not every demand
> or expectation laid on us by other people constitutes an
> obligation, but only demands made in certain ways in cer-
> tain kinds of relationship (for instance, commands of one's
> parents or teachers), and expectations that arise in cer-
> tain ways (for instance, from promises). An unexpressed
> wish is not a command. One is not guilty for anything
> one has not really done. The fact that somebody is an-
> gry does not necessarily imply that an obligation has been
> violated.[5]

Adams suggests that several questions need to be asked
to judge whether a demand is of a sort to create obligation.[6]
First, *who is making the demand?* Is it someone or some
group (e.g., the community) that values the individual? Or
is it someone who is indifferent or hostile to the individual? One cannot be *morally obligated* to be manipulated
or exploited by others, for this is not the path to harmonious relationships. (Of course, people are often made to
feel obligated by manipulative "demanders." But *being* obligated and *feeling* obligated are two different things. Much
psychotherapy aims at helping a person distinguish these
two things in practice.)

Second, *what are the attributes of the demander?* Is
the demander someone I hold in high regard? One reason
God's commands (a form of demand) should be obeyed is
that God is so admirable. Such attributes as *omniscience*
and *moral goodness* must give His demands precedence
over all others. As Adams remarks,

> God is supremely knowledgeable and wise—he is omni-
> scient, after all; and that is very important motivationally.

> It makes a difference if you think of commands as coming from someone who completely understands both us and our situation.[7]

Moreover, it makes a difference that God is both *loving* and *just*; a loving God will always have in mind the long-term best interests of his creatures, and a just God will never treat his creatures unfairly.[8]

In this connection it is worth noting that a society is apt to find its demands fulfilled by its members only to the extent that its members hold it in high regard. The conventions of a society are its most insistent demands. Thus, we cannot ignore the demands embodied in the conventions and still retain a sense of belonging to the group. To disobey the rules which constitute the conventions is to alienate ourselves from society; to comply with the rules is to maintain harmony with the group, and to express our sense of belonging to it.

Finally, Adams observes that the "demandee" must evaluate the demand itself. *Is the demand conducive to ends the demandee himself values? Is it a demand the demandee can meet while meeting the other demands placed upon him? Is it a demand that takes precedence over some (or all) others?*[9]

When we cannot meet all the demands placed on us (and isn't that invariably the case?), we have to set priorities. From the standpoint of the Christian teleological view, the concept of the Kingdom of God is the measuring stick we must use in making such choices. This is not at all the same thing as having a pat formula for moral decision making. One must, above all, keep the vision of God's kingdom before one, and let that ideal inform all decisions. Demands that will be destructive of one's relationship with God rank below all others. "We ought to obey God rather than men" (Acts 5:29).

Normally, the demands of one's society, as expressed in its conventions, create moral obligations *provided* they do not conflict with the demands of God. (I say "normally"

because conventions sometimes place conflicting demands
on us.) As Adams remarks:

> Where community prevails, rather than alienation, the
> sense of belonging is not to be sharply distinguished from
> the inclination to comply with the reasonable requirements
> of the community. A "community" is a group of people
> who live their lives to some extent—possibly to a very
> limited extent—in common. To see myself as "belonging"
> to a community is to see the institution or other members
> of the group as "having something to say about" how I live
> and act—perhaps not about every department of my life,
> and only to a reasonable extent about any department of
> it, but it is part of the terms of the relationship that their
> demands on certain subjects are expected to have some
> weight with me. And valuing such a relationship—loving
> it or respecting it—implies some willingness to submit to
> reasonable demands of the community.[10]

In this connection it is worth noting that social conventions often exist precisely to simplify decision making.
By creating social practices defined in terms of particular rules, we eliminate vagueness and much anxious moral
reflection. However, like other human inventions, social
conventions are imperfect. Sometimes the rules will make
inconsistent demands on us; and sometimes the rules are
oppressive or unjust, and hence must be reformed in the
light of the *telos*—the Kingdom of God.

There is a natural human tendency to seek simple rules
for evaluating demands. And, as I have remarked previ-
ously, rules of thumb can be very helpful in guiding ethical
decision making. But it is interesting to note that much
of the biblical teaching about ethics is given through narrative—stories and parables. In fact, the New Testament
represents Jesus as using parables to a vastly greater extent
than rules and commands; Jesus' parables of the Kingdom
of God give us the most vivid picture of it. Accordingly,
contemporary theologians have made much of the role of
narrative in ethical thought. We seem hardly able to grasp

a statement like, "Love thy neighbor as thyself" apart from parables (such as that of the Good Samaritan) which fill it with meaning.

Biblical narrative is not the only sort of narrative that provides insight into the nature of the Kingdom of God. One reason we value great literature in general is its capacity for moral instruction. McClendon remarks that Henry James

> comes close to the center of the matter in a famous sentence: "What is character but the determination of incident? What is incident but the illustration of character?" So incident (or *plot*) and *character* (and its development) are interdependent narrative elements. If we add to these *setting* (which James certainly did not mean to omit) we have what some recent theorists take to be the necessary and sufficient ingredients of narrative.[11]

Since the virtues and vices are traits of character, a study of great literature has long been regarded as one of the best ways to explore the nature of the virtues and vices. One thinks of the virtuous Alyosha in *The Brothers Karamazov*, of the villainous Iago in Shakespeare's *Othello*, of the worldly Oblonsky in Tolstoy's *Anna Karenin*. So, although biblical materials play a primary role in the formation of a concept of the Kingdom of God, the insight into the virtues and vices found in great literature undoubtedly helps to fill in many gaps in our understanding. The point is that not only moral rules but insightful narratives help us to form a vision of the Kingdom of God.

To sum up the discussion to this point: The Christian teleological view places a high value on relationships, and if we value relationships we must be willing to meet the demands involved in maintaining them. In meeting demands harmony is maintained or achieved. Disharmony is produced not only when demands are not met, but also when demands are inappropriate (unreasonable, hostile, destructive, etc.). Rules of thumb can be helpful in evaluating demands, but it is at least equally important to develop a vivid picture of the *telos*, the Kingdom of God, and to evaluate demands in terms of that *telos*. This picture can be developed through narrative (parable and story) and through philosophical description (as at present).

My remarks concerning demands and obligations in this section connect with the discussion of normative relativism in Chapter 1. There I argued in favor of a universal moral truth, and against the idea that what is right varies as conventions vary. While I certainly stick with that conclusion, we are now in a position to see that a much more restricted relativistic thesis might have merit. If obligations can be created by the demands of others, and if the conventions represent the most stringent demands a society places on its members, there may be some variation in obligation between cultures. For example, modern American culture places a high value on being punctual in many situations. Other cultures do not—it may be understood that an invitation for 7:00 p.m. has considerable "leeway" built into it. Either convention seems reasonable, as long as all parties know what to expect. Now, of course, punctuality is not one of the more pressing moral issues of our day. Nevertheless, it is possible to show considerable disrespect for others by violating the understood obligations about punctuality, and I am suggesting that these obligations might actually vary from culture to culture. It might actually be obligatory to be strictly punctual in America (for many types of events), but not in, say, Malawi. Or again, in case of the death of the mother, some cultures place primary responsibility for raising the child on the father, others on the maternal grandmother. While it is clear that a society without provision for such exigencies would be remiss, is it clear that there is only one correct way of dealing with the problem? It may be that, in such cases, the demands of society fix the particular form the obligation takes. In other words, the question of whom a particular obligation falls on may be settled by convention in some cases.[12]

Have I now fallen into radical moral relativism? Not at all. It should be quite clear that many forms of behavior are ruled out by the *telos*; there can be no harmonious community life if people feel they can kill, steal, lie, cheat, at will. Moreover, from a Christian point of view, God in His omniscience has revealed certain moral truths. These rules are laid down because they are absolutely necessary for human flourishing, e.g., "Don't murder." Other demands He makes, not because they express absolutely essential requirements for human life in community, but to create bonds between Himself and His creatures—e.g., the Old Testament rule, "Keep the Sabbath." Such rules may apply only to certain groups (e.g., the Jews), or even be subject to alteration.

So, the situation seems to be this. We should expect there to be strict rules against killing, stealing, cheating, and lying, and we have a right to demand such things in any cultural setting. (Though even here, of course, we must beware of oversimplification; e.g., what counts as property and therefore what counts as stealing varies to some extent from culture to culture.) From a Christian point of view, the conventions of every culture manifest the fallenness of humanity to some extent, and so stand in need of reform. On the other hand, there are many areas of life in which no one way can be regarded as essential for the kingdom. In such areas, different cultures may make different demands, and such demands may create moral obligations. Humanity is remarkably and gloriously complex, with different peoples establishing differing conventions. And of course it sometimes takes great wisdom to discern whether the differing conventions concern essentials or nonessentials.

In this section I have emphasized that there can be no harmonious relationships unless some demands are met, but I have also insisted that many demands should not be met. One especially noteworthy class of illegitimate demands is the class of *unjust* demands. We shall focus on the issue of justice (and hence of just and unjust demands) in the final chapter.

C. Vocation

One can describe the Kingdom of God as a tapestry of
lives in which the weave is determined by the particular
vocations of individuals. One demand God places on each
person is unique to that person. The great Jewish philosopher Martin Buber has written about vocation in a way that
is at once both illuminating and edifying:

> Rabbi Baer of Radoshitz once said to his teacher, the
> 'Seer' of Lubiin: 'Show me one general way to the service
> of God.'
>
> The zaddik [leader of the Hasidic community] replied:
> 'It is impossible to tell men what way they should take.
> For one way to serve God is through learning, another
> through prayer, another through fasting, another through
> eating. Everyone should carefully observe what way his
> heart draws him to, and then choose this way with all his
> strength.'[13]

And again,

> Every person born into this world represents something
> new, something that never existed before, something origi-
> nal and unique. [Thus everyone] . . . is called upon to fulfill
> his particularity . . . Every man's foremost task is the actu-
> alization of his unique, unprecedented and never-recurring
> potentialities, and not the repetition of something that an-
> other, and be it even the greatest, has already achieved.
>
> The wise Rabbi Bunam once said in old age, when he
> had already grown blind: 'I should not like to change places
> with our father Abraham! What good would it do God if
> Abraham became like blind Bunam, and blind Bunam like
> Abraham? Rather than have this happen, I think I shall try
> to become a little more myself.'
>
> The idea was expressed with even greater pregnancy by
> Rabbi Zusya when he said, a short while before his death:
> 'In the world to come I shall not be asked: "Why were you
> not Moses?" I shall be asked: "Why were you not Zusya?"[14]

The experience of being called by God to be a certain kind of person, or of being called by God to perform a certain task, is a common one in the Judeo-Christian tradition. Some of God's demands are general, applying to all humans, but others are directed at individuals. Perhaps, as Buber suggests, God demands something of each of us that He demands of no one else.

As Robert M. Adams has pointed out, a sense of my vocation "may both impel me and *free me* . . .".[15] For on the one hand, the fact that God demands that I do something, or play a certain role, or be a certain type of person, makes it obligatory for me. But on the other, this demand to be, in a certain sense, myself, can free me from the arbitrary demands of others. I cannot meet their demands if doing so would interfere with the pursuit of my vocation. Of course, I must not conceive my vocation in too narrow a fashion, since each of us is called to help others in many ways. But if one must beware lest "pursuit of vocation" become a code word for selfishness, it is at least equally important to beware lest "service to others" become a way of ignoring God's special call to "be oneself."

Adams supports the idea that there is an important connection between selfhood and vocation. From a Christian point of view, *who I am* is in part a matter of the particular demand God makes on me—a demand, as Adams puts it, with "my name on it." But this is to say that who I am is intimately bound up with my vocation.[16]

How can I know my vocation? So often the demands of God are seen as burdens, as conflicting with our desires and inclinations. But one of the chief ways one discovers one's vocation is precisely by determining what things one cares for most. The difficulty is to avoid the distractions (otherwise known as temptations) that interfere with the pursuit of the vocation. If I find myself persistently drawn to do a certain kind of work or be a certain kind of person (artist, mechanic, politician, scholar, priest, etc.), consistently concerned that a particular injustice be righted or that a particular need be met, then I would do well to take steps toward living out this role.

Of course, it is not uncommon for humans to make mistakes in identifying their vocation. Adams remarks that a

> belief that one has been individually commanded (or even just invited) by God to do something is not one to be accepted uncritically. It is subject to various tests: the test of conformity with what the individual and her community already believe about ethics and God's general purposes, the test of congruence with other facts that are known about her and about the world, and the tests of living it out: Is the sense of vocation strengthened or weakened by prayer? Does it survive tribulation? Is acting on it fruitful?[17]

Although there is no pat answer to the question "What is my vocation?" the history of the Christian church indicates that many have been able to come to a clear sense of vocation. To find one's vocation is to achieve an important form of self-knowledge, and to find a path through the bewildering array of demands placed upon one in the course of a life.

III. ARISTOTLE AND THE VIRTUES

The nearest secular competitor to the Christian teleological view is the approach developed long ago by Aristotle (384–322 B.C.) in his *Nicomachean Ethics*.[18] Comparing (and contrasting) these views will increase our understanding of both.

The Greek philosophical tradition, like the Bible, is filled with the language of virtues and vices. The Greek authors stressed the so-called cardinal virtues—wisdom, courage, moderation, justice ('cardinal' or 'principal' because all other virtues were thought to depend on these).[19] To this list Christians have often added the theological virtues: faith, hope, and love. But in fact both traditions mention other virtues. St. Paul provides a famous list in Galatians 5:22–23: "But the fruit of the Spirit is love, joy, peace, patience, kindness, goodness, faithfulness, gentleness, self-control; against such there is no law." The Beatitudes (Matthew 5:3-11) also constitute a list of virtues.

To connect this talk about the virtues with the Christian teleological view, it will be convenient to begin by summarizing Aristotle's approach to ethics.[20] To grasp this perspective, consider human life from the biologist's point of view. The biologist describes the mode of life characteristic of a given species. Health for a given species (whether of trees, insects, mammals, etc.) is the capacity to live well the life characteristic of that species. The *ergon* (function or work) of a species is the sort of activity most characteristic of that species. For example, the *ergon* of beavers is that of constructing dams and dens out of timber by means of their chisellike teeth. The *ergon* of human beings, according to Aristotle, is activity in accordance with *logos* (reason). The *telos* (goal of ethics) is *eudaimonia* (happiness or blessedness), that is, the human *ergon* done well over a whole life.

The virtues are traits needed to live well the life characteristic of human beings; vices (e.g., cowardice, laziness, self-indulgence) are traits that hinder the life characteristic of humans. It is not entirely clear what Aristotle meant by the phrase "activity in accordance with reason." But I shall follow the Oxford scholar Jonathan Barnes in interpreting it as "the search for knowledge"—"a life of intellectual activity and contemplation."[21] It is clear, however, that Aristotle thought the life characteristic of humans was highly social. For Aristotle, it is in the *polis* (city-state) that human beings flourish, i.e., attain *eudaimonia*. Therefore, among the traits each individual needs in order to flourish are virtues such as *justice* which facilitate human life in groups.

There is much in this Aristotelian scheme a Christian may find attractive—for example, its teleological structure, its conception of the role of the virtues, and its stress on the social nature of human life. But there are aspects of

Aristotle's approach that cannot be accepted by a Christian. First of all, Aristotle's approach is naturalistic. His way of determining what sort of life is characteristic of humans is that of a biologist. One problem with this procedure, from a Christian point of view, is that human beings are sinners, and sinfulness is not something one can determine by empirical observation. Of course, one can determine by observation that human beings treat each other in destructive ways, just as one can determine by observation that bull elephants sometimes fight. But empirical observation will not reveal that human beings are alienated from God by their sin, or that establishing a proper relationship with God is a crucial step towards blessedness. Thus, Christians will claim that Aristotle's description of the *telos* is incomplete or mistaken.

Second, Christians will insist that the true *ergon* is not activity in accord with reason (the search for knowledge), but the cultivation of harmonious relationships with self, others, God, and nature. Can we tell, just by empirical observation, whether the characteristic activity of human beings is the search for knowledge, the cultivation of harmonious relationships, or, say, the search for pleasure? What we can say with certainty is that human beings disagree about this matter, and that having some guidance from revelation ought to be welcome. (An omniscient Being is bound to have a deeper understanding of human nature than we do.) From a Christian point of view Aristotle errs in making intellectual activity the *ergon*, rather than right relationships.[22] This is not to deny that the pursuit of knowledge is central to some vocations. (Keep in mind that the cultivation of a right relation with God, and with oneself, includes pursuing one's vocation.) But, to put the matter in Christian terms (and therefore anachronistically), Aristotle errs in making one particular type of vocation the ideal for everyone, failing to appreciate the diversity of vocations to which God calls human beings.

Theories of ethics involving the epistemological claim that moral knowledge can be acquired in the way Aristotle suggested are called "natural law" theories. Some Christians, such as the great medieval theologian St. Thomas Aquinas, have taken the view that much moral knowledge can be achieved in the way Aristotle suggested—we need only add some items from revelation. But some critics fear that Aristotle's approach leads to normative relativism. Differing conventions (here defined as the customary practices of social groups) are a salient feature of the life characteristic of humans. But the

> confrontation with other ways of life that are incompatible in important respects with our own tends to undermine our confidence. This is often the beginning of moral philosophy when we try to allay our doubts about the way we live. *If we seek support for our values by looking at how things actually are—by studying human life and human nature—what is apt to strike us is the diversity in human life.* Ethical relativism seems the likely outcome of such a naturalistic approach . . .[23]

James Wallace, a philosopher at the University of Illinois, defends Aristotle's naturalistic approach by arguing that a range of virtues is necessary for human life to flourish. Wallace claims that the virtues fall into three main types.[24] First, some virtues are forms of conscientiousness. In order to live together a people must value some conventions, for a human community just is "people sharing a way of life under the same conventions."[25] A conscientious person is one who can be counted on to behave in accordance with the rules (tacit or otherwise) which constitute the conventions. Three especially important conventions in our society are promise-keeping, truth-telling, and paying one's debts. Thus, it is virtuous in such a setting to be a person of one's word, to be truthful, and to be honest.

But if being conscientious involves following the conventions, what if the conventions seem wicked? Now, as we have seen, if conventions differ, it does not necessarily follow that some of them are wicked. Some cultures demand strict punctuality, others do not; some cultures have the convention of driving on the right side of the road, some on the left. In these cases, the old proverb, "When in Rome, do as the Romans do," seems entirely apt. But suppose a culture endorses the vendetta—the practice of revenge killing. This is surely a different sort of case altogether. It may be natural to want to kill someone who has murdered a relative, yet we certainly do not think that blood feuds in Sicily are on a par with driving on the left side of the road in England. In the case of the vendetta, however, it is open to the Aristotelian to argue that the convention is destructive of human society, for history indicates that once the killing starts, it is apt to go on and on. In other words, not all conventions are acceptable, since some are indeed destructive of society, and hence destructive of the life characteristic of human beings. In this way Aristotle's view of ethics allows for some differences in social convention without saying (in effect) "anything goes." And so, on this point, Aristotle's view is similar to the Christian teleological view.

Second, some virtues are forms of benevolence, e.g., generosity and kindness. For to

> value community life, one must see the other members of the community as worthy partners in the enterprise—one must to some extent value other members of the community. Members of a human community will need to have for one another, then, the sort of direct concern that one has for someone or something one values.[26]

Such a direct concern for the good of others creates good will, which binds together the members of a society.

> Third, some virtues, such as courage and moderation, are concerned with the efficacy of an individual's practical reason—the abilities of an individual, first, to mold his feelings and desires into plans that fit with as little discord as possible with one another and with the larger community context, and second, to carry out such plans.[27]

Thus the coward is hampered by fear on occasions when the courageous person would not be. The self-indulgent person is distracted by easily acquired pleasures when the temperate person would not be. The fool is frustrated by his inability to choose good ends (and the best means to those ends) as the wise person is not.

Thus, while Wallace allows that the conventions of different societies may be partially constituted by differing rules, and hence that conscientiousness may involve attachment to one set of rules in society S_1 and to a different set of rules in S_2, still he finds an objective element in ethics, namely, the virtues themselves. No society will function well without the virtues, and nearly everyone will agree that society is to be valued. So, it at least *appears* that we have a strong philosophical defense of the virtues from a purely naturalistic perspective.

Some philosophers have explored the concept of virtue because they thought it would enable them to eliminate moral rules from ethical theorizing.[28] I agree with Wallace's conclusion that this is a vain hope, because some virtues essentially involve attitudes toward moral rules. The forms of conscientiousness (e.g., honesty, truthfulness, fairness, and being a person of one's word) are a case in point. They each involve commitment to a certain type of behavior, be it telling the truth, keeping promises, not cheating, etc. But such types of behavior are readily associated with traditional moral rules: "Tell the truth," "Keep your promises," "Don't cheat," etc. In fact, the rule simply states what form of behavior the virtuous person is committed to.

On the other hand, as Wallace points out, not all forms of virtue involve a similar commitment to rules. Benevolence, for example, seems to be a concern for the long-term best interests of others, and it does not seem at all natural to describe such a concern in terms of a list of specific forms of behavior. The ways of promoting the fulfillment of others are exceedingly numerous, and any attempt to sum them up in a list of rules is probably impossible, and certainly contrary to the spirit of benevolence. Courage also seems incorrectly described as a commitment to certain specific rules or forms of behavior. It is (roughly) a tendency to perform acts the agent considers dangerous, but worth the risk.[29] And again, it does not seem possible or desirable to make a list of rules to which the courageous person is committed.

IV. ETHICS: SECULAR OR RELIGIOUS?

It appears, then, that Wallace provides us with a defense of the virtues—a defense that does not rely on any explicitly religious claims. So, perhaps the most obvious objection to the Christian teleological view is an objection to the theism underlying it. Why build a theory of ethics on the assumption that there is a God? Why not simply endorse a view of ethics along Aristotelian, secular lines, as Wallace suggests? I shall respond to these questions in three stages. First, I contrast the secular and religious perspectives on morality. Second, I explain why I think the moral life makes more sense from the point of view of theism than from that of atheism. And third, I explain how, in practice, secular and religious people can often find common ground for reasoning about ethics.

A. Two Perspectives on the Moral Life

As I conceive it, the modern secular perspective on morality involves at least two elements. First, there is no afterlife; each individual human life ends at death. It follows that the only goods available to an individual are those he or she can obtain this side of death.[30]

Second, on the secular view, moral value is an *emergent* phenomenon. That is, moral value is "a feature of certain effects though it is not a feature of their causes" (as wetness is a feature of H_2O, but not of hydrogen or oxygen).[31] Thus, the typical contemporary secular view has it that moral value emerges only with the arrival of very complex nervous systems (viz., human brains), late in the evolutionary process. There is no Mind "behind the scenes" on the secular view, no intelligent Creator concerned with the affairs of human existence. As one advocate of the secular view puts it, "Ethics, though not consciously created [either by humans or by God], is a product of social life which has the function of promoting values common to the members of society."[32]

By way of contrast, the religious point of view (in my use of the phrase) includes a belief in God and in life after death. God is defined as an eternal being who is almighty and perfectly morally good. Thus, from the religious point of view, morality is not an emergent phenomenon, for God's goodness has always been in existence, and is not the product of nonmoral causes. Moreover, from the religious point of view, there are goods available after death. Specifically, there awaits the satisfaction of improved relations with God and with redeemed creatures.

It is important to note that, from the religious perspective, *the existence of God* and *life after death* are not independent hypotheses. If God exists, then at least two lines of reasoning lend support to the idea that death is not final. While I cannot here scrutinize these lines of reasoning, I believe it will be useful to sketch them.[33] (1) It has often been noted that we humans seem unable to find complete fulfillment in the present life. Even those having abundant material possessions and living in the happiest of circumstances find themselves, upon reflection, profoundly unsatisfied. Indeed, this longing for some good that seems to exceed our grasp is the subject of many great works of literature. Accordingly, if this earthly life is the whole story, it appears that our deepest longings will remain unfulfilled. But if God is good, He surely will not leave our deepest longings unfulfilled provided He is able to fulfill them; and since He is omnipotent, He is able to fulfill them—at least to the extent that we are willing to accept His gracious aid. So, since our innermost yearnings are not satisfied in this life, it is likely that they will be satisfied after death.

(2) Human history has been one long story of injustice, of the oppression of the poor and weak by the rich and powerful. The lives of relatively good people are often miserable, while the wicked prosper. Now, if God exists, He is able to correct such injustices, though He does not correct all of them in the present life. But if God is also good, He will not leave such injustices forever unrectified. It thus appears that He will rectify matters at some point after death. This will involve benefits for some in the afterlife—it may involve penalties for others. (However, the reader will recall the critique of the doctrine of hell in Chapter 2. The possibility of post-mortem punishment does not necessarily imply the possibility of hell *as standardly conceived*.)

We might sum up the main difference between the secular and religious views by saying that the only goods available from a secular perspective are *earthly* goods. Earthly goods include such things as physical health, friendship, pleasure, self-esteem, knowledge, enjoyable activities, an adequate standard of living, etc. The religious or theistic perspective recognizes these earthly goods *as good*, but it insists that there are non-earthly or *transcendent* goods. These are goods available only if God exists and there is life after death for humans. Transcendent goods include harmonious relations with God prior to death as well as the joys of the afterlife—right relations with both God and redeemed creatures.

B. Does Morality Make Sense?

Wallace's defense of the virtues amounts to showing that society cannot function well unless individuals have moral virtue. If we ask, "Why should we as individuals care about society?", the answer will presumably be along the following lines: "Individuals cannot flourish apart from a well-functioning society, so *morality pays for the individual*."

This defense of morality raises two questions we must now consider. First, is it misguided to defend morality by an appeal to self-interest? Many people feel that morality and self-interest are fundamentally at odds: "If you perform an act because you see that it is in your interest to do so, then you aren't doing the right thing *just because it's right*. A successful defense of morality must be a defense of duty for duty's sake. Thus, the appeal to self-interest is completely misguided." Second, *does* morality really pay for the individual? More particularly, does morality always pay in terms of earthly goods? Let us take these questions up in turn.

(1) Do we desert the moral point of view if we defend morality on the grounds that it pays? Consider an analogy with etiquette. Why should one bother with etiquette? Should one do the well-mannered thing simply for its own sake? Do we keep our elbows off the table or refrain from belching just because these things are "proper"?

To answer this question we must distinguish between the *justification of an institution* and *the justification of a particular act within that institution*. (By 'institution' I refer to any system of activities specified by rules.) This distinction can be illustrated in the case of the game (institution) of baseball. If we ask a player why he performs a particular act during a game, he will probably give an answer such as, "To put my opponent out" or "To get a home run." These answers obviously would not be relevant if the question were, "Why play baseball at all?" Relevant answers to this second question would name some advantage for the individual player, e.g., "Baseball is fun" or "It's good exercise." Thus, a justification of the institution of baseball (e.g., "It's good exercise") is quite different from a justification of a particular act within the institution (e.g., "To get a home run").

Now, let's apply this distinction to our question about etiquette. If our question concerns the justification of a particular act within the institution of etiquette, then the answer may reasonably be, in effect, "This is what's proper. This is what the rules of etiquette prescribe." For example, if one is in a new social situation, one may be unsure about which rules of etiquette apply. If one is then informed what the custom is, one may perform it simply because "it's proper." In our daily lives we are not thinking at each moment about the entire institution of etiquette.

But plainly there are deeper questions we can ask about etiquette. Who hasn't wondered, at times, what the point of the institution of etiquette is? Why do we have these quirky rules, some of which seem to make little sense? When these more fundamental questions concerning the entire institution of etiquette are being asked, it makes no sense to urge etiquette for etiquette's sake. What is needed is a description of the human *ends* the institution fulfills—ends which play a justificatory role similar to fun or good exercise in the case of baseball. And it is not difficult to identify some of these ends. For example, the rules of etiquette seem designed, in part, to facilitate social interaction; things just go more smoothly if there are agreed upon ways of greeting, eating, conversing, etc.

If anyone asks, "Why should I as an individual bother about etiquette?", an initial reply might be: "Because if you frequently violate the rules of etiquette, people will shun you." If anyone wonders why he should care about being shunned, we will presumably reply that good social relations are essential to human flourishing, and hence that a person is jeopardizing his own best interests if he places no value at all on etiquette. Thus, in the end, a defense of the institution of etiquette seems to involve the claim that the institution of etiquette *pays* for those who participate in it; it would not be illuminating to answer the question, "Why bother about etiquette?" by saying that etiquette is to be valued for its own sake.

Now, just as we distinguish between justifying the institution of etiquette (or baseball) and justifying a particular act within the institution, so we must distinguish between

justifying the institution of morality and justifying a particular act within the institution. When choosing a particular
course of action we may simply want to know what's
right. But a more ultimate question also cries out for an
answer: "What is the point of the institution of morality,
anyway? Why should one bother with it?" It is natural to respond by saying that society cannot function well without
morality, and individuals cannot flourish apart from a well-
functioning society. In short, defending the institution of
morality involves claiming that morality pays for the individual in the long run. It seems obscurantist to preach duty
for duty's sake, once the more fundamental question about
the point of the institution of morality has been raised.

But if morality is defended on the grounds that it pays,
doesn't this distort moral motivation? Won't it mean that
we no longer do things because they are right, but rather
because they are in our self-interest? No. We must bear
in mind our distinction between the reasons that justify
a particular act within an institution and the reasons that
justify the institution itself. A baseball player performs a
given act in order to get on base or put an opponent out;
he does not calculate whether this particular swing of the
bat (or throw of the ball) is fun or good exercise. A well-
mannered person is not constantly calculating whether a
given act will improve her relations with others, she simply does "the proper thing." Similarly, even if we defend
morality on the grounds that it pays, it does not follow that
the motive for each moral act becomes, "It will pay." For
we are not constantly thinking of the philosophical issues
concerning the justification of the entire system of morality; for the most part we simply do things because they
are right, honest, fair, loving, etc. Nevertheless, our willingness to plunge wholeheartedly into "the moral game"
is apt to be vitiated should it become clear to us that the
game does not pay.

At this point it appears that the institution of morality is
justified only if it pays for the individuals who participate

in it. For if being moral does not pay for individuals, it is difficult to see why they should bother with it. The appeal to duty for duty's sake is irrelevant when we are asking for a justification of the institution of morality itself.

(2) But we must now ask, "Does morality in fact pay?" There are at least four reasons for supposing that morality does not pay from a *secular* perspective. (a) One problem for the secular view arises from the fact that the moral point of view involves a concern for *all* human beings— or at least for all humans affected by one's actions. Thus, within Christian theology, the parable of the good Samaritan is well known for its expansion of the category of "my neighbor." But human societies seem able to get along well without extending full moral concern to all outsiders; this is the essence of tribal morality. Thus, explorers in the 1700s found that the Sioux Indians followed a strict code in dealing with each other, but regarded themselves as free to steal horses from the Crow. Later on, American whites repeatedly broke treaties with the American Indians in a way that would not have been possible had the Indians been regarded as equals. It is no exaggeration to say that throughout much of human history tribal morality has been the morality humans lived by.

And so, while one must agree with Wallace that the virtues are necessary for the existence of society, it is not clear that this amounts to anything more than a defense of tribal morality. (In fact, Wallace says that conscientiousness essentially involves conforming to conventions, and the conventions in a given society may include exceptions regarding outsiders.) From a purely secular point of view, it is unclear why the scope of moral concern must extend beyond one's society—or, more precisely, why one's concern must extend to groups of people outside of one's society *who are powerless and stand in the way of things one's society wants*. Why should the members of a modern industrial state extend full moral consideration to a tiny Amazonian tribe? "Be virtuous, yes! But don't get carried away with the *range* of your concern! Remember that the only reason for being virtuous is that your society won't function well unless its members manifest the virtues."

In terms of the baseball analogy we could put the point like this. If I play baseball for no other reason than that it is fun, and I find another game that is as much (or more) fun that baseball, it is reasonable for me to play the other game in lieu of baseball. Similarly, if tribal morality takes less effort but pays the same dividends (measured in earthly goods) as the relatively idealistic morality endorsed by the great ethicists, why not prefer tribal morality over its more idealistic competitor?

(b) A second problem for secular views concerns the possibility of secret violations of moral rules. What becomes of conscientiousness when one can break the rules in secret, without anyone knowing? After all, if I can break the rules in secret, I will not cause any social disharmony. Of course, there can be no breaking of the rules in secret if there is a God of the Christian type, who knows every human thought as well as every human act. But there are cases in which it is extraordinarily unlikely that any *humans* will discover one's rule breaking. Hence, from a secular perspective, there are cases in which secret violations of morality are possible.

Consider the following case. Suppose *A* has borrowed some money from *B*, but *A* discovers that *B* has made a mistake in his records. Because of the mistake, *B* believes that *A* has already paid the money back. *B* even goes out of his way to thank *A* for prompt payment on the loan. Let us further suppose that *B* is quite wealthy, and hence not in need of the money. Is it in *A*'s interest to pay the money back? Not paying the money back would be morally wrong; but would it be irrational, from a secular point of view? Not necessarily. Granted, it might be irrational in some cases, e.g., if *A* would have intense guilt feelings should he fail to repay the loan. But suppose *A* will not feel guilty because he really needs the money (and knows that *B* does not need it), and because he understands that secret violations belong to a special and rare category of action. Then, from a secular point of view, it is doubtful that paying the loan would be in A's interest.

The point is not that theists never cheat or lie. Unfortunately they do. The point is rather that secret violations of morality arguably pay off from a secular point of view. And so, once again, it seems that there is a "game" that pays off better (in terms of earthly goods) than the relatively idealistic morality endorsed by the great ethicists, viz., one allowing secret "violations."

(c) Even supposing that morality pays for some people, does it pay for *everyone* on the secular view? Can't there be well-functioning societies in which some of the members are "moral freeloaders"? In fact, don't all actual societies have members who maintain an appearance of decency, but are in fact highly manipulative of others? How would one show, on secular grounds, that it is in the interests of these persons to be moral? Furthermore, according to psychiatrists, some people are highly amoral, virtually without feelings of guilt or shame. Yet in numerous cases these amoral types appear to be happy. These "successful egoists" are often intelligent, charming, and able to evade legal penalties for their unconventional behavior.[34] How could one show, on secular grounds, that it is in the interests of such successful egoists to be moral? They seem to find their amoral lives amply rewarding.

(d) Another problem from the secular perspective stems from the fact that in some cases morality demands that one risk death. Since death cuts one off from all earthly goods, what sense does it make to be moral (in a given case) if the risk of death is high?

This point must be stated with care. In many cases it makes sense, from a secular point of view, to risk one's life. For example, it makes sense if the risk is small and the earthly good to be gained is great; after all, one risks one's life driving to work. Or again, risking one's life makes sense from a secular point of view if failing to do so will probably lead to profound and enduring earthly unhappiness. Thus, a woman might take an enormous risk to save her child from an attacker. She might believe that she would be "unable to live with herself" afterward if she stood by and let the attacker kill or maim her child. Similarly, a man might be willing to die for his country, because he could not bear the dishonor resulting from a failure to act courageously.

But failing to risk one's life does not always lead to profound and enduring earthly unhappiness. Many soldiers play it safe in battle when risk taking is essential for victory; they may judge that victory is not worth the personal risks. And many subjects of ruthless tyrants entirely avoid the risks involved in resistance and reform. Though it may be unpleasant for such persons to find themselves regarded as cowards, this unpleasantness does not necessarily lead to profound and enduring earthly unhappiness. It seems strained to claim that what is commonly regarded as moral courage always pays in terms of earthly goods.

At this point it appears that the institution of morality cannot be justified from a secular point of view. For, as we have seen, the institution of morality is justified only if it pays (in the long run) for the individuals who participate in it. But if by "morality" we mean the relatively idealistic code urged on us by the great moralists, it appears that the institution of morality does not pay, according to the secular point of view. This is not to say that no moral code could pay off in terms of earthly goods; a tribal morality of some sort might pay for most people, especially if it were to include conventions which skirt the problems inherent in my "secret violation" and "risk of death" cases. But such a morality would be a far cry from the morality most of us actually endorse.

Defenders of secular morality may claim that these difficulties evaporate if we look at morality from an evolutionary point of view. The survival of the species depends on the sacrifice of individuals in some cases, and the end of morality is the survival of the 'species. Hence, it is not surprising that being highly moral will not always pay off for individuals.

This answer is confused for two reasons. First, even if morality does have survival value for the species, we have seen that this does not by itself justify the individual's involvement in the institution of morality. In fact, it does not justify such involvement if what is best for the species is not what is best for the individual member of the species. And I have been arguing that, from a secular point of view, the interests of the species and the individual diverge.

Second, while evolution might explain why humans *feel* obligated to make sacrifices, it is wholly unable to account for genuine moral obligation. If we did not feel obligated to make sacrifices for others, it might be that the species would have died out long ago. So, moral *feelings* may have survival value. However, *feeling obligated* is not the same thing as *being obligated*. (As I remarked earlier, much psychotherapy is devoted to helping patients differentiate between feeling obligated and actually being obligated.) Thus, to show that moral feelings have survival value is not to show that there are any actual moral obligations at all. George Mavrodes remarks that it is possible

> for one to feel (or to believe) that he has a certain obligation without actually having it, and also vice versa. Now beliefs and feelings will presumably have some effect upon actions, and this effect may possibly contribute to the survival of the species. But, so far as I can see, the addition of actual moral obligations to these moral beliefs and feelings will make no further contribution to action . . . [35]

The point is, the evolutionary picture does not require the existence of real obligations; it demands only the existence of moral feelings or beliefs. Moral feelings or beliefs would motivate action even if there were in actuality no moral obligations. For example, the belief that human life is sacred may very well have survival value even if human life is not sacred. Moral obligation, as opposed to moral feeling, is thus an unnecessary postulate from the standpoint of evolution.

At this point defenders of the secular view typically make one of two moves: (i) They claim that even if morality does not pay, there remain moral truths which we must live up to; or (ii) they may claim that morality pays in subtle ways which we have so far overlooked. Let us take these claims up in turn.

(i) It may be claimed that moral obligation is just a fact of life, woven into the structure of reality. Morality may not always pay, but certain moral standards remain true, e.g., "Lying is wrong" or "Human life is sacred." These are not made true by evolution or God, but are necessary truths, independent of concrete existence, like "1 + 1 = 2" or "There are no triangular circles."

There are at least three difficulties with this suggestion. First, assuming that there are such necessary truths about morality, why should we care about them or pay them any attention? We may grant that an act is correct from the moral point of view and yet wonder whether we have good reason to participate in the institution of morality. So, even if we grant that various statements of the form "One ought to do X" are necessarily true, this does not show that the institution of morality pays off. It just says that morality is a "game" whose rules are necessary truths. While the rules of other games, such as etiquette or baseball, presumably are not necessary, they can be more or less fixed; and this does not prevent us from *reasonably* choosing not to play these games, if playing them is not in our self-interest. To defend the institution of morality simply on the grounds that certain moral statements are necessarily true is to urge duty for duty's sake. And as we have seen, this is not an acceptable defense of the institution of morality.

Second, the idea that some moral truths are necessary comports poorly with the usual secular account. As Mavrodes points out, necessary moral truths seem to be what Plato had in mind when he spoke about the Form of the Good. And Plato's view, though not contradicted by modern science, receives no support from it either. Plato's Form of the Good is not an emergent phenomenon, but is rather woven into the very structure of reality, independently of physical processes such as evolution. So, Plato's view is incompatible with the typically modern secular view that moral value is an emergent phenomenon, coming into existence with the arrival of the human nervous system. For this reason, Plato's views have "often been taken to be congenial. . . to a religious understanding of the world."[36]

Third, it is very doubtful that there are any necessary truths of the form "One ought to do X." We have seen that the institution of morality stands unjustified if participation in it does not pay (in the long run) for individuals. And why should we suppose that there are *any* necessary moral truths if the institution of morality is unjustified? For example, are we to suppose that telling the truth would be obligatory even in a world in which doing so typically led to the destruction of truth tellers? Surely not. The whole drift of our discussion has been toward the idea that there is a necessary connection between moral obligation and self-interest, namely, if living by the moral code does not pay, one is not obligated to live by it. In other words, statements of the form "One ought to do X" are not *necessary* truths, though they may be true *if* certain conditions are met. (Here X stands for such moral terms as "promote harmony" or "tell the truth," not for gerrymandered terms that build special conditions in, such as, "tell the truth if it pays.") Hence, if there are any necessary moral truths, they appear to be conditional (if-then) in form: If certain conditions exist, one ought to do X. Among the conditions, as we have seen, is the condition that doing X pays for the individual in the long run. So, it is very doubtful that there are any necessary moral truths of the form "One ought to do X."[37] The upshot is that morality is partly grounded in those features of reality which guarantee that morality pays; and the secular view lacks the metaphysical resources for making such a guarantee.

Incidentally, these reflections amplify the discussion at the end of Chapter 2 concerning the relation between God and necessary moral truths. I have not shown that there could be no such necessary truths unless God exists, but our discussion indicates that they must be conditional in form. Hence, no obligations fall on us unless the conditions are met, including the condition that morality pays. Thus, our conception of reality must include factors (such as divine activity) which insure that morality pays—otherwise, the moral code is not binding on us.[38]

(ii) But some have claimed that, if we look closely at human psychology, we can see that morality does pay *in terms of earthly goods.* For example, Plato suggested that only a highly moral person could have harmony between the various elements of his soul (such as reason and desire). Others have claimed that being highly moral is the only means to inner satisfaction. We humans are just so constituted that violations of morality never leave us with a net gain. Sure, we may gain earthly goods of one sort or another by lying, stealing, etc., but these are always outweighed by inner discord or a sense of dissatisfaction with ourselves.

There are several problems with this. First, some may doubt that moral virtue is the best route to inner peace. After all, one may experience profound inner discord when one has done what is right. It can be especially upsetting to stand up for that is right when doing so is unpopular; indeed, many people avoid "making waves" precisely because it upsets their inner peace. So it is far from clear that doing what is right is the best or only route to inner peace, from a secular point of view, since being moral implies a lifelong struggle with evil.

Second, how good is the evidence that inner peace *always* outweighs the benefits achievable through unethical action? Perhaps guilt feelings and inner discord are a reasonable price to pay for certain earthly goods. If a cowardly act enables me to stay alive, or a dishonest act makes me wealthy, I may judge that my gains are worth the accompanying guilt feelings. A quiet conscience is not everything.

Third, if inner discord or a sense of dissatisfaction stems from a feeling of having done wrong, why not reassess my standards? Therapists are familiar with the phenomenon of false guilt. For example, a married woman may feel guilty for having sex with her spouse. The cure will involve enabling the patient to view sex as a legitimate means of expressing affection. The point is that just because I feel a certain type of act is wrong, it does not follow that the only route to inner peace is to avoid the action. I also have the option of revising my standards, which may enable me to pursue self-interested goals in a less inhibited fashion. Why drag along any unnecessary moral baggage? How could it be shown, on secular grounds, that it is in my interest to maintain the more idealistic standards endorsed by the great moralists? Certainly, some people have much less idealistic standards than others, and yet seem no less happy.

By way of contrast with the secular view, it is not difficult to see how morality might pay if there is a God of the Christian type. First, God loves all humans and wants all included in his kingdom. So, a tribal morality would violate his demands, and to violate his demands is to strain one's most important personal relationship. Second, there are no secret violations of morality if God exists. Since God is omniscient, willful wrongdoing of any sort will estrange the wrongdoer from God. Third, while earthly society may be able to function pretty well even though there exists a small number of "moral freeloaders," the freeloaders themselves are certainly not attaining harmonious relations with God. Accordingly, their ultimate fulfillment is in jeopardy. Fourth, death is the end of earthly life, but it is not the end of conscious existence, according to Christianity. Therefore, death does not end one's opportunity for personal fulfillment; indeed, if God is perfectly good and omnipotent, we can only assume that the afterlife will result in the fulfillment of our deepest needs—unless we willfully reject God's efforts to supply those needs.

So, it seems to me that the moral life makes more sense from a theistic perspective than from a secular perspective. Of course, I do not claim that I have proved the existence of God, and a full discussion of this metaphysical issue would take us too far from matters at hand.[39] But if I have shown that the moral life makes more sense from a theistic perspective than from a secular one, then I have provided an important piece of evidence in favor of the rationality of belief in God. Moreover, I believe that I have turned back one objection to the Christian teleological view, namely, the allegation that theism is unnecessary metaphysical baggage.

C. Common Ground for Religious and Secular Ethicists

I have just been emphasizing the differences between secular and religious ethics. In order to correct a possible misunderstanding, I need to balance this by explaining why secular and religious people can often agree about moral issues.

The differences between secular and religious ethical theories come most strongly to light when we raise ultimate questions concerning what justifies the institution of morality. These differences do not always make a difference in particular cases. Moreover, even if more ultimate issues do have implications in a given case, this is often overlooked. Thus, I have claimed that Christianity rules out tribal morality, but plenty of Christians have failed to transcend tribal morality. For example, many white American Christians condoned or ignored the pattern of unjust treatment perpetrated by their government against the American Indians throughout the nineteenth century. To illustrate the same point from a different angle, contemporary secular ethicists often claim that all humans are equal, though I have argued that their metaphysics implies a less egalitarian perspective.

Furthermore, the fact that secular and religious people often agree on moral issues is not surprising if—as many Christian theologians have claimed—moral truths are often available through general revelation (i.e., through the cognitive faculties God has given humans in general). Thus, it is readily apparent to most everyone that it is generally wrong to lie, kill, and steal. The destructive effect these types of acts have on human relationships is obvious. So, while I have just been arguing that the institution of morality cannot be adequately defended on secular grounds, I certainly admit that secular and religious people can (and often do) agree in their assessment of particular moral issues.

Of course, they often disagree too. But secular people may very well adopt a moral perspective that has much in common with the Christian teleological view. This view may remain intuitive and unformulated, or it may be clearly formulated and consciously adopted. For example, it might be claimed that an act is right if and only if it promotes harmonious relations between *human* persons. While this view leaves God out, it plainly leaves room for plenty of agreement with Christians on how things should go here and now, this side of death. So, in principle, there can be much collaboration between secular and religious ethicists.

V. Utilitarianism and the Christian Teleological View

I have tried to respond to the charge that the Christian teleological view is burdened by an indefensible commitment to theism. But even if (CT) can be defended from this charge, important questions remain. For (CT) is, like act utilitarianism, a consequentialist view. Will (CT) fall prey to objections raised against (AU) in Chapter 3? In this section we shall discuss the "Deathbed Promise" case and the supererogation issue. Problems regarding justice will be treated in the next chapter.

A. Deathbed Promise Case

In outline, the "Deathbed Promise" case is one in which *A* makes a promise to *B*, *B* then dies, and *A* discovers that keeping the promise will not maximize utility. The problem for act utilitarianism is that it casts aside important moral rules (such as, "Keep your promises") whenever breaking the rules maximizes utility. It seems especially problematic that even a *slight* advantage in utility should be thought to override a solemn promise.

Will a similar objection work against the Christian teleological view? What if we can promote the Kingdom of God best by violating standard moral rules? The reply to this question is as follows: standard moral rules are either social conventions—and hence, demands society makes on us—or divine demands (or both). Since meeting such demands is a vital aspect of maintaining harmonious relationships, we must generally show respect for traditional moral rules. But in conflict situations we may have to break a conventional rule in order to meet God's demands, or view one societal demand as having priority over another.

Should we keep promises made to a person who is now dead, if keeping such a promise will not maximize utility? Yes, *if keeping such promises is demanded by society or by God*. And it is not surprising that society should want our agreements with the dead to be kept for the most part. Most of us want our legal wills to be kept, for example, and this indicates that we want certain demands made while we are alive to be satisfied when we are dead. But it is hardly fair for me to demand that others keep pre-death agreements with me unless I am willing to satisfy similar demands made by others. Thus, (CT) is able to give moral rules a special status which (AU) cannot; for traditional moral rules express a type of demand—whether a divine command or a social convention—and legitimate demands must be met, on pain of rupturing harmonious relationships. Furthermore, any notion that the promise can be broken secretly is ruled out, if God is omniscient.

B. Supererogation

(AU) is also vulnerable to the objection that it can make no place for supererogation. (Recall that an act of supererogation is one that is morally praiseworthy but not obligatory.) According to (AU), if an act maximizes utility, then it is obligatory, no matter how strenuous or how far "beyond the call of duty" it seems.

It must be said that Christians often speak as if apparently supererogatory acts were obligatory. "Go the second mile" is a phrase often employed among Christians, and it is often meant to indicate that a certain strenuous task is a moral duty. Yet it also seems that, in subtle ways, Christians teach their children to distinguish between duty and supererogation. If a child asks, "Must I give my allowance to the poor?", she probably will not be told, "Yes, you must, for that is what God demands. It's your duty." In all likelihood she will be told something more like, "You don't have to give your allowance to charity—it's up to you. If you want to give the money to the poor, that would be a good thing. But if you want to save it or spend it some other way, you may." Such parental instruction seems to rest on a distinction between *what is obligatory* and *what is praiseworthy but not obligatory.*

Feinberg has pointed out that, where conventions are sufficiently precise, a clear meaning can be given to the term 'supererogation.'[40] For example, one convention in our society is that a person should work the number of hours agreed upon with his employer. A custodian may have a duty to spend eight hours a day cleaning offices. If he occasionally spends more time cleaning the offices than this, he has (in one clear sense) gone beyond his duty. Thus, the Christian teleological view can make room for a concept of supererogation. And given the strong tendency humans have to make intrusive demands upon one another, the concept of supererogation can be an important one for the protection of the individual.

However, the problem of supererogation may arise in a more pressing form. If an act promotes the Kingdom of God, it is a moral requirement. Thus, if donating a kidney to a perfect stranger promotes the Kingdom of God, I am required to donate it. Yet, as we discussed in Chapter 3, such an act seems (intuitively) beyond the call of duty. Does it follow that (CT), like (AU), makes supererogatory acts duties? To answer this question, we must first ask another: "Would donating a kidney to a stranger *in fact* promote the Kingdom of God?" Donating a kidney would of course meet the stranger's demand and thus promote harmonious relations with the stranger; the question is whether the stranger's demand is appropriate (or whether it takes priority over other demands). It may not be possible, however, to answer this question in a perfectly general way. For example, it could conceivably be part of someone's vocation to donate a kidney to a stranger. However, I suspect that such a vocation would be the exception rather than the rule, for three reasons (corresponding to the three questions we must ask about demands in general). First, who is making the demand? It is a stranger—not a spouse, close friend, or relative—and one measure of the appropriateness of a demand is the intimacy of the relationship between demander and demandee. The more intimate the relation, the more appropriate a major demand would be.

Second, what are the stranger's attributes? Is he someone whose contribution to society is especially vital and admirable? If so, his demand might take on more weight. Is he an especially violent or wicked person (e.g., a convicted criminal)? If so, his demand might be entirely out of place. In a more typical case, the stranger's attributes probably neither count strongly against nor strongly in favor of his demand.

Third, we must ask, "Is the demand reasonable?" It is
plain that risks are involved for the donor; removing a kidney is no minor operation. Moreover, should the donor's
remaining kidney fail, he may die or find himself in need
of costly and painful medical assistance. But perhaps the
potential donor's best indicator is this question:"Do I feel
that I would have the right, if I were in need of a kidney,
to demand that a stranger donate one to me? Would I feel
that this is too much to ask of a stranger?" If I believe that
I would be asking too much if I asked a stranger to donate
a kidney to me, then, in all probability, my sincere belief
is that the stranger's demand for my kidney is inappropriate. And, indeed, it seems to me that in nearly every case a
stranger's insistent demand for one of my kidneys would be
highly inappropriate. Once again, then, it appears that (CT)
has resources for handling certain objections which have
commonly been regarded as refutations of utilitarianism.
What maximizes utility and what promotes the Kingdom
of God may be quite different things in a given case.

But a further question about supererogation and Christianity remains. However one interprets the New Testament, and especially the teachings of Jesus (such as the
Sermon on the Mount), it is clear that the Christian life is
a demanding one. It involves denying oneself, taking up
one's cross, going the second mile, etc. How are we to understand such teachings? Did Jesus, as represented by the
Gospel writers, make into duties acts most people would
regard as supererogatory? It seems to me that the answer
to this question cannot be a simple yes or no.

First, it is important to keep in mind that Jesus Himself
condemned the Pharisees for laying heavy burdens of obligation on ordinary people—burdens which the Pharisees
themselves would not bear (Matthew 23:4). Second, Jesus'
explicit teaching was "Love thy neighbor *as thyself*." The
qualification "as thyself" is crucial. While Jesus insists that
we promote the Kingdom, each individual's ability to do
so is limited by the quality or extent of his or her self-love.

I am not promoting the Kingdom in the appropriate sense if my acts of "sacrifice" are making me bitter or resentful, or if they leave me with a feeling of being unfulfilled.

Now, this may seem a dangerous teaching:"Don't make a sacrifice if doing so will make you deeply frustrated or resentful." Couldn't people use this as a rationalization for remaining at a very low level of spiritual and moral maturity? No doubt they could—but then, it is often the case that truths can be used by ill-intentioned people to rationalize their selfishness or to justify their hardness of heart. The fact that a principle can be misused is therefore no indication of its falsehood. What I am saying is this: Whether an act promotes the Kingdom depends, in part, on whether *the agent* can perform it without growing deeply resentful or bitter. This implies, for example, that an act might be a duty for St. Francis, because he has the spiritual resources to pull it off with contentment, while it would not be a duty for me, because I could not make the sacrifice without feeling deeply resentful. Thus, acts that many ordinary people would regard as supererogatory (because they go beyond the demands of convention) might indeed be duties for some saintly persons. "To whom much is given, much is required." And Jesus' teachings can be taken as challenges to grow spiritually, in order that we might find ourselves increasingly able to extend ourselves for others without feeling cheated, bitter, or frustrated.

But what about a very cruel or selfish person who is resentful because he is not allowed to hurt and exploit others? Is it then not his duty not to hurt others? I am of course assuming that normal humans are able to rise above this level. When they do not, it is not because they are unable. Rather, when they do not, it is because they do not wish to. People who *literally* cannot rise above such insensitivity are radically defective and must simply be restrained if they cannot be treated.

Perhaps it needs to be said that there are many cases in which one can grow spiritually by doing something that is not at all attractive, and in meeting such challenges one very often discovers inner resources one was unaware of, or divine grace one did not realize was available. So, I am not suggesting that one avoid difficult moral tasks until such time as one feels fully "up to the challenge." Rather, I am merely saying that some apparently praiseworthy acts may not in fact promote the Kingdom of God, and hence may not be duties, because the agent is unable to perform them without becoming resentful.

Did Jesus make into duties acts most people regard as supererogatory? Yes, in the sense that some acts which go beyond the demands of convention are *required* of those who have sufficient spiritual resources to perform them without growing deeply resentful or frustrated. But "Love they neighbor *as thyself*" militates against the kind of "living for others" that ends in resentment born of the feeling that "it has been all give and no take."

In this chapter I have expounded the Christian teleological view and contrasted it with its nearest secular competitor, Aristotelian naturalism. Along the way I have considered and responded to a number of objections to (CT). Thus, I argued that the Kingdom of God is a nonmoral good in the sense needed to qualify as a *telos*. I also argued that the existence of God is not a meaningless addition to moral theory, but rather that morality makes more sense if God exists than if He does not. Finally, I argued that (CT) provides a better account of promise keeping and supererogation than (AU) can. We must now ask what sort of theory of justice is implied by the Christian teleological view.

Appendix to Chapter 5:
The Prisoner's Dilemma

Is it rational to be moral? Contemporary philosophers use a special type of situation called the "prisoner's dilemma" to get at this question. In this appendix I want to offer some brief reflections on the prisoner's dilemma from the Christian teleological perspective.

Let us suppose that the Secret Police of the Occupational Forces have taken two citizens into custody, Jules and Simone, mistakenly accusing them of working for the resistance. (In fact, though neither would collaborate with the occupational forces, neither works for the resistance.) Each prisoner is given two alternatives: to confess to working for the resistance or not to confess. They are offered the following, rather complicated deal. If one confesses and the other does not, the "confessor" goes scot free while the "nonconfessor" gets ten years in prison; if both confess, both go to prison for five years; if neither confesses, both go to prison for one year.

We can represent this situation by means of a payoff matrix, as follows:

Assume that the prisoners have the following preferences. First preference = go scot free; second preference = go to prison for one year; third preference = go to prison for five years; fourth preference = go to prison for ten years.

Let us suppose that Jules and Simone think the matter over and make an agreement *not* to confess. The question is, is it to the advantage of each to keep this agreement? Is it, in other words, rational for Jules and Simone to be conscientious (moral) in this situation?

Much depends on whether Jules and Simone can confess in secret, without the other's knowledge. For if Jules finds out that Simone has confessed, Jules will presumably confess also, to avoid the worse case from his point of view, viz., Jules gets ten years and Simone goes scot free. Similarly, Simone will confess if she finds out that Jules has, to avoid getting ten years while Jules goes scot free. Thus, if each knows what the other is doing, and if each is prudent, it seems assured that they will each keep the agreement (thus getting one year in prison apiece), in order to avoid the case in which both confess and both get five years.

But suppose the two can confess secretly. For example, imagine they are put in separate cells, so that Jules's decision is independent of Simone's, and vice versa. The reason prisoner's-dilemma type situations have received much attention from philosophers of late is that there is a plausible argument to the effect that it is to the advantage of each prisoner to confess, thus breaking their agreement. Look at it from Jules's point of view: "Either Simone will confess or she won't. If she confesses, I must confess to avoid the ten year sentence. If she doesn't confess, then again it is advantageous for me to confess, for I'll go scot free. Either way, confession is most advantageous for me." And, of course, an exactly similar argument will lead to the conclusion that it is to Simone's advantage to confess. If it is indeed prudent for each prisoner to confess, thus breaking the agreement, being moral is not prudent in this case, i.e., not to the advantage of each individual.

Two points are worth noting. First, prisoner's-dilemma cases are not possible if there is a God of the Christian type, for the payoff matrix does not reflect the costs of violating God's demands. (I take it for granted that God would demand that one keep the agreement not to confess.) Therefore, prisoner's-dilemma cases may represent a special sort of problem for secular moral theories. That is, cases of this type may underscore a point I have tried to make in Chapter 5—that secular moral theories have a difficult time showing that it pays to be moral.

Second, does it matter if being moral pays for the individual? I have argued (Chapter 5, Section IV) that there are no genuine moral obligations if being moral does not pay for the individual. And if being moral does not pay for individuals, then, in my estimation, morality is most likely nothing more than a mechanism for keeping social order, i.e., a means by which individuals are made to act in the interest of the collective rather than in their own best interests. From this perspective, those who preach duty for duty's sake are promulgating (consciously or unconsciously) a kind of propaganda for the collective.

For more about the prisoner's dilemma, see R. Duncan Luce and Howard Raiffa, *Games and Decisions* (Harvard University Press, 1958), pp. 94-102; and David P. Gauthier, "Morality and Advantage," in *Morality and Rational Self-Interest*, ed. David P. Gauthier (Prentice-Hall, 1970), pp. 166-180.

Justice and Human Rights 6

Justice demands that each individual receive his or her due. But what is due an individual? According to a venerable tradition, one is due one's rights. But what is a "right"? And, assuming there are such things as rights, how do we know which rights are ours? Furthermore, does the talk about rights have a natural place in a Christian ethical theory?

It is important to be clear that our inquiry is not into the subject of legal rights, but moral rights. Whether one has a legal right to something can be settled simply by examining the statute books of the relevant country or state. Of course, it is natural to suppose that there is a relation between legal and moral rights, namely, that legal rights are meant to be based on moral rights. But, notoriously, the laws in a given society tend to be biased in favor of the powerful members of that society. This usually means that some legal rights are in conflict with moral rights; for example, some people may be given the legal right to own slaves, to pay starvation wages, or to discriminate against the members of another race or sex.

So, some legal rights are not morally justifiable. But a further reason for distinguishing legal and moral rights needs to be recognized, namely, that most of us do not want the legal code to reflect the moral code in every respect. Most of us, for example, think it is wrong to lie, and think we have a right not to be lied to. But do we want lying to be made illegal in *every* case? Do we want to be able to haul people into court for relatively harmless lies? Few, if any, want this. It appears, then, that most of us want the law to protect us only from the more serious types of violations of our rights. But in saying this we are once again recognizing a distinction between legal and moral rights.

I. What Is a Right?

Taking a lead from Alan Gewirth, one of the foremost contemporary rights theorists, we can say that one has a right to *X* (e.g., life or liberty) if and only if (a) one is *entitled* to *X* and (b) some other person or group has a *correlative duty* either to *provide* one with *X*, or to *assist* one in obtaining or maintaining *X*, or *at least to refrain from interfering with one's having X.*[1] Both parts of this analysis—(a) and (b)—deserve elaboration.

Let's begin with (a), the notion of entitlement. A crucial difference between an appeal to justice, as opposed to an appeal to charity or goodwill, consists in the claim to entitlement. If one asks for charity or makes a plea to the goodwill of another, it seems that one is admitting a lack of entitlement. For example, suppose Mary, a needy student, has asked me to help fund her college education. Since Mary is intelligent and hard working, and since I have some extra funds, I feel that I ought to help out. From the fact that I ought to help her out, does it follow that she is entitled to the money, that she can demand it as a right? It seems not; she could not claim to be wronged if I used the money in some other fashion. By way of contrast, suppose someone has stolen a large sum of money from Mary. Then she will not appeal to the culprit for repayment (assuming he has been apprehended) on the basis of charity or goodwill. She will claim that she is *entitled* to the money as a matter of justice, that it is hers *by right*. So, one key aspect of Gewirth's analysis of the concept of a right is this: it does not guarantee the validity of the inference from

"You ought to do X for me" to "I have a right to X." If A ought to provide B with something, it does not *necessarily* follow that B is *entitled* to it.

However, the second part of Gewirth's analysis (i.e., (b)) points out that if I have a right to something, then there must be a respondent—some person or group of persons who have a correlative duty. This duty can take at least three forms. (1) At minimum, it involves refraining from interfering with one's having the good in question. Thus, if I have a right to liberty in some area of my life, then others have a duty not to force me to do their will in that area. And if I have a right to life, then others have a duty not to kill me. (2) Furthermore, if I have a right to liberty, then others have some obligation to *assist me in maintaining* that liberty, e.g., by calling the police if my right to walk about freely is being infringed by ruffians. And if I have a right to life, others also presumably have *some* obligation to assist me in staying alive—at least in circumstances where their doing so is not very difficult, costly, or time-consuming. (3) Finally, at least in some cases, if I have a right to X, others have a duty to provide X. For example, if you have made a promise to me, then, other things being equal, I am entitled that you keep it.[2] It is my right that you should provide what you promised.

If I have a right to liberty, do others have a duty to provide me with liberty? I think so. For example, if I have been unjustly imprisoned by a tyrant, I think my fellow citizens have a duty to secure my release (if they can). But although I have a right to life, it makes little sense to suppose that others have a duty to *provide* me with life. (Except perhaps in very unusual cases—e.g., I am clinically dead and a doctor can bring me back to life—we can assist others in maintaining life but we cannot *provide* it. And I do not think it makes sense to say that we have duties to "nonexistent persons" to provide them with life. I take it that, as regards procreation, we are not to suppose that prior to conception there is a person—a "possible person"?—to whom life is owed.) But in many cases we have a duty to *provide* goods to which another is entitled.

Part (b) of Gewirth's analysis leaves open the much-debated question of whether rights are negative or positive (or which rights are negative and which positive). America's founding fathers were primarily concerned with negative rights, and hence with the duties others have *not to interfere* with one in certain ways, e.g., the duty not to interfere with one's liberty. But contemporary debates, such as the debate about welfare, often focus on rights alleged to be positive, and hence concern the duty to assist or provide others with some good, e.g., sustenance. Does my right to sustenance imply only that you must not interfere with my efforts to obtain food, clothing, and shelter, or does it mean you have some sort of duty to help me obtain these things—particularly if I am unable to obtain them myself? It seems that, at least in some cases, negative rights are almost worthless apart from positive rights. In modern society, what good is the negative right not to be assaulted unless it is backed up by the positive right to police protection? Or what good is the right of an impoverished defendant to legal counsel if the state will not pay legal fees? But again, for the moment, the point to notice is that Gewirth's analysis of the concept of a right leaves these issues open. Hence, his analysis of *what a right is* can be accepted by persons who have widely varying views about which rights humans actually have. It can even be accepted by those who hold that human beings have no rights. ("Yes, that's what rights are, but no one has any of them.")

According to Gewirth, the full structure of a claim to have a particular right can be given in the following formula:

A has a right to B against C by virtue of D.

The key elements here are the *subject* A of the right, i.e., the person who has it; the *object* B of the right, i.e., what it is a right to (e.g., life); the *respondent* C of the right, i.e., the person or persons who have the correlative duty (e.g., not to kill); and the *justifying basis or ground* of the right, **D**.³ Various justifying bases or grounds have been offered for rights. Nowadays the most common claim is that we have certain rights simply by virtue of being human. But in medieval times, for example, the rights of a lord were thought to be grounded, not in his humanity (which the serfs shared), but in the special status he enjoyed as a nobleman. This special status was not thought of as earned or acquired, but as natural and hence God-given. A lord was simply born to a higher position in the "great chain of being" than the serf, and hence his authority and privilege were not thought of as a matter of social convention, but as a part of the created order.

II. RIGHTS AND CHRISTIAN THEOLOGY

Some Christians are suspicious of the idea that human beings have rights. They may point out that the Bible does not discuss justice in terms of human rights, or they may claim that, since Christ told us to deny ourselves, take up our crosses and follow Him, that we can claim no rights (that is, it may be claimed that "denying oneself" involves denying that one has any rights). I think that this denial of rights rests on a serious misunderstanding of what a right is. As Gewirth's analysis indicates, if I deny that I have a right not to be assaulted, then I must either (a) deny that I am entitled not to be assaulted, or (b) deny that others ought to refrain from assaulting me (or both). But surely it is clear that, except in very special circumstances, others *ought* to refrain from assaulting me. Any serious moral theory will endorse this. So, these Christians must be saying, by implication, that (a) others ought to refrain from assaulting me, but (b) I am not entitled to their so refraining. But why am I not so entitled? Is it because I must think of the restraint of others—in not assaulting me—as a matter of charity? Imagine someone saying, "It's awfully nice of them not to assault me, but I am hardly in a position to demand it." Is *that* the Christian attitude?

I submit that this is neither the response of a psychologically healthy person nor a biblical response.[4] If one has a proper self-image—as a being God has endowed with marvelous capabilities and whom He loves dearly—can one pretend that one is not entitled *not* to be assaulted? It is plain that psychologically healthy persons feel entitled *not* to be assaulted, for if assaulted, they react with indignation. For example, in Acts 16:19-39 St. Paul frightens some magistrates who have had him beaten unjustly by informing them of his Roman citizenship (as a Roman citizen he enjoyed numerous rights not accorded to others). On another occasion, to avoid being unjustly beaten, St. Paul reminded the authorities of his Roman citizenship. And in the Old Testament, when Nathan the prophet confronts King David for his treachery in the matter of Uriah and Bathsheba, the moral of Nathan's parable is naturally described in terms of rights. In the parable, the rich man, who has "many flocks," flagrantly violates the rights of the poor man by stealing his one and only sheep in order to entertain a guest.[5]

The fact that the biblical writers do not explicitly employ the language of rights does not mean that the notion is alien to the biblical scheme. For if we accept Gewirth's analysis of the concept of a right, then we can see that the biblical emphasis on justice tacitly includes a claim to rights. For example, consider the following passages from Amos:

> Thus says the Lord: "For three transgressions of Israel, and for four, I will not revoke the punishment; because they sell the righteous for silver, and the needy for a pair of shoes—they trample the head of the poor into the dust of the earth, and turn aside the way of the afflicted" (Amos 2:6-7).

> Hear this, you who trample upon the needy, and bring the poor of the land to an end, saying, "When will the new moon be over, that we may sell grain? And the sabbath, that

we may offer wheat for sale, that we may make the ephah small and the shekel great, and deal deceitfully with false balances, that we may buy the poor for silver and the needy for a pair of sandals, and sell the refuse of the wheat?" The Lord has sworn by the pride of Jacob: "Surely I will never forget any of their deeds. Shall not the land tremble on this account. . . "? (Amos 8:4-8)

But let justice roll down like waters, and righteousness like an everflowing stream. (Amos 5:24)

It is hard to see how one would be distorting Amos's view if one took such passages to imply that the poor are *entitled* not to be cheated through sharp business practices. In fact, it is hard to imagine that Amos would quarrel with the idea that the poor have a *right* not to be cheated. The language of rights is not his mode of expression, but the idea that people are entitled to just treatment is not foreign to his thought. Nicholas Wolterstorff has suggested that the

> Old Testament prophets. . . sometimes had their eye on what we now call human rights. They did not, however, think of them as grounded in the imago dei [the image of God]. They thought of them rather as grounded in the purpose of God for his human creatures—what he wants for them. What God called *shalom*. What God wants for his human creatures is that they be participants in a shalom community—such participation comprising both sharing the goods of such a mode of flourishing and fulfilling the responsibilities appropriate thereto. Natural human rights are then the legitimate claims persons have qua human persons, to the goods of such a community; and the ultimate grounding of such rights is the purpose of God.[6]

In short, something like the modern concern for human rights seems to be implied by the emphasis on justice found in various parts of the Bible. Therefore, if some contemporary Christians are suspicious about rights-claim, this suspicion has nonbiblical sources. There are at least three such nonbiblical sources.

First, the great theological wars within American churches in the first half of this century divided Christians into liberals and conservatives. It is fair to say that the liberal wing of the church maintained a much greater emphasis on social justice (and hence on human rights). This social concern was suspect to conservatives, because it seemed to them to be accompanied by a lack of concern for devotional piety and for salvation from sin. From the conservative point of view, this concern for justice amounted to a "social gospel," i.e., an ethical version of Christianity, long on love for neighbor but short on love for God. From this perspective, a concern for social justice seemed to be in competition with a form of religion centered on personal piety and salvation from sin. Of course, as an argument, this has obvious weaknesses. Is a concern for social justice really in competition with the love for God? Can one love God without sharing his passionate concern for the poor and oppressed? Surely true spirituality involves balancing a range of important concerns—not simply jettisoning some of them because the balance proves difficult to maintain.

Second, historically speaking, talk about human or natural rights came into prominence with the great contractarians, Thomas Hobbes (1588–1679), John Locke (1632–1704), and Jean-Jacques Rousseau (1712–78).[7] The contract tradition is commonly regarded as supporting individualism, the idea that the chief justification of the state is that it provides a haven for the pursuit of self-interest. So, historically speaking, talk about natural rights has been associated with self-interest. We shall have to see whether the connection between rights and self-interest is merely one of historical association, or whether the connection is logical, and therefore ineradicable. But it is undeniable that some contractarian claims can be readily used to justify a selfish individualism. On Locke's view, for example, rights are given by God for *self-preservation*. It is especially significant that Locke regards *property rights* as a vital instrument for self-preservation. As Diana Meyers remarks,

> Part of the trouble is that Locke derives natural rights from the wrong source. Since he defends natural rights as props to survival, right-holders can point out that grave misfortunes can unexpectedly reduce vast wealth to meager proportions, and they can insist that these familiar hazards justify their proclivity for precautionary accumulation.[8]

Thus, Lockean property rights can easily be used as a rationalization for laying one's treasures up on earth. While such forms of individualism are rightly rejected as un-Christian and remain a significant barrier to community spirit in some countries, I believe Meyers is correct in identifying the problem as lying in Locke's stress on self-preservation, rather than on the concept of rights itself. My attempt to justify this claim is given in Section IV, in which I offer an alternative derivation of rights.

Third, I think the *proliferation of rights-claims* in this century has caused some Christians to suspect that rights-talk is nothing more than a form of rhetoric designed to put a moral veneer on self-interest. Rightly or wrongly, many feel that so many different groups are claiming so many different rights, that "I have a right to X" is too often, on examination, simply a misleading way of saying "I want X, and I want society to provide X for me." Because of the stress of the founding fathers on negative rights, which demand that others not interfere with one in certain ways, I think that Americans are especially suspicious of claims to positive rights, which demand that others provide one with or assist one in having certain things. And claims to positive rights, such as the right to welfare, to medical care, or to funding for abortion, are common nowadays.

The charge that the language of rights is but a form of the rhetoric of self-interest is a serious one. It has been leveled by critics as ideologically diverse as Bentham, Burke, and Marx, and I think it would be hard to deny that talk about rights *is* in some cases a mask for mere self-interest.[9]

But surely this is not so in all cases. Is our talk about the right to life, to free speech, and to association merely a verbal screen hiding self-interest? Aren't such rights a vital aspect of the social fabric, part of what holds us together? So it would seem. That some people have misused the language of rights is hardly surprising. That others have taken this misuse as a reason for rejecting rights-claims altogether is surely unfortunate. But I think the best way to lay these concerns to rest is to provide a theory of rights—a strategy for sifting through rights-claims in an intelligent, systematic fashion.

III. How Are Rights Determined?

To determine what our legal rights are we need only look at the statute books. But we must now ask, "What is the 'moral analogue' of statute books?"[10] There are five main views about how rights are to be determined.

First, there is the *intuitionist* position. On this view, some beliefs of the form "Humans have a right to _____" are *properly basic*, i.e., such beliefs are taken to be rational even though they are not based on any evidence. This position is assumed in the American Declaration of Independence, which speaks of certain rights as being self-evident. In other words, on this view, it is just obvious that humans have certain rights; we do not need evidence for this any more than we need evidence for "$1 + 1 = 2$" or "Nothing can be red all over and green all over at the same time."

There are at least two problems with intuitionism. (a) If it is just obvious or self-evident that humans have certain rights, then why is there so much disagreement about which rights they have? Indeed, if it is obvious that humans have rights, how can so many intelligent people doubt that humans have any rights at all? Intuitionism fails to explain the phenomenon of massive disagreement about human rights. (b) Intuitionism provides no means of adjudicating conflicting rights-claims. If one person thinks it obvious

that humans have a right to free speech, that women have
a right to equal pay for equal work, that gays have a right
to sexual fulfillment, or that whales have a right to life, and
another person finds these claims dubious or even outra-
geous, the intuitionist can offer no means for resolving the
dispute, *not even in principle*. Of course, given the cantan-
kerousness of human beings, it would be unfair—indeed,
utterly ridiculous—to demand that a moral theory actually provide a way to secure agreement between all parties
on every ethical question! But intuitionism is a counsel of
despair for ethical reasoning. It simply leaves disputants
staring at one another, each claiming that he or she intuits
the truth.

A second view about how rights are determined alleges
a close connection between rights and *interests* (needs
and desires). Thus, a contemporary philosopher, Michael
Tooley, suggests that " '*A* has a right to *X*' is roughly syn-
onymous with 'If *A* desires *X*, then others are under a
prima-facie obligation to refrain from actions that would
deprive him of it.' "[11] The attempt to link rights closely
with interests (in the sense of needs and desires) is problematic for at least three reasons:

(a) How does one move logically from need (or desire)
to entitlement? Suppose I need a car to get to work. Is it
supposed to follow from the fact that I need a car that I
am entitled to one? To put it mildly, the connection between needing (or desiring) something and being *entitled*
to it is not obvious. Historically speaking, many factors
other than needs and desires have been regarded as the
basis for rights-claims. For example, rights have been attached to one's contribution or merit. Thus, a worker's
right to a promotion or higher pay is typically based on
her merit, not on demonstrated need. The point is that the
connection between needs (or desires) and rights must be
demonstrated, not merely assumed.

One could put this point another way by saying that Tooley's analysis of rights is a reflection of political liberalism,

which involves the claim that humans have equal rights because they have similar basic needs. This view seems to imply a right to equal distribution of basic necessities, regardless of the individual's willingness to work. After all, needs and desires remain even if one is unwilling to work to meet them. Notoriously, this view collides with an alternative view, that goods should be distributed according to merit, as rewards for one's contribution. A philosophical analysis of right which reflects only one pole in the contemporary dispute about distributive justice can be of little help in adjudicating that dispute.

(b) Any view that connects rights closely with interests may fall prey to the objection that rights-talk is just a mask for self-interest. After all, on Tooley's view one's right to X can be reduced to one's interest in X in cases where one's pursuit of X should not be interfered with by others. This is not apt to comfort a person who suspects that rights are a rhetorical cover-up for self-interest.

(c) Does a person have a right to X if she does not desire X but others have a prima facie obligation not to interfere with her having X? If the answer is "Yes," then the connection between desire and rights has been broken. Tooley himself is much concerned with the case of comatose persons who plainly have no occurrent desire to go on living. He accords such persons a right to life on the grounds that they would desire to go on living if they were not temporarily unconscious.[12]

But the problem also arises in cases where the subject is not temporarily unconscious. Consider an immigrant who has never so much as dreamed of having a right to free speech. He can hardly desire what he has not even dreamed of! Would such a person lack the right simply because he did not desire free speech? Surely not. Granted, he could not consciously exercise the right until he became aware of it, but he would still have it. If by chance he were to voice a criticism of the current administration, he should still be protected. Or how about a person who has no desire to go on living? For example, suppose she has decided, on philosophical grounds, that life is not worth living. And suppose she is not brainwashed or distraught or seriously ill; rather she has held the view for some time, carefully considering alternatives, and simply does not desire to go on living. Does such a person have a right to life? I assume that the correct answer is, "Yes," and that one would violate that right if one were to kill her. But then again it appears that the connection between desire and rights has been broken.

Third, there is Rawls's theory of rights.[13] Essentially, Rawls claims that if we were to choose a structure for our society from behind the veil of ignorance, we would include rights for each person. (Recall that, behind the veil of ignorance, we lack knowledge of all our particular qualities—race, status, age, IQ scores, career, etc.) Gewirth points out that Rawls's position,

> viewed as giving a justificatory answer to the question whether humans have equal moral rights . . . may be convicted of circularity. For the argument attains its egalitarian conclusion only by putting into its premises the egalitarianism of persons' universal equal ignorance of all their particular qualities. This ignorance has no independent rational justification, since humans are not in fact ignorant of all their particular qualities. Hence, apart from an initial egalitarian moral outlook, why should any actual rational informed person accept the principle about equal moral rights that stems from such ignorance?[14]

In other words, Rawls begs the question. Equality seems to be built into the veil of ignorance, and hence the step to equal rights is short and easy. But we want to know what grounds such equality. In virtue of what do people have rights?

Fourth, some have claimed that rights are *conventional*, i.e., that entitlements are generated by social custom. The problem here is that some conventions are morally objectionable. For example, the vendetta entitles a relative of a murdered person to kill the murderer (without due legal process). We cannot assume that moral rights are identical with the rights actually recognized in any given culture; in fact, as we have seen, it is plausible to suppose that the conventions of every society are in need of reform.

Fifth, theologians often claim that rights are grounded in the fact that humans are made in the image of God. Among philosophers a similar idea is sometimes expressed, namely, that human beings have intrinsic worth or dignity. It is interesting to note that, while the Bible does say that humans are made in God's image (Genesis 1:26), it nowhere suggests that this is the ground of equality. Nevertheless, since the idea that humans are in God's image plays a significant role in the moral thinking of some Christians, let us examine this idea. What does it mean to be in the image of God? Presumably, it means that humans are like God in certain important respects. But in what respects? What relevant qualities or capacities do we share with God? This is a crucial question, for a dilemma threatens:

> To insure that all human beings have the rights in question, the capacities singled out must be elementary; but then it proves to be the case that animals have them as well, so that we have not so much grounded human rights as animal rights. Alternatively, to insure the distinctiveness of human rights, the capacities singled out must be sophisticated; but then it proves to be the case that not all human beings have them, so that we have grounded something narrower than human rights.[15]

For example, if we choose rationality or the capacity to love as the capacity by virtue of which humans have rights, we must admit that not all humans have these qualities, e.g., fetuses, day-old babies, the severely mentally deficient, and the comatose. If—recoiling from the implications of our first suggestion—we try to select some capacity that more nearly all humans seem to have, like the ability to experience pain and pleasure, we must admit that many nonhuman animals have this quality too.

At this point someone may suggest that what all humans have in common is just this: that they are human. But what does the word 'human' mean here? Is it being used in a purely biological sense, so that 'human' means 'member of the species *homo sapiens*'? This is not a trivial question, for the word 'human' means different things in different contexts. For example, suppose we are discussing abortion and someone asks, "Is the fetus a human being?" It would be uncharitable to interpret this question as, "Is the fetus a member of the species *homo sapiens*?" This latter question is a purely biological one, and the answer to it can be determined by examining the fetus's chromosomes. Naturally, the fetus of any two members of *homo sapiens* will itself be a member of *homo sapiens*. Rather, in the context of the abortion debate, when someone asks "Is the fetus human?" he is usually asking a question which could be put more clearly as follows: "Is the value of the life of a human fetus equivalent to that of a normal human adult?" This is plainly an ethical question, not a biological one, and the answer is in dispute.

If we say that, "Humans are in God's image" means "Humans have special value," we must ask, "What gives them that special value?" And here we have to avoid a problem similar to the problem of arbitrariness discussed in connection with the divine command theory. For if we say that humans have this special value because God loves us more dearly than other animals, we must ask, "Could God have given the same value to other animals had He so chosen? Could He, for example, have poured out his love on hawks or horses, leaving humans without a special value?" Surely the value of human beings is based on some property or properties that we have. It is not simply a matter of God's giving us value by fiat. But then what is the property (or set of properties) by virtue of which humans have such worth, such value?

Occasionally it is suggested that humans have a special value because they have immortal souls and hence will live forever (either in heaven or in hell), whereas nonhuman animals cease to exist once and for all at death. There are several problems with this proposal. (a) How is it known that nonhuman animals cease to exist at death? The fact that the Bible does not specifically mention an afterlife for animals is no proof that they have no afterlife. And some theologians have hypothesized an afterlife for animals as a means of dealing with one aspect of the problem of evil.[16] (b) What is the connection between having an afterlife and having rights of any sort? Why should anyone suppose that the fact that humans survive death gives them the rights to free speech, to freedom from assault, to freedom of association, etc.? The connection between rights and having an afterlife is no more obvious than that between rights and desires. It is even difficult to find any logical connection between having an afterlife and having a right to *life*. Indeed, someone might suggest that having an afterlife removes the right to life; after all, if it is true that a person is going to live forever anyway, why shouldn't he be killed? Killing him will only end his *earthly* life, and maybe his earthly life is not so important anyway. Perhaps one would even be doing him a favor by sending him along to a higher mode of existence! Those who accept a traditional view of hell may claim that in killing someone one risks consigning him to eternal misery. But can the value of human life really boil down to this negative possibility? Surely the value of life must rest on something more positive than the possibility of damnation. Moreover, even if this negative possibility did ground a right to life, it is difficult to see how it would ground any other rights.

If we say that being in God's image is just a matter of belonging to the species *homo sapiens*, a similar problem arises. What is the connection between having a certain type of gene structure and having special moral worth? A bit of science fiction can make the point of this question vivid. Suppose space travelers run into extraterrestrials who are intelligent and have the capacity for moral choice—but belong to another species. Wouldn't such creatures have the rights of humans without having human biology? Surely we would have a duty not to kill, enslave, or torture such nonhuman creatures.

Or again, imagine our reaction were someone to claim that being in God's image is just a matter of belonging to a certain *race*. For example, suppose a white racist theologian claims that only whites have a right to life. Surely we would find this claim philosophically puzzling as well as morally repugnant. Why would anyone suppose that a purely biological property, such as race, confers special moral status? One might as well claim that being blond or blue-eyed confers such status. But if racism is implausible, so is "speciesism" (the *arbitrary* preference for one's own species), since both attempt to ground rights on a purely biological property.[17]

Thus, it appears that the attempt to base a theory of rights on the idea that humans are made in the image of God is fraught with difficulties. And we are left with our original question, "Where do rights come from and how are they to be determined?"

IV. THE FUNDAMENTAL RIGHT

The solution I propose is in terms of the Christian teleological view. From this viewpoint, it is our duty to promote the Kingdom of God. However, in general, if it is one's duty to do X, then one has a right to do X. For example, if I have a duty to keep a promise in a given case, then I certainly have a moral right to keep it. Thus, from the Christian teleological point of view, we have a right to promote the Kingdom of God.

These logical points may seem trivial. Almost any moral theorist will agree that one has a right to do one's duty; e.g., a utilitarian will grant us the right to maximize utility. But that is not much of a right, since as we have seen, utility is often maximized at the expense of individuals. To apply this to the Framed Tramp Case of Chapter 3, one's right to maximize utility could take the form of a right to be framed for a crime one did not commit! But rights are supposed to provide a sphere of protection for individuals.[18]

However, we have already had occasion to note that utility is a very different *telos* than the Kingdom of God. If I have a duty to promote the Kingdom of God, then I have a duty to participate in that Kingdom. And I am failing in my duty to promote the Kingdom to the extent that I personally resist harmonious relations with God and neighbor. But harmonious relations are impossible apart from a respect for the rights of the individual. In particular, we must respect the rights of others to participate in the Kingdom of God, to find and follow their vocations, to love and serve God and His creatures. Indeed, from a Christian standpoint, it would clearly be wrong to interfere with anyone's participation in the Kingdom of God. So, according to the Christian teleological view, the fundamental right is the right to participate in the Kingdom of God.

If one has a right to participate in the Kingdom of God, then one has a right to the goods necessary for such participation, otherwise the right to participate in God's Kingdom is vacuous. And we must keep in mind that the earthly stage of the Kingdom of God involves an embodied existence. Hence, certain material goods are necessary for participation in the Kingdom in its earthly stage. This means that human beings have a right to life, i.e., a right not to be killed. It also means that humans have a right to basic necessities, such as food, shelter, and clothing. For one's capacity to participate in the Kingdom of God in its *earthly* stage is plainly tied to one's degree of physical well-being. Beyond such physical necessities, humans need a certain kind of freedom if they are to participate fully in the Kingdom of God—freedom to discover and to live out their vocations, freedom to express their love for God and neighbor. So, in order to participate in the Kingdom of God, one must be able to make uncoerced choices, to reflect on one's purposes, and to pursue one's purposes. Obviously, if one is tied down, locked in a cage, or under constant physical harassment, one will lack the necessary freedom. Thus, we may summarize the goods necessary for participating in God's kingdom, as *well-being* and *freedom*.[19]

This fundamental conception raises a number of urgent questions which cry out for attention. If rights are derived from duties, what about those humans who lack the mental capacity for moral agency, and who therefore have no duties? Are such humans without rights? And do any nonhuman animals have rights? Or are they utterly without moral entitlement? Furthermore, are rights negative or positive? And, finally, are rights absolute or can they be overridden by other moral factors?

V. Humans Lacking the Agapic Capacity

Thus far I have spoken of rights as grounded in the duty to promote the Kingdom of God. This seems to me the strongest argument in favor of rights from a Christian point of view. However, it implies that rights are at least partly grounded in the capacities necessary for moral agency. For in order to participate fully in the Kingdom of God, a human being must be able to make free choices, to reflect to some degree on her purposes, and to form loving relationships with other humans and with God. Let us call this cluster of capacities the *agapic capacity. (Agape* is the ancient Greek word for altruistic love.) The agapic capacity is enormously important from a Christian point of view, since it is presupposed in the central Christian story of love between God and His human creatures.

But it seems that fetuses, week-old babies, the severely mentally deficient, and the permanently comatose lack the agapic capacity. Let us say, for short, that these humans are *nonagapic*. Do nonagapic humans have rights?

Now, before plunging into a discussion of whether nonagapic humans have rights, it should be understood that even if such humans lack rights, it does not necessarily follow that they can be wantonly killed or mistreated. Logically speaking, it is possible that we ought to treat these humans with great care, even if they cannot properly be said to have the *right* to such care. As we have seen, every right implies a corresponding duty, but not every duty implies a corresponding right (held by someone besides the agent). The demands of charity can fall upon us even when the demands of justice do not. But a theory that leaves all nonagapic humans without moral protection of some sort would be unacceptable.

It is often suggested that some nonagapic humans have rights because they have the *potential* to be normal human adults. For example, a fetus or week-old baby may be regarded as having a right to life by virtue of this potential. Very often the concept of potential is left inexplicit. But it is roughly this: to say that *A is potentially B* is to say that *A* presently has some property *P*, and that there is a natural law connecting *P* with *B*. Thus, to say that a zygote is potentially an adult human is to say that (a) the zygote presently has some property *P* (e.g., the full human genetic code), and that (b) since the zygote has this property it will one day be an adult human, assuming nothing interferes with the normal biological processes. Let us refer to the thesis that nonagapic humans have rights by virtue of their potential as "the potential principle."

The main defense of the potential principle, as a ground for the right to life, is as follows. Normal adult humans have capacities which make an especially rich and remarkable kind of life possible—a life of a distinctly higher sort than that of other animals. For Christians, this especially valuable kind of life includes the fulfillment of an earthly vocation, a life devoted to knowing and serving God. This earthly life is regarded as having a value of its own, not merely as a prelude to life after death. Now, killing an adult human is, generally speaking, wrong, not because it destroys that part of life already lived—obviously it does not—but because it destroys the prospect of future (earthly) life. Killing a fetus or baby destroys this same prospect.[20]

The appeal to potential is not without difficulties. First, some humans do not have the potential to be normal human adults. For example, severely mentally defective infants lack this potential, as do the permanently comatose. Are we to say that such humans lack a right to life? Apparently so, if potential is all we can appeal to.

Second, if it is wrong to terminate the potential to be a normal adult human, then it is wrong to practice contraception. Let us suppose that a woman uses a spermicidal foam on an occasion in which pregnancy would have occurred had she not used the foam. This is to say that one of the millions of sperm in question would have fertilized the egg in question. Now consider that egg-sperm pair as an entity. (Not a "fused" entity, like a zygote, but a disjoint entity like a dinette set or an arrangement of flowers.) That egg-sperm pair had adult-human potential. For if the normal biological processes had not been interfered with, it would have become a zygote, and a zygote plainly has adult-human potential. So, if there is something wrong with terminating adult-human potential, there is something wrong with using a contraceptive that terminates or obviates that potential. Both contraception and killing destroy the prospect of future life.[21]

It is sometimes objected that since the unjoined egg and sperm are not a human organism, contraception is not wrong because it does not involve killing a human. This misses the point. If cutting off the prospect of future life is wrong, contraception is just as wrong as killing. We are left with the conclusion that the potential principle is false if contraception is permissible.

Third, the potential principle fails to account for the widespread judgment that an early abortion is less problematic (morally speaking) than a late abortion. This judgment is common even among those who take a conservative view of abortion. For example, many conservatives find abortion permissible in the case of pregnancy due to rape. But they would insist that such abortions be performed early on, as soon as possible after discovery of pregnancy. And, indeed, most people would regard it as perverse to delay an abortion *intentionally and without good reason* until late in the pregnancy. However, these judgments make no sense if the potential principle is true. An early abortion terminates the prospect of future life just as surely as a late abortion does. So, the potential principle has some very dubious implications.

Let us now consider a second proposal concerning the rights of nonagapic humans. This proposal is based on the principle that how we should treat a creature depends, at least in part, on what it may one day be. We have all heard the fairy tale about a frog who turns into a prince upon being kissed by a beautiful princess. Within the tale, those who mistreat the frog are seen as callous and lacking in insight. Such tales bring out our conviction that the way we should treat a creature can depend on what it may become, not merely on the capacities it currently possesses.[22] And this idea—I shall call it *the principle of future dignity*—differs from the potential principle in three ways. First, if *A* is potentially *B*, then *A* becomes *B* as a matter of *natural law*. But frogs do not become princes as a matter of natural law. The transformation occurs through the gracious act of the beautiful princess.

Second, the potential argument is concerned only with creatures which may become normal human adults. Now, the principle of future dignity certainly tells us not to mistreat those creatures who are likely to become normal adult humans. Normal human adults have the dignity conferred by the agapic capacity. But if Christian theology is correct, abnormal humans will one day have the agapic capacity too—not in this life, but in the world to come. For example, permanently comatose and severely mentally defective humans will be turned into glorious creatures in the afterlife by a gracious act of God. Our present treatment of them must reflect this fact.

Third, while the argument from potential rules out any act that cuts off the *prospect* of normal adult human life, such as contraception, the principle of future dignity rules out the *mistreatment* of creatures *presently susceptible to abuse*. Within the world of the fairy tale, the principle of future dignity tell us not to mistreat frogs who may become princes. But it does not tell us that it would be wrong to limit the birth rate among frogs via contraception. Talking frogs are things that can be mistreated and abused. Egg and sperm cells are not. So, unlike the potential principle, the principle of future dignity apparently does not rule out contraception.

This last point is important and needs to be developed, as it may have implications for the abortion debate. Although space does not permit a systematic discussion of abortion, a sketch of some possible implications may be useful. If it is correct to say that one cannot abuse egg and sperm cells, then it seems correct to say that one cannot abuse a zygote either. It seems that we cannot speak intelligibly of abusing a thing unless it has attained a certain state of development. Of course, the phrase "certain state of development" is extremely vague. Let us approach the topic indirectly.

In some cases we may speak of abusing an inanimate object, e.g., of abusing an object of art. This use of the word seems metaphorical. The offense is against the artist, the owner, or others who prize the work. Similarly, if we speak of "abusing" a mountain or a river, we are speaking metaphorically. The offense is surely against the living things who depend upon the physical environment, or perhaps against the Creator. It is slightly more natural, I think, to speak of abusing or mistreating plants. A child who wantonly stomps on flowers may be said to abuse them. But even this is, in my judgment, a nonstandard use. We do not think that a person who goes about pulling up weeds is mistreating them. This suggests that the offense in "abusing"' plants has to do with the interests of humans or other higher creatures.We may speak of destruction as abuse if a plant is needed by (or appreciated by) humans or other animals. But as our attitude toward weed pulling indicates, the interests of higher creatures are involved. By way of contrast, when we come to the case of animals capable of feeling pain, i.e., sentient creatures, the language of abuse or mistreatment is entirely natural. One can clearly abuse a sentient creature by wantonly inflicting pain upon it, or by wantonly killing it.[23]

Now, I do not claim that these brief remarks about the concept of abuse are definitive. But if they are on the right track, the principle of future dignity has quite different implications for the abortion debate than the potential principle. If the language of abuse becomes appropriate only when applied to sentient creatures, contraception is clearly permissible from the standpoint of the principle of future dignity, while the potential principle rules it out. Moreover, an early abortion, prior to the development of the nervous system, would not count as mistreatment from the standpoint of the principle of future dignity, since there can be no pain until the nervous system is in place. So, unlike the potential principle, the principle of future dignity may permit very early abortions. Of course, once mistreatment of the fetus becomes possible, the principle of future dignity would weigh heavily against abortion.

Let us now examine four objections to the principle of future dignity. First, some may argue as follows: "It is plainly immoral for a woman who knows she's pregnant, and who knows the effects of alcohol on the fetus, to drink heavily *early* in pregnancy. Hence, it is possible to abuse insentient humans (zygotes, embryos, etc.). Therefore, contrary to what has been alleged, the principle of future dignity puts early abortions on the same moral par as late ones."

This argument is fallacious. From the fact that it is immoral for a pregnant woman to drink heavily early in pregnancy it does not follow that such a woman is *abusing* the zygote, embryo, or insentient fetus. A mad scientist who irradiated egg and sperm cells in order to produce birth defects would be doing something very immoral, but it would not make sense to describe his action as *abuse* of egg and sperm cells. I shall suggest an alternate way of understanding why these acts are wrong momentarily.

Second, some may claim that we cannot base our treatment of a creature on what it *may* one day be. Outside fairy tales, who knows what frogs may one day be? We cannot take far-fetched possibilities into account each day of our lives.

In response it must be admitted that the principle of future dignity is utterly impractical unless we can form reasonable beliefs about the long-term future of the creatures we encounter on a daily basis. Of course, Christian theology claims that such reasonable beliefs are available. I cannot defend this claim here, but merely allude to it.[24] Naturally, an argument which depends on belief in the afterlife will be of limited value in the public debate about abortion. But my chief purpose in this book is to work out a Christian view of the issues.

Third, it may be claimed that the principle of future dignity rules out relatively late abortions in the case of fetal abnormality, such as spina bifida. For once the fetus is sentient, the principle of future dignity equates abortion with infanticide or euthanasia. Further, it may be alleged, any view implying that abortion is wrong in these cases is mistaken.

In this context, "relatively late abortions" can only mean abortions involving sentient fetuses, i.e., fetuses capable of feeling pleasure and pain. The precise time at which the fetus achieves sentience is not yet known. It is clear that the zygote is not sentient, since it has no nervous system. First trimester fetuses are probably not sentient, for while it is true that the fetus will flinch in response to certain stimuli late in the first trimester, given the state of its brain development this is probably an automatic response that does not signal the experience of pain. On the other hand, it is very probable that third trimester fetuses are sentient. Thus, given the current state of medical knowledge, it appears that sentience is probably attained sometime in the second trimester. (Unfortunately, present methods of testing for abnormality, such as amniocentesis and ultrasound, cannot be employed until the second trimester.)[25] Vague as the phrase "sometime in the second trimester" is, it does have some clear implications. For example, if the fetus becomes sentient sometime in the second trimester, the principle of future dignity equates abortions late in the second trimester (and thereafter) with infanticide or euthanasia. However, I fail to see that such an admission is a philosophical embarrassment for the principle of future dignity. In fact, I find it plausible to suppose that a late abortion is morally on a par with infanticide or euthanasia (in the case of a newborn baby).

Fourth, and more radically, it may be claimed that *painless* killing is not mistreatment if the victim will go on to attain a higher form of existence. In this respect, it may be claimed, the fairy tale is misleading: killing the frog would cut it off from its princely future, but killing nonagapic humans will not cut them off from their glorious futures, assuming Christian theology is correct (they will be raised from the dead). So, far from extending rights to nonagapic humans, the principle of future dignity entirely removes the barrier against killing them as long as the killing is done painlessly!

This objection is devastating if correct. However, the principle that it is permissible to transfer a creature painlessly to a higher mode of existence is very dubious. If we could somehow cause fetuses to skip childhood and move painlessly to mature adulthood, would that be a good thing to do? I doubt it; the persons in question would have lost out on the joys of childhood. And it can be wrong to bring about the loss of one type of good *even if* a greater good is thereby made available. Perhaps you could provide me with a better sculpture than the one I presently have by chiseling it into a smaller but more beautiful figure. But unless you have my consent, you will have done something wrong in thus depriving me of my original sculpture—even if you have left me with a better one. And earthly life can be regarded as analogous to childhood or to my original sculpture. Thus, depriving me of my earthly existence would be wrong, other things being equal, even if it would transfer me to a higher mode of existence.

Admittedly, some childhoods are so miserable that skipping them would plausibly be better than living through them. Similarly, it might be claimed that some lives are so miserable or so lacking in value that killing would not be wrong, if a better mode of existence awaits. Of course, this raises the whole issue of euthanasia, and I cannot here discuss euthanasia in a detailed fashion. But I can say this: the principle of future dignity does not by itself imply that euthanasia is always wrong. For we are here bringing in the further factor of a radically miserable life, or of a life having no value to the person who must live it, and such factors can arguably outweigh even a right to life based directly on the agapic capacity. Consider the example of a pilot who has crashed and is trapped beneath the burning wreckage of his airplane. He is burning to death, and in terrible pain. He begs a lone bystander to put him out of his misery. The bystander is unable to remove the pilot from the wreckage, and finally kills the pilot with a blow to the head, using a bit of metal from the wreckage. This is plainly euthanasia, and may well be justified in such circumstances.

In terms of the fairy tale we could put the point like this. The frog in the fairy tale is not in irreparable, debilitating pain—nor is his present frogish life of no value to himself. Thus, the principle of future dignity does not straightforwardly apply to cases involving these factors. For example, it does not necessarily imply that it would be wrong to "pull the plug" on a severely and irreparably brain-damaged accident victim. For, assuming the brain damage is such as to render the person permanently unconscious (this side of death), "pulling the plug" could hardly be construed as *mistreatment.*

But, then, doesn't the principle of future dignity allow for some shocking practices? For example, wouldn't it permit the factory farming of *insentient* humans ("human vegetables") for medical research? Perhaps by itself it would. But the principle of future dignity is not the only principle governing the treatment of nonagapic humans. There remains, for example, the duty to try to bring healthy humans (if any) into the world. And "human vegetables" are not healthy, i.e., they are unable to live well the life characteristic of their kind. Deliberately to cause a human organism to be nonagapic throughout its earthly life is to cut it off from participating in the earthly stage of God's kingdom in the way appropriate to its kind. So, while the principle of future dignity is not adequate as the *only* moral principle regarding nonagapic humans, the Christian teleological view has supplementary principles in reserve, such as the duty to try to bring healthy humans (if any) into the world. It is this duty which accounts, in my estimation, for our disapproval of the pregnant woman who drinks heavily even though she knows it will harm her fetus.

To sum up: the fundamental right, from the Christian teleological point of view, is the right to participate in the Kingdom of God. This right is grounded in the agapic capacity, either directly or indirectly through some further principle, such as the potential principle or the principle of future dignity. It seems to me that the principle of future dignity accords with our reflective moral judgments better than its rivals. Most notably, it is superior to the potential principle, which is commonly appealed to in contemporary debates about the right to life.

VI. DO NONHUMANS HAVE RIGHTS?

If we allow that nonagapic humans have rights, it is natural to ask whether nonhuman animals have rights. For the Kingdom of God consists not only in *human beings* following their vocations; it also involves other creatures and the Creator. That is, the *telos* consists in creatures of all kinds relating harmoniously under God's authority. And while I believe that the strongest argument for rights derives them from the agapic capacity, there is another possible ground for rights from the Christian teleological point of view. For although only creatures having the agapic capacity can have vocations (which involve moral choices), all creatures have a *role* to play in the creation order. From a Christian point of view, it is wrong to interfere with such roles at will, i.e., without good reason. For example, it is wrong to torture or kill an animal without good reason. Could some nonhuman creatures have *entitlement* based on the role God wants them to play in the creation order?

It is true, of course, that creatures without the agapic capacity cannot be said to have a duty to fulfill their roles, and hence we cannot derive their rights from their duties. But could it be that some nonhuman creatures are *entitled* to be treated in a certain way because of the God-intended role they play?

I am certainly *not* suggesting that everything which plays a role in creation has rights. Rocks, stars, and grains of sand play a role in the creation order, but surely they do not have rights. In fact, as we have already seen, the concept of abuse or mistreatment does not come into its own until we are speaking of sentient creatures. And I do not see how we can speak intelligibly of a thing as having rights if we cannot speak intelligibly of its being liable to abuse or mistreatment. So, my suggestion is that *sentient* creatures have rights based on their God-intended roles. In particular, they have the right not to be abused, i.e., not to be wantonly subjected to pain or destruction. And it is very probable that higher animals, such as chimps, dogs, and dolphins, are sentient. On the other hand, it is probable that lower animals, such as insects, spiders, and slugs, are not sentient. Their nervous systems are complex enough for automatic responses, but not for the conscious experience of pain and pleasure.

Some may claim that animals cannot have rights, because they are incapable of asserting their rights. But, if the argument of the previous section is correct, some nonagapic humans have rights even though they cannot assert their rights. So, the ability to assert or claim a right is not a necessary condition for having it. Furthermore, while animals cannot assert their rights, there are identifiable respondents—namely, human beings.

But how do we know what God intends for animals? The best evidence seems to be the capacities associated with each kind—something we determine empirically. Presumably God did not make creatures with special capacities only to have those capacities thoroughly frustrated. Clipping the wings of all the eagles or pulling the teeth of all the beavers would be very wicked actions, and violations of the rights of these creatures. Of course, we must not treat nonhuman animals as if they were human. Nonhuman animals probably do not make moral choices; they presumably do not relate to God in a personal way. Yet, they constitute an important part of the physical environment in which humans find themselves, and the role of stewardship given to humans in the Bible strongly suggests that relationships between humans and nonhuman animals are meant to be as harmonious as possible.

It may be objected that animal nature is fallen, and hence that we cannot know the proper roles of the animals. For example, some of the early Christian theologians held that God did not create the carnivores as carnivores; rather, that all animals were originally herbivores, but some animals (e.g., tigers and wolves) began eating other animals as a result of the fall of Adam and Eve. However, this view is not taught in the Bible. Moreover, the fossil evidence provides us with strong support for the view that some carnivores predated human beings. The fangs of a saber-toothed tiger are hardly designed for grazing! In all probability animals preyed upon other animals millions of years before *homo sapiens* was brought into existence. So, it is reasonable to suppose that a careful study of nature can reveal the roles of the various species. Of course, we have much to learn about such matters, and our knowledge is far from infallible, e.g., we have only recently learned of the high intelligence of dolphins and of the ability of chimpanzees to learn sign language.

If animals have a right not to be abused, is it wrong to eat animals? In saying that higher animals have a right to participate in the creation order (in the way appropriate to their capacities), it may seem that I am giving them a vastly more exalted role than Christians traditionally have. Not so. I *have* accorded them a right to life, in a sense. That is, it follows from the fact that animals have a right to participate in the "creation community" that it is wrong to kill them wantonly. It does not necessarily follow that it is wrong to kill them for food, for it may be part of their role in the larger scheme of things to serve as food for humans.[26] Throughout the food chain it is common for the role of one species to involve its serving as food for another, and I have grounded the rights of sentient, nonhuman animals in their God-intended roles.

VII. SUSTENANCE RIGHTS AS POSITIVE

The right to participate in the Kingdom of God entails the right to various goods necessary for such participation. Among these goods are food, shelter, and clothing. We may summarize this by saying that persons have *sustenance* rights. But are these rights positive or negative? In other words, are those who lack food, shelter, and clothing entitled to assistance in having these goods? Or are they only protected from interference with their own efforts to obtain these goods?

I do not see how it can be avoided that these rights are positive, from the Christian teleological point of view. All humans having the agapic capacity, as well as those covered by the principle of future dignity, have a right to well-being. (For the moment, let us refer to humans who are either agapic or covered by the principle of future dignity as *persons*.) Now, suppose that a given person is unable by her own effort to secure adequate food, shelter, or clothing. Is she not entitled to some assistance from those who have plenty? Is she to be cut off from the Kingdom of God (in its earthly stage) for lack of ability to obtain sustenance? Surely God has not given a surplus to some in order that they might hoard it to themselves. As St. John Chrysostom (345?–407), one of the fathers of the Greek-speaking church, pointed out long ago: a rich Christian who withholds money from the needy is like an official in the imperial treasury who is given money to distribute it as ordered, but instead hoards it or spends it on his own pleasure. So "also the rich man is a kind of steward of the money which is owed for distribution to the poor. He is directed to distribute it to his fellow servants who are in want."[27] In short, we do not have the right to hoard surplus wealth or to squander it on extravagant, needless luxuries. It is given us that we might use it to advance the Kingdom of God. What we have in abundance is therefore not ours by right. The poor and needy are entitled to it, because they have a right to participate in the Kingdom of God.

I must hasten to add that this does not imply, for example, that "throwing" money at famine-stricken countries is the best way to provide assistance. We have plenty of evidence that throwing money at social problems is ineffective and wasteful. So, providing assistance has to involve something more creative than simply sending money. It may mean providing an agricultural education, or contraceptives, for example. But the failure of some poorly designed programs is not a good excuse for neglecting the poor; the surplus wealth is not ours to keep or to waste.

In this way sustenance rights differ dramatically from Lock-ean property rights, which permit hoarding in the interest of self-preservation.[28]

But how does one define 'surplus wealth'? Here the demand for precision is misguided if not disingenuous. No one can seriously deny, for example, that many Americans indulge themselves in extravagant luxuries. And most Americans have some discretionary income left over after their needs have been met. From a Christian point of view this surplus should be used in a way that shows due respect to the right to well-being, and hence for the right to sustenance. Surely this implies that most American Christians have a duty to give some of their income to responsible organizations devoted to improving the lot of the impoverished.[29]

VIII. RIGHTS AGAINST GOD?

My remarks about sustenance rights may raise the following questions: "Is God a respondent to our right to sustenance? Does God have a duty to supply us with our basic physical needs? And, more generally, do humans have any rights against God?"

I think we can say with certainty that if God has as duty to provide us with sustenance, then He has at times failed to live up to it. Many individuals have died of famine in the history of the world, and in most cases those famines have been due to natural causes, which are directly in God's control. But if God has failed in any duty, then He is not perfectly good. However, according to Christian theology, God *is* perfectly good. I conclude that He does not have a duty to provide us with sustenance.

Nevertheless, a Creator has no right to create a being and then wantonly frustrate its attempts to fulfill the very nature He has given it. A deity who made creatures for the express purpose of frustrating them eternally would be unjust in the extreme, and would violate the rights of his creatures. Moreover, to place volitional creatures in a permanently hopeless situation, in which all their best efforts to find fulfillment were doomed to failure, would be a particularly insidious form of abuse. Accordingly, I believe that God is under an obligation to make fulfillment *possible* for His agapic creatures in the long run.[30]

But I do not think that all creatures must be given an opportunity for fulfillment. For example, the larva which is eaten by a bird has surely not been wronged by its Creator. Nor, in my judgment, is such a larva entitled to a full insect life after death, as compensation for its early death. Such creatures are not even sentient, and so they are without rights. Furthermore, as far as I can see, merely sentient creatures, such as birds and rodents, are generally fulfilled by the rudimentary pleasures afforded them in the natural setting. And while it would reflect badly on a creator if he wantonly abused his merely sentient creatures, I see no good reason to suppose that a creator owes each merely sentient creature a pleasant life of, say, average length for the species in question—or, failing that, compensation in the afterlife. Such creatures have a right not to be abused, but I think it doubtful that they have a right to fulfillment, for as we have already seen their God-intended roles seem to include the function of serving as food for other animals. But be that as it may, the point I wish to emphasize is that agapic creatures fall into a special category, because it seems abusive to endow a creature with a capacity of free choice and a capacity to seek *consciously* for fulfillment, and yet to deny that creature the very possibility of fulfillment.

I am not suggesting, however, that a creator has a duty to *insure* his agapic creatures' fulfillment in the long run. According to Christianity, the fulfillment of agapic creatures depends in part on the choices they make. And the situation is that they—at least, the *human* agapic creatures—have turned away from their Creator, thus rejecting their only source of true fulfillment. But if fulfillment involves a free response of love on the part of creatures, those creatures who choose to reject their Creator have rejected fulfillment, and it is logically impossible that they should be *forced* by God to choose *freely* what is best for them. So, agapic creatures are entitled to an opportunity for fulfillment, but fulfillment is not necessarily guaranteed.

Further, apart from special agreements such as promises or covenants, I can see no reason to suppose that a creator has a duty to sustain agapic creatures in existence indefinitely. As I see it, a creator has very strong rights over his creatures, based on the fact that he not only invented them but brought them into existence out of nothing. On what grounds can a creature claim to *deserve* continued existence *vis-à-vis* its creator? If an agapic creature has achieved fulfillment, or if it has had ample opportunity for fulfillment, I cannot see that God is obligated to sustain it in existence. Continued existence is a gift from God, not an entitlement, apart from special agreements. Of course, if God *has* promised the creature everlasting life, then He is bound by His promise, and the creature has a right that God should keep His promise. So, creatures have some rights against their Creator. But for the most part a theory of rights must be concerned with rights having human respondents, such as sustenance rights, the right to liberty, and the right to life.

IX. Enforcement and Punishment as Positive Rights

Sinful human nature being what it is, we know that violations of rights will occur. And if criminals know they can violate rights with impunity, they will be encouraged in their criminal activities. Furthermore, if victims know that no action will be taken when their rights are infringed, talk about rights will rapidly come to be regarded as empty verbiage. Hence, as Diana Meyers points out, if we take no action when rights are violated, rights fall into disrespect; but from a moral point of view it is intolerable for rights to fall into disrespect. Therefore, we fail in our moral commitments if we take no action when rights are violated.[31]

But what action should we take when rights are violated? In many cases social sanctions, such as vocal disapproval, are sufficient to insure respect for rights. But we know from experience that social sanctions are not always sufficient; some people will violate rights at will unless they are hindered by force or the threat of force. And since criminals will not take threats seriously unless force is actually used on some occasions, rights will go unrespected unless force is sometimes actually used. We therefore have the right to *enforce* our rights.

However, for at least two reasons, this right must be waived by the individual *on condition that* her rights are enforced by society. First, individuals are typically incapable of effectively enforcing their rights. Most people lack the time and ability to catch criminals and to bring them to justice. Second, history makes it plain that vigilantee groups are much more prone to cruelty and injustice than officially sanctioned police operating in conjunction with a system of courts presided over by legal authorities. These considerations lead us to the conclusion that the right to enforcement is *positive*. For it should now be clear that if society does not provide enforcement for individual rights, the rights of many individuals will go unrespected. Moreover, even those able to enforce their own rights are apt to lapse into cruelty and injustice in doing so. Such outcomes are intolerable from the moral point of view. This means that humans living in modern societies have a positive right to police protection.

Does the right to enforcement require that we take action, not only to prevent crime, but also to punish it when it occurs? Nowadays many would say *no*, on the grounds that punishment is merely revenge. Psychiatric treatment and/or rehabilitation are therefore urged by many as civilized alternatives to the more "barbaric" institution of criminal punishment.[32] However, while systems of criminal punishment have often been cruel and unjust, it is by no means obvious that the concept of punishment has a place only in "barbaric" conceptual schemes. And we ought to keep in mind that so-called mental health institutions have at times promoted apparently cruel treatments too, such as shock therapy.

Herbert Morris, professor of law and philosophy at UCLA, has suggested a promising justification of the practice of criminal punishment.[33] In a just society the laws are, in part, designed to secure a fair distribution of benefits and burdens. Laws against killing and assault, for example, are designed to provide us with well-being and with freedom from a certain kind of fear. Laws against theft and sharp business practices are designed to provide us with security in the possession of material goods. But the legal code in a given society is fair only if it benefits *all* who must conform to it. For example, a code that proscribed theft from the rich but permitted theft from the poor would be grossly unfair to the poor. Indeed, in such a society one could hardly blame the poor for refusing to obey the law. Accordingly, the laws must

> define a sphere for *each* person . . . which is immune from interference by others. Making possible this mutual benefit is the assumption by individuals of a burden. The burden consists in the exercise of self-restraint by individuals over inclinations that would, if satisfied, directly interfere or create a substantial risk of interference with others in proscribed ways.[34]

Thus, the laws against murder, assault, theft, etc., place a burden of self-restraint on each member of society. Hence, these laws restrict liberty in the name of liberty, for they require that each individual suppress certain impulses.

What are we to do when the laws are broken? Well, what state of affairs has the crime brought about? Morris points out that

> if a person fails to exercise self-restraint even though he might have and gives in to such [criminal] inclinations, he

renounces a burden which others have voluntarily assumed and thus gains an advantage which others, who have restrained themselves, do not possess.[35]

So, the criminal has failed to take on a burden that the rest of us continue to carry; he has tried to take unfair advantage of us, by benefiting from the law without obeying it. And as Morris remarks, "Fairness dictates that a system in which benefits and burdens are equally distributed have a mechanism designed to prevent a maldistribution in the benefits and burdens."[36] Hence, one can view criminal punishment as the attempt to shift an appropriate burden back onto the criminal, thus restoring a just distribution of burdens and making it plain to the criminal that violations of rights will not be tolerated. From this perspective, the practice of criminal punishment seems just.

Therefore, it seems that our basic rights of freedom and well-being imply not only a positive right to law enforcement, but also a positive right to the punishment of lawbreakers. However, as George Sher has pointed out, Morris's theory of punishment provides us with a *purified* version of retributivism. Retributivist views are typically associated with the claim that "The guilty should suffer," a view which threatens to equate criminal punishment with institutionalized revenge. But on Morris's account the point of punishment must be to secure fairness, not to make the wrongdoer suffer. (Of course, any punishment may cause some suffering, but that should not be its purpose.) How is fairness to be secured? By removing a liberty proportionate to the liberty unfairly taken by the criminal. And according to Sher, the best measure of the degree of liberty unfairly taken by the criminal (and hence the best measure of liberty to be taken as punishment) is the degree of seriousness of the moral prohibition which has been violated. Thus, in the interests of fairness, the state typically has not only a right but a duty to take more liberty from a murderer than from, say, a thief.[37]

Of course, it is a long way from an abstractly described system of punishment, such as Morris's, to the practice of criminal punishment in any actual society. Most societies, if not all, have some unjust laws on their statute books. Sometimes the injustice is blatant. For example, in some countries approximately 5 percent of the population possesses nearly all of the land, and hence nearly all of the wealth, while the other 95 percent is destitute, reduced by necessity to working the land for starvation wages. In such countries laws permitting the accumulation of vast holdings serve to maintain a system that stacks the cards heavily against the poor. In such a situation, punishing the poor for stealing from the rich becomes a means of perpetuating structural evil.

Furthermore, the justification of criminal punishment does not justify an unwillingness to correct the social factors that abet crime. It is remarkable that political candidates in America continue to get votes through "law and order" rhetoric, without any suggested program for eliminating the factors in American society that breed crime. America has a higher rate of violent crime than any western European country. Is this because America gives less attention to enforcement or punishes crime less severely? Hardly. It is rather the case that Americans have been unwilling to confront the factors which abet crime, such as ghettos and child-rearing practices (e.g., neglect, permissiveness, and abuse). These problems are often lamented, and many Americans wax moralistic about them, but constructive programs designed to address such problems receive little support in the way of votes and tax dollars.

Finally, even if punishment is justifiable, a given method of punishment may not be. For example, a good case could be made—has often been made—that American prisons make their inmates worse. Criminals come out more likely to commit crimes than when they went in. If we know that a given form of punishment tends to harden criminals, and if we know of alternative forms of punishment

that do not have this effect (but still serve in other respects
as adequate sanctions), then obviously we ought to prefer
the more benign forms. Presently, electronic surveillance
for nonviolent offenders and "boot camp" style programs
for youthful offenders show promise of providing a creative alternative to the often demoralizing prison system
in America.

It is sometimes argued that criminal punishment must be
very harsh to be "effective." The idea is that would-be criminals will be deterred if and only if criminal punishment is
perceived to be very harsh. This idea is questionable, to put
it mildly. Deterrence depends at least as much on the perceived likelihood of getting caught as on the severity of the
punishment. Thus, few people will commit a crime while
a policeman is watching, even if the punishment is not
severe. But the fact is that in the vast majority of cases in
America, criminals are never apprehended. We simply do
not have enough police to catch them. In fact, the attempt
to curb crime via enforcement—apart from a corresponding attack on the social causes of crime—is almost certainly
doomed to defeat. We probably could not afford the massive police force this would require, but even if we could
afford it, creating such a police force would be risky in the
extreme. For by creating a sufficiently large police force
we would almost certainly create a monster—the familiar
modern police state.

The main point is that punishment has little deterrent
value unless would-be criminals think it is likely that they
will be caught. And in the contemporary American scene
criminals know they have a very good chance of avoiding
arrest altogether. So, we cannot achieve deterrence simply
by insuring that prisons are harsh and brutal environments.
Ironically, a more likely result would be increased recidi-
vism. Thus, although criminal punishment seems justifiable
from the Christian teleological point of view, Christians
ought to be among the first to demand a creative approach
to punishment that will further the Kingdom of God. More-

over, they ought to be among the first to emphasize the importance of addressing the social factors that perpetuate crime.

X. ARE RIGHTS ABSOLUTE?

I said earlier that the structure of a rights-claim is as follows: A has a right to B against C by virtue of D (where A is the subject, B is the object, C is the respondent, and D is the ground of the right). This schema, however, gives us no indication of the stringency of the right, and since rights can and often do conflict, we must have some idea about their relative stringency.

One factor relevant to conflicts of rights is the *manner of possession* of the right, i.e., is the right absolute or can it be overridden by other moral considerations? Is it merely prima facie or is it somehow retained even when overridden? Is it inalienable or can it be separated from the subject (right-holder) under certain circumstances?

If a right is *absolute*, it can never be overridden by other moral considerations. There is at least one absolute right from the Christian teleological point of view, namely, the right to promote the Kingdom of God. But this general right tells us very little, really, since the interesting cases involve conflicts between particular rights. For example, in case of a food shortage, A's right to well-being may conflict with B's right to well-being. If there just is not enough food for everyone, then some cannot be fed, and hence (assuming "ought implies can") there can be no obligation to feed everyone. But if we cannot feed both A and B, whose right is to be denied? Similarly, the right to life seems not to be absolute. If A attacks B with a lethal weapon, B may be permitted to kill A in self-defense. Furthermore, conflicts between one person's liberty and another's are quite common. Thus, A's freedom to hunt a deer may conflict with B's freedom to photograph it. Finally, conflicts between the right to liberty and the right to well-being are also common. For instance, an entire family may be quarantined because a child has an infectious disease. In such a case the family's right to liberty is infringed in deference to the right of others to well-being.

To these examples it might be replied that the rights in question have exception clauses built in. It might be said, for example, that the right to life does not extend to an attacker who intends to kill his victim. Or it might be said that the right to photograph an animal does not apply when the animal is being hunted for food, or that liberty does not extend to those who are carrying or may be carrying life-threatening, infectious diseases. The trouble with this suggestion is that it makes describing the rights in question hopelessly difficult. It is doubtful that we have sufficient insight to list all the exception clauses needed to describe rights in this way. But even if we could produce a complete list of exceptions, it would probably be very complicated, making the right in question virtually impossible to remember. On the other hand, most any particular right *described in reasonably simple terms* can be overridden by others in some cases. Thus, plausible candidates for "absolute right" status are hard to find.[38]

Probably the most plausible candidate is the right not to be tortured.[39] But I doubt that even this right is absolute. Suppose the police have caught a terrorist who has planted an atomic device in the middle of a large city. The device is timed to explode in an hour, and is bound to kill millions, but the terrorist refuses to tell us where it is. Now torture is an awful thing, but it is not clear to me that it would be wrong to torture such a terrorist, if it were the only hope of getting the necessary information from him. So, although general rights (such as the right to promote the Kingdom of God or to do one's duty) may be absolute, particular rights do not seem to be absolute.

The frequency of conflict between rights has led some philosophers to hold that all rights are prima facie rights. On this view one has a right to X in a given case only if no conflicting moral considerations of greater stringency apply. This suggestion fails to capture the ordinary concept of a right, for it implies that in the case of a conflict of rights, the less stringent right really is not a right at all. But one can possess a right, even if the object of the right must be denied due to shortage or conflict. This is reflected in the fact that respect for a right can be shown even when its object must be denied. Compensation is one way to show respect for a right, even though its object must be denied; apologizing is another way. For example, suppose a family has been quarantined due to a child's illness, i.e., their liberty has been denied for the sake of the well-being of others. It does not follow that the members of the family have lost their *right* to liberty for the period in which they are quarantined, for we may show respect for their right to liberty by compensating them in some way (e.g., financially). The fact that we feel compensation to be appropriate is an indication that we think their right to liberty should be recognized even if an important freedom must be denied. In an imperfect world the object of a right must sometimes be denied, but the right itself does not necessarily vanish in such cases.[40]

So, it seems to me that particular rights are best regarded as neither absolute nor prima facie. They are not absolute because they can be overridden, in the sense that the object of the right can be denied for adequate moral reasons in some cases. They are not prima facie, because they do not simply vanish when they are overridden.

Rather than thinking of human rights as absolute or prima facie, some authors regard them as inalienable. While different authors define the term 'inalienable' in different ways, the usual idea is that a right is inalienable if and only if it cannot be separated from the subject by being transferred, waived, revoked, renounced, or forfeited. By way of contrast, alienable rights can be separated from the subject in any of these ways. Some examples, borrowed from Diana Meyers, may help to clarify these concepts.

(a) If I am standing near the front of a long line at the theater, I presumably have a right to my place in line. But such a right is alienable, for if someone asks me for my place in the line, I can *transfer* my right to her, and go to the back of the line myself. (b) A parent may *waive* her right to demand that her rowdy children go to their rooms on the condition that they play quietly. She is not transferring her right or renouncing it, for she reserves the option to claim it if the condition is not met. (c) A driver's license may be *revoked* by the governing authorities, e.g., if the holder is found guilty of driving while intoxicated. (d) A king may *renounce* his right to the throne, thus initiating a competition for power. To renounce is neither to transfer nor to waive, for transferring involves specifying a new subject, and waiving involves specifying the conditions upon which the right may be reclaimed. Renouncing simply separates the right from the right-holder. (e) The right to return merchandise may be *forfeited* if one violates the conditions of return, e.g., by keeping the merchandise beyond the specified trial period.[41]

Many people deny that there are any inalienable rights. Perhaps the most common reason for this denial is the claim that one can forfeit one's rights through wrongdoing. Thus, it is often said that a murderer forfeits her own right to life, or that a thief forfeits (in some degree) her right to property. However, as Joel Feinberg has pointed out, the general thesis that *A* can forfeit her right to *X* by violating *B*'s right to *X* is very dubious.[42] Suppose *A* tortures *B* for the fun of it. Does it follow that *A* alienates her own right not to be tortured, so that *B* (or perhaps anyone) is permitted to torture *A*? Surely not. While *A* no doubt deserves to be punished, we would regard torturing her as cruel and unusual punishment. Apparently, then, the fact that *A* has tortured *B* does not legitimate torturing *A* in return. And so the common belief that a criminal *always* forfeits the very right he has violated seems false.

Nevertheless, in some cases it is plausible to suppose that rights can be forfeited. As Meyers remarks, a right is forfeited when the qualifications for possessing it are no longer met.[43] And it seems to me that the qualifications for possessing a right can include volitional states of the right-holder. For example, I find it plausible to suppose that a person who could work *but won't* forfeits his sustenance rights, for as long as he refuses to work. As St. Paul remarks, "If any one won't work, let him not eat" (2 Thessalonians 3:10).[44] And I am also inclined to think that if *A* violates *B*'s right not to be confined, e.g., by locking *B* up in a cage, then *A* forfeits his own right not to be confined, and so may be imprisoned for a time.

Admittedly, it can be difficult to tell whether a right has been forfeited or merely overridden by a more stringent right. For example, one could claim that a refusal to work does not imply forfeiture of sustenance rights, though it does create a circumstance in which the right can be over-ridden by some other right, such as the right to demand that others pull their own weight (when they can). And it might be claimed that one who violates another's right not to be confined retains his own right not to be confined *even though it is overridden* by society's right to punish criminals.

But I think that two important considerations support the thesis that many particular rights (and perhaps even all) are forfeitable. First, in many cases we do not think that we owe compensation, or even an apology, when the object of a right has been denied. This is most obvious in the case of criminal punishment, for we routinely deny liberty to criminals by imprisoning them. If they have retained their full right to liberty during the time of imprisonment, then we would owe them compensation or at the very least an apology. But surely it would be ludicrous to suppose that we owe criminals either compensation or an apology; it is more plausible to suppose that criminals forfeit their liberty (in some degree), at least temporarily. Similarly, I do not think we owe compensation, or even an apology, to those denied welfare payments (i.e., sustenance) if they could work but won't. It is more plausible to suppose that the right is forfeited for as long as the person refuses to work.

Second, we have already seen that there are two opposing conceptions of justice in our culture. One of these conceptions is *meritarian*, i.e., it says that justice consists in treating people according to their deserts or merits. The other is *equalitarian*, and says that justice consists in treating people according to their basic needs, which happen to be roughly equal (e.g., we all need food, shelter, and clothing). Confronted with a question regarding the distribution of goods, a meritarian is apt to claim that the goods should be awarded to those who have earned them or made the greater contribution. The equalitarian will stress that the meritarian view leads to inequalities, and that it is ultimately arbitrary since a person's merit is apt to be closely linked with factors over which he has little control, such as intelligence, upbringing, or quality of education. So, the equalitarian will urge us to distribute goods so as to make an equal contribution to the fulfillment of individual needs. This may mean more for the disabled or deprived person, and less for the gifted or fortunate, regardless of individual merit.

If rights are forfeitable, then I believe we have a way of reconciling the meritarian and equalitarian views, in the sense that we can preserve the partial truth in each of them. From the Christian teleological point of view, equality is based *not* on an alleged similarity of need, but on the fact that all agapic humans have the *same basic rights*. (I say *basic* rights, because some rights are specific to one's role, status, or situation; e.g., a woman's right not to be impregnated against her will—a right obviously not shared by men—is derived from a more basic right to liberty which is held by men also.) Now, the Christian teleological view accords each agapic human the right to participate in the

Kingdom of God, and hence a right to the goods necessary for such participation, such as freedom and well-being. In this way the Christian teleological view shows a concern for the human needs which are the focus of the equalitarian view. However, if a right is forfeitable, possessing it depends on meeting the relevant qualifications. So, if a right is forfeitable, one can be said to *merit* the object of the right by virtue of meeting the relevant qualifications. Obviously, this has a meritarian ring to it.

From our present vantage point, the debates between meritarians and equalitarians can be regarded as debates about the qualifications for having rights, rather than as debates between fundamentally irreconcilable views about the very nature of justice. Of course, I am not suggesting that disputes about justice are apt to go away simply because the two positions are in principle reconcilable. But getting clear about the true locus of the disagreement is obviously an aid to mutual understanding, and may suggest a more fruitful way to approach the issues.

It is noteworthy that the qualifications for possessing rights vary significantly from one right to another. For example, the right to a promotion in the workplace surely depends on demonstrating one's ability and willingness to do the job well, and the right to perform surgical operations depends on the satisfactory completion of adequate medical training. By way of contrast, many philosophers hold that one does not have to *do* anything to possess the right to life. I myself have argued that all agapic humans as well as all humans covered by the principle of future dignity meet the central qualifications for this right. But it may be that even the right to life can be forfeited if one is sufficiently callous in one's treatment of others. For example, it is not implausible to suppose that serial murderers have forfeited their own right to life. So, it may be that one's right to life depends in part on one's *not doing* (or on one's refraining from) certain things. Moreover, it is noteworthy that in some cases one can even forfeit a right *inadvertently.* For example, by forgetting to return merchandise on time one may forfeit one's right to return it. Finally, I think that one can forfeit even a right grounded in the agapic capacity if one intentionally destroys one's own agapic capacity, e.g., by intentionally taking a drug which one knows will destroy one's higher brain functions. Perhaps, in such a case, one would subsequently be covered by the principle of future dignity, but one would have deliberately removed one's qualifications for certain rights, e.g., the right to liberty (which presupposes a capacity of free choice). My point is that in a great many cases one can forfeit a right by doing or failing to do something. In these cases there is a clear sense in which one must *merit* the object of the right, either by performing acts to meet the relevant qualifications or by refraining from acts which result in the loss of the qualifications.[45]

So, there are theoretical advantages in regarding many rights as forfeitable, including such basic rights as the right to liberty and the right to sustenance. First, if rights are forfeitable, we have a clear explanation of why compensation is not always owed when the object of a right is denied, viz., the right has been forfeited. Second, if rights are forfeitable, we have a way of combining, at least in principle, the central insights of the meritarian and equalitarian conceptions of justice.

If a right is forfeitable, then it is not inalienable *in the standard sense.* But I believe that a modified concept of inalienability is important for ethics. For the remainder of the discussion let us say that a right is *inalienable* if and only if it cannot be separated from the subject by being transferred, waived, revoked, or renounced. (This is the same as our earlier definition, except the word 'forfeited' has been deleted.) The debate about euthanasia illustrates one important application of the concept of an inalienable right. For voluntary euthanasia, or euthanasia by consent, has sometimes been defended on the grounds that any right can be waived.[46] Obviously, if all rights can be waived, all are alienable—including the right to life. Hence, if I waive my right to life, it becomes permissible to kill me.

But it is implausible to suppose that all rights can be waived. For example, can I waive my right to liberty, thus making it morally permissible for others to enslave me? However sincere I might be in saying, "I waive my right to liberty," it does not seem possible for me to legitimate your owning me, demanding that I work without pay, forcing me to obey your dictates, etc. Similarly, I cannot waive my right not to be assaulted; I cannot make it morally permissible for you to assault me just by (sincerely) uttering some words to the effect that I waive this right. If, upon hearing my words, you proceed to assault me, simply because you assume my utterance removes my right, you will have done something immoral. And one's right to life is more like one's right to liberty or one's right not to be assaulted than like, e.g., one's right to fire an employee (which may be waived on condition that her work improves). So, the concept of an inalienable right can be used to expose some dubious moves in ethical reasoning.

We come now to a final, and rather messy, issue. Whether rights are inalienable or not, they can conflict. How do we decide which right is overriding when two or more rights conflict?

Those who are asking for hard-and-fast rules here are asking the wrong questions. The problem (as examples throughout this book indicate) is that a given right will have a different stringency in different circumstances. Therefore, simple rules will inevitably run roughshod over the complexities of the moral life. It is no accident that Jesus typically used stories and parables, rather than rules, to characterize the Kingdom of God. For the important thing is to have a vision of creatures related harmoniously under God's authority. Still, some general principles, as opposed to absolutes or algorithms, can be given. These draw attention to the most important things to keep in mind when adjudicating conflicts of rights.

The most general principle is the *greater demand* principle. When two rights conflict, one can be accorded only at the expense of the other. Often one right protects a demand which can be satisfied at the cost of denying a lesser demand. The demands may be placed on us by God or by other humans. The greater demand principle says we ought to give preference to the right protecting the greater demand. To take a trivial case, if your right to life conflicts with my right to move my limbs freely, because we are standing in close proximity to the edge of a cliff, then your right overrides mine, for your well-being can be preserved by a minor restriction on my freedom. There is no difficulty in deciding between your loss of life and my loss of a very minor freedom. Needless to say, difficulties arise when the two rights protect roughly comparable demands. We shall examine such a case momentarily.

Two secondary principles are worth making explicit. First, the *levels of kinds* principle. On this principle, the flourishing of some kinds of things is more important than the flourishing of other kinds of things. For example, suppose I come upon the scene of an automobile accident. A dog and a human are both injured, and let us imagine that I know they are both dying—will die unless I render aid. But I have medical supplies only for one. What should I do? Is it mere speciesism to save the human? Not if there are good reasons to suppose that the lives of humans are normally more important than the lives of dogs. And as we saw in Sections V and VI, such reasons exist.

Second, the *vocation* principle. Those who are called by God to be a certain kind of person, or to perform a certain kind of task, have the right to fulfill their calling. For example, if God has called one to be a medical doctor, then it would seem clear that one is not required to give the money one has saved for tuition expenses to the poor. Obviously, the concept of vocation can be used to rationalize selfishness, but this is not an adequate reason for refusing to employ the concept, only a reason for caution and humility in identifying one's vocation. Moreover, unless one gives due attention to one's vocation, and to the conditions necessary for following that vocation, Christian living can too easily become "living for others" in a way that, in effect, denies the injunction, "Love thy neighbor *as thyself*." Our lives are not to be spent merely in pleasing others or in servile obedience to the demands of others, as though everyone's purposes and goals but our own mattered. Rather, we must live out the roles and tasks God calls us to as individuals.

It will be instructive to examine a case of conflicting rights in the light of the principles discussed above. Clearly, normal adult humans have a right to life, for they cannot participate in the Kingdom of God in its earthly stage if they are killed. But what if one's right to life conflicts with another right? An American philosopher, Judith Jarvis Thomson, has described such a case. Thomson's case is somewhat fanciful, but has generated an enormous amount of discussion because of its relevance to the abortion issue. Suppose

> you wake up in the morning and find yourself back to back in bed with an unconscious violinist. A famous unconscious violinist. He has been found to have a fatal kidney ailment, and the Society of Music Lovers has canvassed all the available medical records and found that you alone have the right blood type to help. They have therefore kidnapped you, and last night the violinist's circulatory system was plugged into yours, so that your kidneys can be used to extract poisons from his blood as well as your own. The director of the hospital now tells you, 'Look, we're sorry the Society of Music Lovers did this to you—we would never have permitted it if we had known. But still, they did it, and the violinist now is plugged into you. To unplug you would be to kill him. But never mind, it's only for nine months. By then he will have recovered from his ailment, and can safely be unplugged from you.' Is it morally incumbent on you to accede to this situation? No doubt it would

be very nice of you if you did, a great kindness. But do you *have* to accede to it? What if it were not nine months, but nine years? Or longer still?[47]

Do not be distracted by the fact that the case is not medically realistic. Instead ask, "What *would* be my rights and obligations if I *were* in such a situation?" As an adult human being, it seems clear that the violinist has a right to life. Does his right to life entitle him to the use of your kidneys for nine months, or even nine years? Can it be *required* of you, as a matter of *justice*, that you lie there for nine months, or nine years? Most people have the intuition that he does not have this right, this entitlement. Perhaps out of benevolence or goodwill you might make this sacrifice, but it is not something the violinist (or his advocates) could demand as his *right*.

But doesn't the right to life override all others? Several factors must be kept in mind in answering this question. First, the right to life is not the fundamental right; it is derived from the right to participate in the Kingdom of God. Second, we may be obligated not to kill when we are not obligated to save. Thus, someone might claim that there is an important difference between disconnecting oneself from the violinist and, say, shooting him in the head. For if you disconnect yourself and he somehow (miraculously) survives, it would plainly be wrong for you to shoot him. The right to disconnect—if it is a right—is not the right to guarantee the death of the other. The point is that it is one thing to say that the violinist has a right to life, and another to say that he has the right to be kept alive at any cost. If you could save the violinist at no danger to yourself by connecting with his circulatory system for nine minutes, it would seem to be a violation of his right to life if you refused. Surely he is entitled to that minimal amount of assistance. But nine months lying in bed is a different matter, and nine years is surely unthinkable. Lying in bed for nine months or nine years represents an enormous restriction on your freedom.

Of course, it is possible that some people would be called to save the violinist—that lying in bed for nine months would be an aspect of their vocation. But there is no reason to suppose that this would be true of everyone. In fact, lying in bed for that long would in all likelihood significantly interfere with the pursuit of one's vocation. So, my own inclination is to say that the violinist does not have the right that you should remain connected to him for nine months, let alone nine years.

Thomson's "famous violinist" case is analogous to abortion in the case of pregnancy due to rape. In both cases the life of one human A is made dependent on that of another human B without B's consent. In both cases B's freedom to control her own body is infringed. True, an ordinary pregnancy does not entail lying in bed for nine months, but this does not destroy the force of Thomson's analogy for two reasons. First, the fact that a woman must be confined to her bed for medical reasons throughout pregnancy is not typically accepted as a justification for abortion among conservatives, who insist that killing the innocent is murder. (Incidentally, this equation of murder with killing the innocent is dubious. If one is attacked by an insane person one may have to kill in self-defense, even though the attacker, being insane, is morally innocent. And killing in self-defense is not murder.) Second, the invasion of one's body represented by an unwanted pregnancy is, if anything, a greater infringement of one's freedom than being confined to bed for nine months. Now, occasionally this is denied—usually by men. I therefore offer the following case to jog intuitions. Suppose that scientists have invented a "pregnancy pill" that will make men pregnant. Someone slips one of the pills into Mr. Jones's drink at a party. Shortly thereafter his doctor informs him that he is pregnant. Would carrying the fetus to term be at least as great an infringement of Mr. Jones liberty as being confined to bed for nine months? I must leave the answer to the reader. (Delivery will be by Caesarean section, of course!)

Plainly, conflict cases can be excruciatingly difficult to decide. The point of this section has been that, in such cases, we must seek to respect the right which is such that, if accorded, the Kingdom of God will be fulfilled, i.e., the right protecting the most pressing demand. Disagreements about this are possible because the concept of the Kingdom of God is not precise. We must accept the fact that moral concepts do not always have precise boundaries, and hence that a clearly correct answer is not available in every case.

*   *   *   *   *

In this chapter I have tried to develop a theory of justice based on the Christian teleological view. Justice consists in giving individuals their due, and individuals are due their rights. The fundamental right is the right to participate in the Kingdom of God. For human beings, this right is grounded in the agapic capacity, either directly or indirectly through the principle of future dignity. In general, such rights as a creature has are grounded in the capacities it has to participate in the life characteristic of its kind. The right to participate in the Kingdom of God entails the right to the goods necessary for such participation. These goods can be summarized as well-being and freedom. Thus, the fundamental right entails a right to life, the right to freedom from assault, the right to sustenance, and the right of society to punish criminals.

XI. Concluding Note

In this book I have tried to approach ethical theory from the standpoint of Christian theology. I hope my efforts suggest the fruitfulness of combining ethical and theological reflection. I have written in the belief that progress can be made in ethics; thus, I have argued that certain views are preferable to others on rational grounds. The popular moral subjectivism of our time, which equates one moral opinion with the next, is in my view the result of slipshod thinking rather than an authentic response to the complexity of the moral life. Ours is an impatient age, with little tolerance for the vital intellectual work of noticing significant differences and drawing distinctions. I have written in the hope that the construction of systematic perspectives can give us a measure of freedom from the intellectual vicissitudes of our day. And I shall feel amply rewarded for my efforts if what I have written serves in some small way to encourage those who seek clarify amidst the present confusion.

Notes

Notes to Introduction

1. Alasdair MacIntyre, *After Virtue*, rev. ed. (Notre Dame, Ind.: University of Notre Dame Press, 1984), pp. 6-22.

2. For an insightful summary of the history of ethics, see Alasdair MacIntyre, *A Short History of Ethics* (New York: Macmillan, 1966).

Notes to Chapter 1: Relativism and Subjectivism

1. James Rachels, "The Challenge of Cultural Relativism," in *Taking Sides: Clashing Views on Controversial Moral Issues*, ed. Stephen Satris (Guilford, Conn.: Dushkin, 1988), p. 13.

2. Ibid.

3. William K. Frankena, *Ethics*, 2nd ed. (Englewood Cliffs, N.J.: Prentice-Hall, 1973), p. 109.

4. Rachels, "Challenge of Cultural Relativism," pp. 16-17.

5. William Graham Sumner, "Folkways," in Satris, *Taking Sides*, p. 4.

6. Fred Feldman, *Introductory Ethics* (Englewood Cliffs, N.J.: Prentice-Hall, 1978), p. 166.

7. The formulation owes much to Feldman (ibid.).

8. For this argument I am indebted to Peter Singer, *Practical Ethics* (London: Cambridge University Press, 1979), p. 6.

9. See for example Alfred Jules Ayer, *Language, Truth, and Logic* (New York: Dover, 1952).

10. The reader may note that this accident victim example not only refutes the claim that "You ought to keep your promises" *is true by definition*, but it also refutes the claim that we ought

always to keep our promises. We shall examine this and related issues in Chapter 4, Section III.

11. Perhaps the most famous advocate of subjective naturalism is the Finnish philosopher Edward Westermarck. See his *Ethical Relativity* (London: Kegan Paul, Trench, Trubner, 1932). It must be said, however, that the version of subjective naturalism which I discuss in the text involves a much less subtle analysis of the moral emotions than Westermarck's version. In spite of this, I think that Westermarck's view falls prey to essentially the same objections.

12. G. E. Moore, *Philosophical Studies* (London: Routledge and Kegan Paul, 1960), p. 333.

13. A. C. Ewing, *The Definition of Good* (New York: Macmillan, 1947), pp. 5-6.

14. It is no doubt an anachronism to regard hedonism, a tradition with roots in ancient Greece, as a view about the analysis of moral terms. Nevertheless, such an interpretation is both natural and useful in the current analytic climate. For a scholarly discussion of ancient Greek hedonists, see J. C. B Gosling and C. C. W. Taylor, *The Greeks on Pleasure* (Oxford: Clarendon Press, 1982). We shall examine traditional hedonism (the view that pleasure is the primary good) in Chapter 3.

15. J. L. Mackie, *Ethics: Inventing Right and Wrong* (New York: Penguin, 1977), chap. 3.

16. Ibid., pp. 55-56.

17. Brand Blanshard, *Philosophy and Phenomenological Research* 9 (1949): 504-511. The article is also in Satris, *Taking Sides*, pp. 28-33.

18. Feldman, *Introductory Ethics*, pp. 221-222.

19. More precisely, a proposition is a bearer of a truth value. There is a debate among philosophers about the nature of propositions. Some hold that propositions are just sentences, i.e., linguistic entities (in this case there would be no truth if there were no language). Others hold that propositions are thoughts or judgments, i.e., mental entities (in this case there would be no truth if there were no thinkers). Still others hold that propositions are platonic or abstract entities, existing independently of concrete existing things (mental or physical). On this view, sentences or judgments are not propositions, but merely express propositions.

Notes to Chapter 2: God and Ethics

1. Some may respond: "But neither hell as reform nor hell as annihilation is biblical." There is an obvious reply. The Bible speaks of "eternal punishment" (Matt 25:26). Those who claim that hell is separation rather than punishment obviously think it unnecessary to read such passages literally. And if "eternal punishment" can be taken metaphorically, how can we dogmatically rule out alternative interpretations such as "eternal destruction" (annihilation) or an indefinitely long period of reform?

2. What I say here is necessarily brief, and owes a debt to Marilyn McCord Adams's, "Hell and the God of Justice," *Religious Studies* 11 (1975): 433-447. Those inclined to accuse me of oversimplifying the issues should find her treatment satisfyingly thorough.

3. Some may argue that the view under consideration has properly to do with nothing like social status but with moral greatness. Thus, it may be claimed that a mugger who roughs up Mother Teresa sins more greatly than a mugger who roughs up some "morally average" human. But even if we grant that it is worse to offend against a good person than a morally average (or bad) person, it is still a long way to the conclusion that each sin against God merits eternal punishment since it remains clear that there are greater and lesser offenses against Mother Teresa. Moreover, our horror vis-à-vis the attack on her may stem in part from something other than her goodness, viz., her vulnerability. But God is not vulnerable if He is omnipotent.

4. Kierkegaard is a possible exception to the rule. He may have held that Abraham, in being called to kill Isaac, was required by God to commit an unethical action. In other words, he may have held that religious obligations can conflict (and override) ethical obligations. See his *Fear and Trembling and the Sickness unto Death*, trans. Walter Lowrie (Princeton, N.J.: Princeton University Press, 1941), pp. 64-91.

5. Plato, *Five Dialogues*, trans. G. M. A. Grube (Indianapolis: Hackett, 1981), pp. 5-22.

6. It is only fair to point out that a variety of philosophical views have gone by the name of 'divine command theory'. I am here treating the view I regard as paradigmatic. For alternatives, see Robert Merrihew Adams, "A Modified Divine Command Theory of Ethical Wrongness," in *Divine Commands and*

Morality, ed. Paul Helm (Oxford: Oxford University Press, 1981), pp. 83–108; and Philip L. Quinn, *Divine Commands and Moral Requirements* (Oxford: Oxford University Press, 1978).

7. See MacIntyre, *Short History of Ethics*, pp. 121–124; and Satris, *Taking Sides*, pp. 38–44.

8. I do not mean that torture could never be right in a special case. I mean that in the actual world torture is usually wrong and that its wrongness in a specific case would not go away by divine fiat. In Chapter 6, Section X, I will describe a putative case of permissible torture.

9. For a concise discussion of arguments from authority, see Wesley C. Salmon, *Logic*, 3rd ed. (Englewood Cliffs, N.J.: Prentice-Hall, 1984), pp 97–101.

10. See Richard G. Swinburne, "Duty and the Will of God," in Helm, *Divine Commands and Morality*, pp. 120–134. I have adapted Swinburne's ideas for my own use, so I must be held responsible for any mistakes in the reasoning.

11. Ibid., p. 124.

12. Ibid., pp. 124, 130–131.

13. The doctrine of the Trinity is often regarded as logically incoherent or hopelessly mysterious. For a brief discussion of these metaphysical issues see C. Stephen Layman, "Tritheism and the Trinity," *Faith and Philosophy* 5 (1988): 291-298.

14. However, in Chapter 5, Section IV, I shall have to amplify what I say here about "certain conditions." This amplification will carry with it a problem for those who seek to ground morality *merely* in necessary moral truths.

15. Frankena, *Ethics*, p. 44.

Notes to Chapter 3: Consequentialism

1. See Cicero, "The Ethics of Epicurus: Egoism," in *Introductory Readings in Ethics*, ed. William K. Frankena and John T. Granrose (Englewood Cliffs, N.J.: Prentice-Hall, 1974), pp. 42–49.

2. My formulation is indebted to that of Fred Feldman. See his *Introductory Ethics*, p. 82.

3. Not all philosophers accept the principle that "ought implies can." See *Moral Dilemmas*, ed. Christopher W. Gowans (New York: Oxford University Press, 1987), pp. 20ff.

4. See Michael A. Slote, "An Empirical Basis for Psychological Egoism," in *Egoism and Altruism*, ed. Ronald D. Milo (Belmont, Calif.: Wadsworth, 1973), pp. 100–107.

5. Feldman, *Introductory Ethics*, p. 87.

6. Again my formulation owes a debt to Feldman, pp. 16–29.

7. J. J. C. Smart, "An Outline of a System of Utilitarian Ethics," in Satris, *Taking Sides*, p. 75.

8. More precisely, to allow for cases in which two alternatives are equal in utility and higher than all the rest, it is our moral duty to take a course of action *which has at least as much utility as any alternative*.

9. The main outlines of this case are borrowed from H. J. McCloskey, "A Non-Utilitarian Approach to Punishment," in *Philosophical Perspectives on Punishment*, ed. Gertrude Ezorsky (Albany, N.Y.: State University of New York Press, 1972), p. 127.

10. The scarequotes here are in deference to the common claim that it is logically possible to punish only the guilty, but of course one can give the innocent the same sort of harsh treatment the guilty are given, which is what matters in the present case.

11. Frankena, *Ethics*, p. 42.

12. The essentials of this case are borrowed from John M. Taurek, "Should the Numbers Count?" *Philosophy and Pubic Affairs* 6 (1977): 293–316.

13. Among them, perhaps, J. S. Mill and R. B. Brandt. See John Rawls, *A Theory of Justice* (Cambridge, Mass.: Harvard University Press, 1971), pp. 161–162.

14. J. S. Mill, *Utilitarianism*, ed. Oskar Piest (Indianapolis: Bobbs-Merrill, 1957), p. 31.

15. John Rawls, "Two Concepts of Rules," *Philosophical Review* 44 (1955): 3–32.

16. For a defense of rule utilitarianism, see Richard B. Brandt, "Toward a Credible Form of Utilitarianism," in Frankena and Granrose, *Introductory Readings in Philosophy*, pp. 154–165.

Notes to Chapter 4: Deontological Views

1. Immanuel Kant, *Groundwork of the Metaphysic of Morals*, trans. H. J. Paton (New York: Harper and Row, 1964), p. 88.

2. The story about hypothetical and categorical imperatives is more complicated than this paragraph suggests and requires

230 *The Shape of the Good*

a much more technical treatment than space here permits. See Philippa Foot, "Morality as a System of Hypothetical Imperatives," in *Virtues and Vices and Other Essays in Moral Philosophy* (Berkeley: University of California Press, 1978), pp. 157–173, and Thomas E. Hill, "The Hypothetical Imperative," *Philosophical Review* 82 (1973): 429-450.

3. The examples given here are inspired by Frankena. See his *Ethics*, p. 32.

4. Foot, "Morality as a System," p. 161.

5. Kant, *Groundwork of the Metaphysic of Morals*, p. 96.

6. For a more positive evaluation of Kant (which I do not, however, find convincing in the last analysis), see Alan Donagan, *The Theory of Morality* (Chicago: University of Chicago Press, 1977).

7. Thomas Hobbes, *Leviathan* (New York: Penguin, 1968), pp. 186, 188. For John Locke's account of the state of nature, see chaps. 2 and 3 of his *Second Treatise of Government*, ed. C. B. MacPherson (Indianapolis: Hackett, 1980), pp. 8–16.

8. John Rawls, *Theory of Justice* (Cambridge, Mass.: Harvard University Press, 1971).

9. My exposition of Rawls owes a debt to Feldman. See his *Introductory Ethics*, pp. 135–148. It should be noted that Feldman does not endorse the contractarian view, he merely explicates it.

10. See Rawls, *Theory of Justice*, pp. 118-161 for a detailed discussion of the points listed in this rough summary.

11. Ronald Dworkin, *Taking Rights Seriously* (Cambridge, Mass.: Harvard University Press, 1977), pp. 150-183. It should be noted that Dworkin himself ultimately employs this objection, not to reject Rawls's theory, but to support an interpretation of it which diverges radically from the one provided in this text. On Dworkin's view, Rawls's theory is not fundamentally contractarian, but rights-based. I do not wish to take up the issue of the correct interpretation of Rawls here, except to say that I have tried to provide an interpretation which is, I believe, more or less standard. What I have to say about theories of rights appears in Chapter 6.

12. Ibid., p. 151.

13. Ibid.

14. For more information about biblical covenants, see G. E.

Mendenhall, "Covenant," *The Interpreter's Dictionary of the Bible*, ed. George Arthur Buttrick (Nashville: Abingdon, 1962).

15. Peter Singer, *Practical Ethics* (London: Cambridge University Press, 1979), pp. 48–71. Also see Rawls, *Theory of Justice*, pp. 504–512.

16. Rawls, *Theory of Justice*, pp. 14, 302.

17. Ibid., pp. 14–15, 302.

18. Ibid., pp. 534-541.

19. Ibid., pp. 150–161.

20. Robert Nozick, *Anarchy, State, and Utopia* (New York: Basic Books, 1974), p. 198. Emphasis added.

21. Ibid. Emphasis added.

22. The Ten Commandments are recorded in the Old Testament book of Exodus. See Exodus 20:17.

23. William David Ross, *The Right and the Good* (Oxford: Oxford University Press, 1930), chap. 2.

24. Ibid., p 41.

25. Donagan, *Theory of Morality*, p. 23.

26. Feldman, *Introductory Ethics*, pp. 157–158.

27. Ibid., p. 159.

28. Norman L. Geisler, *Ethics: Alternatives and Issues* (Grand Rapids, Mich.: Zondervan, 1971), esp. pp. 114-136.

29. I do not mean to suggest that this is Geisler's own hierarchy. He does not use Ross's terminology. Moreover, as we shall see, Geisler's own list of norms is radically incomplete, which is why I have not reproduced it in the text.

30. Geisler, *Ethics*, p. 114.

31. Ibid., pp. 115-121.

32. Feldman, *Introductory Ethics*, p. 154.

33. Ibid.

Notes to Chapter 5: Ethics and the Kingdom of God

1. Or, at any rate, after some new and radical intervention by God. If anyone wishes to insist on a premillennial view, in which the Kingdom of God is fulfilled this side of death, he can easily modify the presentation to suit.

2. The phrase is borrowed from Francis A. Schaeffer, *The Church Before the Watching World* (Downers Grove, Ill.: Inter-Varsity Press, 1971).

3. Robert Merrihew Adams, "Divine Commands and the Social Nature of Obligation," *Faith and Philosophy* 4 (1987): 262-
275. Adams is defending a version of the divine command theory
in this article. Thus, he does not think obligation can be adequately explained in terms of social requirements unless God is
a member of the "society." I should also say that, since Adams
rejects teleological views of ethics, I am using the material from
his article for my own purposes, and thus I must take full responsibility for any shortcomings in the discussion.

4. Ibid., p. 268.

5. Ibid.

6. Ibid., pp. 272-273.

7. Ibid., p. 272.

8. Ibid.

9. Ibid., p. 266. The emphasized questions are paraphrastic.

10. Ibid., Ibid., p. 265.

11. See James W. McClendon, Jr., "Narrative Ethics and Christian Ethics," *Faith and Philosophy* 3 (1986): 390. The quotation
from Henry James is taken from "The Art of Fiction," in *Henry
James: Literary Criticism, Essays on Literature, American Writers, English Writers* (New York: Library of America [Viking],
1984), p. 55. Authors who have made much of the role of narrative in ethical thinking include MacIntyre and Hauerwas. See
MacIntyre, *After Virtue*, esp. chap. 15, and Stanley Hauerwas,
The Peaceable Kingdom (Notre Dame, Ind.: University of Notre
Dame Press, 1983), esp. chaps. 2 and 7.

12. It might be replied that it is not different societal demands, but different situations, that create different obligations
in this case. For example, in American society the maternal
grandmother often lives far away from the father, so it would
be wrong to make her primarily responsible for the child, since
this would involve separating the child from its father. In general
I grant—indeed, I insist—that situations place limits on what a
society can rightly demand. However, in societies in which the
extended family lives together, I see no situational barrier to placing primary responsibility on either the father or the maternal
grandmother *other things being equal*. In such cases, societal
demand creates moral obligation, in the sense of determining
who is primarily responsible for the child's upbringing.

13. Martin Buber, *The Way of Man (According to the Teaching of Hasidism)* (Secaucus, N.J.: Citadel Press, 1950), p. 15.

14. Ibid., pp. 16–17.

15. Robert Merrihew Adams, "Vocation," *Faith and Philosophy* 4 (1987): 448. Emphasis added.

16. Ibid., pp. 454–458.

17. Ibid., p. 458.

18. *The Ethics of Aristotle*, trans. J. A. K. Thomson (New York: Penguin, 1955).

19. A discussion of these four virtues is already present in the first great work in Greek ethics, Plato's *Republic*. (See *Plato's Republic*, trans. G. M. A. Grube [Indianapolis: Hackett, 1974], esp. book 4.) Christian theologians have not been reluctant to learn from the Greek philosophical treatment of the virtues. Thus Aquinas discusses the cardinal virtues in his *Summa Theologicae*. The parts of the *Summa* concerning virtue are neatly bound up in the *Treatise on the Virtues*, trans. John A. Oesterle (Notre Dame, Ind.: University of Notre Dame Press, 1984). See pp. 108–117 for Aquinas's discussion of the cardinal virtues.

20. My summary of Aristotle owes a debt to James D. Wallace, *Virtues and Vices* (Ithaca, N.Y.: Cornell University Press, 1978), esp. chap. 1.

21. Jonathan Barnes, *Aristotle* (Oxford: Oxford University Press, 1982), p. 2.

22. It seems to me that the Christian thinkers most influenced by Aristotle, namely Aquinas and those in the Thomist tradition, tend to import Aristotle's error into Christian theology. The very phrase, "beatific vision," used by thinkers in this tradition to describe the final state of the blessed, suggests that one's relation to God is more like perceptual contemplation of an object than like an I-thou (interpersonal) relationship. See Aquinas, *Summa Contra Gentiles (Book Four: Salvation)*, trans. Charles J. O'Neil (Notre Dame, Ind.: University of Notre Dame Press, 1975), pp. 35-38.

23. Wallace, *Virtues and Vices*, p. 159 (emphasis added). Wallace is not endorsing this argument, but only stating it.

24. Ibid., p. 160.

25. Ibid.

26. Ibid.

27. Ibid., pp. 160-161.

28. Ibid., p. 9. G. E. M. Anscombe suggested the possibility of such elimination in "Modern Moral Philosophy," *Philosophy* 33 (1958): 1-19. This paragraph and the next owe much to Wallace.

29. It may also be important that most people would find the act difficult to perform in the circumstances. See Wallace, *Virtues and Vices*, p. 79.

30. It can be argued that, even from a secular perspective, some benefits and harms are available after death. For example, vindicating the reputation of a deceased person may be seen as benefiting that person. See, for example, Thomas Nagel, *Mortal Questions* (London: Cambridge University Press, 1979), pp. 1-10. But even if we grant that these are goods for the deceased, it is obvious that, from the secular point of view, such post-mortem goods cannot be consciously enjoyed by the deceased. They are not available in the sense that he will never take pleasure in them.

31. George Mavrodes, "Religion and the Queerness of Morality," in *Rationality, Religious Belief, and Moral Commitment*, ed. Robert Audi and William J. Wainwright (Ithaca, N.Y.: Cornell University Press, 1986), p. 223.

32. Singer, *Practical Ethics*, p. 209.

33. For an excellent discussion of arguments for immortality, see William J. Wainwright, *Philosophy of Religion* (Belmont, Calif.: Wadsworth, 1988), pp. 99-111.

34. My source for these claims about "happy psychopaths" is Singer, *Practical Ethics*, pp. 214-216. Singer in turn is drawing from Hervey Cleckley, *The Mask of Sanity, (An Attempt to Clarify Some Issues About The So-Called Psychopathic Personality)*, 5th ed. (St. Louis, Mo.: E. S. Cleckley, 1988).

35. Mavrodes, "Religion and the Queerness of Morality," p. 219.

36. Ibid., p. 224. I am borrowing from Mavrodes throughout this paragraph.

37. Those acquainted with modal logic may have a question here. By a principle of modal logic, if p is a necessary truth and p necessarily implies q, then q is a necessary truth. So, if it is necessarily true that "certain conditions are met" and necessarily true that "If they are met, one ought to X," then, "One ought to do X" is a necessary truth. But I assume it is not *necessarily true* that "certain conditions are met." In my judgment it would be most implausible to suppose, e.g., that "Morality pays for humans" is a necessary truth.

38. At this point some readers may fear that I have lapsed into ethical egoism. If we say that morality must pay for the

agent, aren't we endorsing (EE)? No. (EE) describes the *telos* in terms of pleasure. On the Christian teleological view, individual fulfillment consists in harmonious relationships. In other words, the *telos* remains the Kingdom of God. I am arguing that morality must pay, but I deny that it must pay in terms a hedonist would accept. However, I do admit that if promoting the Kingdom of God is the only way to promote one's own interests, then "An act is right if and only if it promotes one's own best interest" is materially equivalent to the Christian teleological view.

39. Two fine discussions of moral arguments for theism are Robert Merrihew Adams, "Moral arguments for Theistic Belief," in *Rationality and Religious Belief*, ed. C. F. Delaney (Notre Dame, Ind.: University of Notre Dame Press, 1979), pp. 116–140, and J. L. Mackie, *The Miracle of Theism* (Oxford: Oxford University Press, 1982), pp. 102–118.

40. Joel Feinberg, *Doing and Deserving* (Princeton, N.J.: Princeton University Press, 1970), pp. 3-24. The example employed here is Feinberg's.

Notes to Chapter 6: Justice and Human Rights

1. Alan Gewirth, *Human Rights: Essays on Justification and Applications* (Chicago: University of Chicago Press, 1982), p. 41.

2. I say "other things being equal" because it might be that one is no longer able to keep the promise, or that it was a wicked promise in the first place, or that keeping the promise is incompatible with some more stringent duty.

3. Gewirth, *Human Rights*, pp. 2-3.

4. For a careful discussion of the relationship between claiming one's rights and self-respect, see Thomas E. Hill, Jr., "Servility and Self-Respect," *Monist* 57 (1973): 87-104. This article is also found in *Today's Moral Problems*, ed. Richard Wasserstrom (New York: Macmillan, 1975), pp. 137-152.

5. See Acts 22:22-29 and 2 Samuel 12:1-15.

6. Nicholas Wolterstorff, "Reply to C. Stephen Layman," *Christian Scholar's Review* 17 (1987): 199.

7. See Hobbes, *Leviathan*; Locke, *Second Treatise of Government*; and Jean-Jacques Rousseau, *The Social Contract*, trans. Maurice Cranston (New York: Penguin, 1968).

8. Diana T. Meyers, *Inalienable Rights: A Defense* (New York: Columbia University Press, 1985), p. 193.

9. *Nonsense Upon Stilts (Bentham, Burke, and Marx on the Rights of Man)*, ed. Jeremy Waldron (London and New York: Methuen, 1987), pp. 190-209.

10. For this way of putting the question and for the summary of "analogues" which follows, I am indebted to Gewirth, *Human Rights*, pp. 42-45. I am, however, adapting the materials to my own use, and so must take responsibility for it.

11. Michael Tooley, "Abortion and Infanticide," in *Applied Ethics*, ed. Peter Singer (Oxford; Oxford University Press, 1986), p. 64. It should be noted that Tooley recognizes that this initial analysis of rights is problematic and offers more sophisticated versions of it later in the paper. But I do not think the more subtle versions assist us in understanding the link between interests and rights.

12. Ibid., pp. 74-82. It is, however, interesting to note that Tooley does not regard the fetus as temporarily unconscious. As a being which has never had a desire to live, it lacks a right to life.

13. Here the reader may want to review section II in Chapter 4, which contains a summary of Rawls's position.

14. Gewirth, *Human Rights*, p. 44.

15. Nicholas Wolterstorff, "Christianity and Social Justice," *Christian Scholar's Review* 16 (1987): 222.

16. For example, see C. S. Lewis, *The Problem of Pain* (New York: Macmillan, 1962), pp. 129-143.

17. The term is borrowed from Peter Singer. Speciesists "give greater weight to the interest of members of their own species when there is a clash between their interests and the interests of those of other species." See Singer, *Practical Ethics*, p. 51.

18. For a penetrating discussion of the difficulty utilitarians have in making room for rights, see David Lyons, "Utility and Rights," in *Theories of Rights*, ed. Jeremy Waldron (Oxford: Oxford University Press, 1984), pp. 110-136.

19. That freedom and well-being are goods necessary for action is a point much stressed by Gewirth, *Human Rights*, pp. 45-51. I have borrowed heavily from him throughout this paragraph.

20. This defense of the potential principle is borrowed from Philip E. Devine, *The Ethics of Homicide* (Ithaca, N.Y.: Cornell University Press, 1978), p. 95.

21. This argument is borrowed from L. W. Summer, *Abortion and Moral Theory* (Princeton, N.J.: Princeton University Press, 1981), pp. 103–105.

22. Perhaps some would argue that the frog in these tales already has "princely capacities," but cannot manifest them. However, I have no need or desire to digress into fairy tale interpretation. I am interested only in a story in which frog-status implies the lack of the specifically princely capacities. In "my story" the frog, though able to talk, has never before been a prince. For an insightful interpretation of "The Frog King" that sticks closely to the original, see Bruno Bettelheim, *The Uses of Enchantment (The Meaning and Importance of Fairy Tales)* (New York: Random House, 1975), pp. 286–291.

23. A technical point may be helpful here for metaphysically alert readers. Note that sentience is a dispositional property, i.e., a power, tendency, or capacity. One can have such a dispositional property even though manifestations of it are temporarily blocked. For example, one does not lose the *capacity* of rationality simply by going to sleep, even though manifestations of it are temporarily suspended. Similarly, one can have the *capacity* to feel pain at time *t* even though manifestations of the capacity are blocked at time *t*. This could happen, for example, if one were given a large dose of morphine. Wantonly inflicted bodily damage done to a person so drugged would count as abuse, i.e., as mistreatment of a sentient being, even though manifestations of the capacity for sentience were temporarily blocked by the morphine. Otherwise, all manner of damage could be done to persons *without mistreating them*, provided one gave them painkillers in advance.

24. I have, however, sketched two arguments for life after death in Chapter 5, section IV.

25. My source for this summary of the state of our knowledge about fetal sentience is Summer, *Abortion and Moral Theory*, pp. 146–154.

26. Genesis 9:1-3 indicates that it is permissible for humans to eat nonhuman animals. Genesis 1:26-28 indicates a stewardship role for humans over the rest of creation.

27. St. John Chrysostom, as quoted in Wolterstorff, "Christianity and Social Justice," p. 223.

28. I owe this point about the contrast between sustenance

rights and Lockean property rights to Meyers, *Inalienable Rights*, pp. 193–194.

29. Provocative discussions of the entitlements of the impoverished include Garrett Hardin, "Lifeboat Ethics: The Case Against Helping the Poor," in Satris, *Taking Sides*, pp. 280–287, and Louis Pascal, "Judgment Day," in Singer, *Applied Ethics*, pp. 103–123.

30. Some have held that God is bound by no duties, since one cannot be said to have duties unless one can fail to perform them, and God can do no wrong. But those who accept this line of argument can still hold that God's goodness consists, in part, in His *acting in accord* with duty even though He is not *bound* by duty. See Thomas V. Morris, *Anselmian Explorations: Essays in Philosophical Theology* (Notre Dame, Ind.: University of Notre Dame Press, 1987), chap. 2.

31. The idea that law enforcement and criminal punishment can be regarded as ways to *respect rights* I owe to Meyers, *Inalienable Rights*, pp. 152–169.

32. See for example Karl Menninger, "Therapy, Not Punishment," in *Punishment and Rehabilitation*, ed. Jeffrie G. Murphy (Belmont, Calif.: Wadsworth, 1985), pp. 132–141.

33. This paragraph and the next owe much to Herbert Morris. However, I am adapting his ideas for my own purposes and so must be held responsible for any mistakes in the presentation. See Herbert Morris, "Persons and Punishment," *Monist* 52 (1968): 475–501. The article is anthologized in Wasserstrom, *Today's Moral Problems*, pp. 302–323. (Subsequent page numbers refer to Wasserstrom.)

34. Ibid., p. 304. Emphasis added.

35. Ibid.

36. Ibid.

37. George Sher, *Desert* (Princeton, N.J.: Princeton University Press, 1987), pp. 74–84.

38. This paragraph owes a debt to both Joel Feinberg and Diana Meyers. Feinberg's detailed discussion of conflicts between rights indicates the enormous difficulty of listing all the "exception clauses" for a given right. See his *Social Philosophy* (Englewood Cliffs, N.J.: Prentice-Hall, 1973), pp. 68–97. Meyers makes the point that the complete list of exceptions would be impossible to remember (*Inalienable Rights*, p. 10).

39. For example, Feinberg argues that the right not to be tortured is absolute (*Social Philosophy*, pp. 87, 96).

40. That rights can still be respected even when the object of the right must be denied is a point I owe to Meyers (*Inalienable Rights*, pp. 143-152). Feinberg makes a similar observation (*Social Philosophy*, p. 74-75). This seems to require a slight modification of the analysis of the concept of a right offered in Section 1. In cases of conflict, we may not have a duty to refrain from interfering with an individual's possession of a good, since we may *have* to interfere with it. In such cases, our corresponding duty may take the form of doing the next best thing, e.g., compensating the subject (insofar as that is possible) or at least apologizing.

41. I owe the conception of an inalienable right provided in this paragraph to Meyers, *Inalienable Rights*, pp. 1-28.

42. See Feinberg, *Social Philosophy*, pp. 79-93 and 94-97.

43. Meyers, *Inalienable Rights*, p. 13.

44. This does not necessarily imply, however, that those who refuse to work should be denied welfare. When welfare is denied a person, it is often his or her children who suffer most.

45. This paragraph owes a debt to Meyers's insightful discussion of the various ways in which rights can be lost. However, I am adapting this material for my own purposes, and must bear the responsibility for any mistakes in the reasoning. See Meyers, *Inalienable Rights*, pp. 9-15. The striking observation that some rights can be forfeited inadvertently or involuntarily occurs on p. 14.

46. See Baruch Brody, "A Non-Consequentialist Argument for Active Euthanasia," in Satris, *Taking Sides*, pp. 108-113.

47. Judith Jarvis Thomson, "A Defence of Abortion," *Philosophy and Public Affairs* 1 (1971). It has been often anthologized. The quotation here is from Singer, *Applied Ethics*, pp. 38-39.

INDEX

241